RUSSIA OBSERVED

Advisory Editors
HARMON TUPPER   HARRY W. NERHOOD

THIRTY-FIVE YEARS IN RUSSIA

George Hume

ARNO PRESS & THE NEW YORK TIMES
New York • 1971

Reprint Edition 1971 by Arno Press Inc.
LC 79-115548
ISBN 0-405-03082-7

Russia Observed
ISBN for complete set 0-405-03000-2

Reprinted from a copy in
the Harvard College Library

Manufactured in the United States of America

THIRTY-FIVE YEARS IN RUSSIA

THIRTY-FIVE YEARS IN RUSSIA

BY
GEORGE HUME

WITH ILLUSTRATIONS AND MAP

LONDON: SIMPKIN, MARSHALL,
HAMILTON, KENT & CO., LTD.

Copyright. First published 1914

LONDON: SIMPKIN, MARSHALL, HAMILTON, KENT & CO., LTD.

CONTENTS

INTRODUCTION . . . . pp. xv–xxiii

CHAPTER I
EARLY LIFE

Parentage—Birth—Christening—St. Giles—Stage-coach travelling—Spartan discipline in childhood—A mother's influence—Cousin Anne—Removal to Feltham—Greenwich Fair and Hospital—Infant-school life—Miss Phillips—Hunting incident—Methods of education—School at Egham House—Incidents of school life—Drilling—A girl's trick—Mr. Tom—Frequent punishments—The German master and gift of snuff—Cricket accident—Close of schooldays—Dates of principal historical events during boyhood—Observations on Education . . . . pp. 1–20

CHAPTER II
APPRENTICE DAYS

Apprenticed at Ipswich—Unhappy experiences—Evening studies—Charles Freeman—Typhus fever—Colchester Brewery incident—Effects of lack of ambition in workmen—Close of apprenticeship — Enter Penn's — Examination for Naval Engineers — Narrow escape from death—Work on men-of-war—*Warrior*, the first ironclad — Narrow escape on *Duke of Wellington*—The *Mithridates*—Severe tempest in Bay of Biscay—Failure of superheating apparatus—Arrival at Odessa—Transferred to Russian Steam Navigation Company—Formation of Steam Navigation Company—Object of same—Repudiation of clause of Treaty of Paris *re* Black Sea . . . . . pp. 21–33

CHAPTER III
ODESSA AND SEBASTOPOL

Refit of vessel—Odessa and its history—Mr. Melville—Purchase of socks—Learning Russian—Introduction to Mr. Wagner—State of Odessa streets—Easter Sunday festival—My first visit to Sebastopol—Journey of Grand Duke Constantine—Description of Sebastopol Harbour—Colonel Gowen—Visits to battlefields—Accident on Plains of Inkerman—The cemetery and Balaclava . pp. 34–42

CONTENTS

CHAPTER IV

FURTHER SEA EXPERIENCES

Transfer to *Gounib*—Meaning of the name—Transport of pilgrims to Jerusalem and Mecca—Exciting incident at sea—Fight between pilgrims—Storm at Jaffa—Imminent destruction of ship—Algiers and Lisbon—Discharge cargo at Waterford—Arrival at Odessa—Appointed superintendent of company's repairing shops—Supersession and disagreement with a Colonel—Interview with Admiral—Offer of resignation refused—Unpleasant position and final resignation—Voyage to Constantinople in s.s. *Alexander II*—Storm in Black Sea—Meeting Mr. Graham in Constantinople—Decision to introduce steam thrashers and reaping machines into Russia .   .   .   . pp. 43–50

CHAPTER V

INTRODUCTION OF REAPING MACHINE INTO RUSSIA

Arrival at Berdiansk—Desiccation of Sea of Azov—Phenomenon illustrating drying of Red Sea before Moses—Shooting excursions—A narrow escape—Mr. Hahn—Meeting after many years—A wedding trip—Terrific storm and cloud burst—Mennonite worship—First visit to German colonies—Their origin—Settlement by Catherine II—Windmills of mediæval type—Great hospitality—" Bees "—Introduction of reaping machine—Mr. Dick—Opinion of village blacksmith—" The Grasshopper and the Locust "—Stampede of horses—Success of machine—Amazement of peasants—Desire to see demon in reaper—The Mennonites—Their origin—Main tenets—Opposition to military service—Comparison with Quakers and Plymouth Brethren—Emigration to America—Arrangement with General Todleben—Their present number—The Stundists—The unrighteousness of Mammon—Compulsory baptism .   .   .   . pp. 51–66

CHAPTER VI

INTRODUCTION OF STEAM THRASHER

First hire of thrashing machine—The police inspector—Nature of contract—Transport of machines—Work begun on old corn—Infringement of agreement—Peasants fascinated by the machines—M. Popoff—His hospitality—Granaries for storing corn—Sleeping under tarpaulins—Watch for robbers of stored wheat—The thieves trapped—M. Popoff's help—Interview with and assault on inspector—Work for M. Popoff—Reconciliation with the inspector—Our subsequent meeting .   .   . pp. 67–75

CONTENTS

CHAPTER VII

LIFE ON THE OPEN STEPPE

Successful year closed—New machines ordered—Disastrous harvest in 1862—Drought—Absence of means of irrigation—M. Popoff—Proclamation of freedom of serfs—Their disappointment—Emperor's tea—Charles Pope—Life on Steppe near Wassilefka—Deportation of Crimean Tartars—Shooting on Steppe—Bustard hunting—Opinion of Russian peasant—Migration of peasantry during harvests—Amusing racial quarrels—Bargaining—Picnics on Steppe—Beautiful nights—Steppe cooking—Tartar servant—Religious instincts of peasants—Superstitions—Financial difficulty—Unexpected settlement—Journey to Ekaterinoslav—Snowstorm—Hospitality of great Russian landowner   pp. 76-92

CHAPTER VIII

THE STEPPE: ITS POPULATION, CHARACTER, AND FAUNA

Extent of Crimean Steppe—Nomad tribes—Herds of horses—Black earth soil—Underground water supply—Ravines and hills due to water-action—Kurgans, or Scythian burial places—Comparison of climates in South Russia and England—Good effects from rain—Sheep pasturage—Sheep dogs—Abundance of wild flowers—Cloud effects—Enemies of agriculture—Hessian fly and Hungarian beetle—Marmot (Souslik)—Jerboa—Bird life—The mirage—History of Steppe—Locusts—Tarantula—Serpents

pp. 93-108

CHAPTER IX

LIFE IN POLTAVA AND KHARKOV

Marriage—Third failure of harvest—Removal from Berdiansk to Poltava—Visit to German colonies—Incident of river crossing—Establishment at Poltava—Steppe journey to Novo-Moskovsk from Keitchkass—Perilous position in snowstorm—Kharkov—Distillery contract difficulty—Country tracks in winter—Inability to obtain workmen—Friendships formed in Poltava—Establishment of mill at Kharkov—Mill burnt down—Agency for Messrs. Marshall, Sons & Co. arranged—Partnership with Mr. Lister—Improvements in machines—Prosperous times—The Baron incident—The carriage incident .   .   .   .   . pp. 109-135

CONTENTS

CHAPTER X

LAW COURTS AND NIHILIST CONSPIRACIES IN KHARKOV

Introduction of trial by jury—First case—Basis of Russian laws—Amusing case in the Courts—Origin of Nihilism—The *Kolokol* or *Bell* newspaper—Results, incendiarism and assassination—The Emperor's speech—Establishment of martial law—Appointment of German Governor—Riots at Kharkov—Wholesale deportations of peasants—Imposition of fines on us by Governor—Incident of English governess — M. Jukovsky— Petition of Zemstvos for national education—Attitude of Tchinovniks—Petition refused—Causes of student discontent—Zemstvos' action paralysed — Triumph of arbitrary government — Contrast in political status of Bulgaria and Russia—Ferment among students in Kiev—Building of sugar factory—Yard man, or Dvornik, in Russia—Dvornik shows unexpected abilities—Visit of police inspector—Arrest of Dvornik—Police placed at gates—Discovery of dynamite—Method adopted to dispose of same without discovery—Artel system at Kiev and Kharkov—Accuracy of Russian carpentry . . . . . . pp. 136–151

CHAPTER XI

RUSSO-TURKISH WAR AND PENJDEH INCIDENT

Origin of Russo-Turkish War—Effects on money exchange—Negotiations with English firm—Final decision—Purchase of wheat and storage—Failure of transport—Severity of winter of 1877–78—Osman Pasha and Turkish prisoners—Precautions taken to preserve wheat at stations—Incident of purchase from Prince L.—Final settlement—Penjdeh incident—Anxious moments—Volunteer fleet—Incident with Chief of Custom House—Reasons of unpopularity of police—Introduction of universal military service—The old system—Length of service based on education—Terms of service—Cossacks—Comic incident connected with Cossack's purchase of machine—Co-operative purchases of machines by Cossack—The Zaporozhski—Russian Army as fighting force—Importance of religious or racial motive . . . pp. 152–170

CHAPTER XII

JOURNEY FROM LONDON TO KIEV

Incidents of stormy passage—Cologne incidents—Sociability of Continental traveller—Arrival in Berlin—Methodical arrangement for vehicles—Hotel Kaiserhof, Berlin—Methods of Berlin advertisement—Beaconsfield's room at Kaiserhof—Ambassador's ball—Predominance of military element—A feature of militarism—Impressions of Berlin—Method of visiting new places—What a

CONTENTS

German working man found interesting—The opera—Emperor William I—Tipping in Germany—The start for Breslau—The forgetful clerk and the obsequious conductor—My travelling companions—Breslau—Cracow—Wieliczka salt mines—Conversation on Cologne—Plague and quarantine—Method of isolating epidemics—Apathy of officials in Russia . . pp. 171–197

CHAPTER XIII

THE TRAGEDY OF KIEV

Failure of important firm—Meeting of creditors—Our firm and Mr. Leiste appointed liquidators—Meeting at Dessau—Return to Kiev—Suicide of Mr. Leiste . . . . pp. 198–204

CHAPTER XIV

AN ADVENTUROUS JOURNEY HOME IN 1881

Family temporarily removed to England—Settled in Cheltenham—Education of my two sons—Business delays at Kiev—Intention to reach home at Easter—General inquisitiveness of Russian travellers—My fellow-passengers—Sluggishness of Russian railways—" Dead-heads "—Rise of blizzard—Train stopped by snow in middle of forest—Yelping of wolves at midnight—Difficulty of obtaining provisions—Sixty hours' stoppage—Train service dislocated—Starving third-class passengers—Arrival at Warsaw in early morning—Food obtained under difficulties—Arrival in England by night boat—Failure of connections—Stay night in Gloucester . . . . pp. 205–213

CHAPTER XV

EVENTS LEADING TO DEATH OF ALEXANDER II

Autocratic character of Nicholas I—Military insurrection, December, 1825—Effects of Crimean War—Alexander II ascends throne—Transformation of principles of government—Emancipation of serfs—Difficulties with peasants and land distribution—Opposition of proprietors—Appointment of committee by Emperor—Methods adopted—Village communes and their powers—The Zemstvos—Usual limitations of autocracy—Emancipation of serfs directly due to Emperor—Start of Nihilism in 1877—Reign of terror—Attempt on General Trepoff—Acquittal of Vera Zasulitch —Prince Krapotkin's murder—Attempts on life of Emperor—His assassination, March 13th, 1881—His character—No advantage accruing from his death . . . . pp. 214–222

CONTENTS

CHAPTER XVI

RUSSIAN POLITICAL PROBLEMS. PART I. THE JEWISH QUESTION

Jewish question perplexity for Russian Government—Relations between Jews and dominant power—Characteristics of Jews—Extent of Jewish pale—Sections of Jewish race—The Sephardim—The Karaim—The Ashkenazim—Congestion not the cause of problem—Basis of antagonism between Jew and peasant—Non-intolerance of peasantry—Economic causes—" The cry of Christendom "—Origin of special laws—Smuggling—Universal military service—Remedial laws by Alexander II—Their effect—Evasions of law—Oppression of peasantry by the Jew—Jewish colonies—Their failure—Jewish jargon—Jews in London—East End Ghetto—Summary—Kotlinski incident—Conversion for purposes of gain
pp. 223-237

CHAPTER XVII

RUSSIAN POLITICAL PROBLEMS. PART II. RUSSIA AND THE POLES

Warsaw, the capital of Poland—Moral depression of city—Poland treated as conquered—Permanent martial law—Russian language obligatory in Universities—Oppressive land laws—Prohibition of public meetings—Economic neglect of city—Military disabilities—Racial and religious differences between Poles and Russians—Revolution of 1863—Deportation of Poles—Causes of downfall—Internal dissensions and election of kings—Insincerity of Poles
pp. 238-245

CHAPTER XVIII

A GEOLOGICAL TOUR IN SOUTH-WESTERN RUSSIA

Aim of journey—Berditchev—Jewish metropolis in Poland—Dubious methods by hotel-keepers—Incident on previous visit, and its sequel—Zhitomir—Visit cathedral and city—Labradorite quest accomplished—Hospitable invitation by Bohemian quarry-owner—Russian surprised at our visit—Journey by post-wagon—Character of quarry—Sudden storm on return journey—Interesting conversation with postmaster, and kind entertainment—Journey to Kiev by diligence—Our fellow-passengers—Terrible storm—Attitude of companions—Tree struck by lightning with terrific crash—Coach embedded in mud—Arrival at Kiev—Picturesque city—Mother-church of Russia—Centre of sugar industry—Mazeppa—Dnieperian Cossacks—Pilgrimages to shrines—Pechersk monastery and catacombs—St. Sophia Cathedral—The monasteries—Visit to a monk—Incident of loan to Emperor—Nestor—Russian classical authors . . . . . pp. 246-261

CONTENTS

CHAPTER XIX

GEOLOGICAL JOURNEY FROM KIEV TO DONETZ MINERAL BASIN

Leave Kiev—Plan of journey—River Dnieper—Methods of landing—Sandbanks—Visit to Belgian ironworks—Hospitable reception—Krivoi Rog, great iron ore quarries—Original discoverer—New Russia Company—Mr. Hughes—Jealousy of mining department—Visit of Grand Duke Constantine to works—Local newspaper comments—Prosperous career—Vast iron ore resources—Folding of strata—Krementchug—Alexandrovsk—Scene of my first Russian experience—Original reaper still preserved—Meet two sons of early acquaintances—Arrival at Kharkov—Leave for Slaviansk—Borki, scene of disaster to Imperial train, 1888—Monastery of Svyatogorski (Holy Hill)—Great pilgrim centre—Apparition of holy pictures—Kharkov Virgin—Procession—Nicholas I forbids appearance of holy pictures—Order obeyed—Visit friends—Yasinovataya—Coal and iron region—Hughesovka and the works—Visit to Stiela iron ore region—Bakhmut rock salt industry—Alabaster Hill—Nikietovka cinnabar (mercury ore) mines—Return to Kharkov—Close of journey . . . . pp. 262–275

CHAPTER XX

INCIDENTS OF TRAVEL: FROM KHARKOV TO TIFLIS ACROSS THE CAUCASIAN MOUNTAINS

Programme of journey—Slaviansk salt springs—Borki—Enthusiastic reception of Emperor after accident—Taganrog—Silting up of Sea of Azov—Scene of death of Alexander I—The Don Cossacks—Land held subject to military service—Cossack horses—Feats of horsemanship—Cossacks a frontier guard—Rostov—Circassia entered—Various races at station—Armenian fellow-passenger—Armavir—Change in scenery—Plains replaced by hills—Mineral spring centres—Nizoblania and its horse fair—Picturesque tribesmen—Armed escort at Kavkaz—Train robberies—Vladikavkaz—" Ruler of the Caucasus "—Caucasian tribes—Burnous—Hôtel de France—The Elbruz—German brewery—Beer not forbidden by Koran—Revelry of Circassian Prince—Quaint notice—Scotch colony—Russian dissenters—Special passport—Varieties of dialects—Insecurity in the mountains—Surrender of Schamyl—Principal tribes—The Ossitinski—Descendants from Crusaders—Procession to Table Mountain—Blood feuds. *Through the Caucasian Mountains :* Military road—Russian troika—Station of Lars—Special luxuries—Balta station—Grandeur of Darial defile—River Terek—Devil's Bridge—Post-boy's impressions—Cossack fortification—Castle of Tamara—Lermontov's " Demon "—Table Mountain—Kazbek—Prometheus legend—Young Englishman and Bass's beer—Mountain road from Kazbek—Danger from

xii   CONTENTS

snow avalanches—Cossack fort—Kobi—Chalybeate spring—Caucasian chamois—Gudaur—Magnificent view—Avalanche—Boundary between Europe and Asia—Apex of watershed—Zigzag road to Mleti—Passanaur—Orchards, honey, and bears—Ananúr—Fortified church of Kitobel—Mtzkhet, the " Meeting of the Waters "—Cathedral and Georgian regalia—The seamless robe . . . . pp. 276–291

CHAPTER XXI

INCIDENTS OF TRAVEL : FROM TIFLIS TO BAKU, BATOUM, AND SEBASTOPOL

Arrival at Tiflis—Capital of Georgia—Hotel London—Bazaars—Zion Church—Mount Ararat—Depressing railway journey to Baku—Kurdish raids—Capture of bandits—Copper works of Ekhptala—Locusts stop train—Arrival at Baku—Its railway station—Increase in population—Its harbour—Black and White Towns—Balakhani—Artesian oil fountains—Burning of wells—Temple of Zoroaster—Fire-worshippers—Firm of Nobel—Visit to gas geysers in Caspian Sea—Return journey to Batoum—Lower Caucasian Range Mountain Railway—Mud volcanoes—Liquorice factory—Tremendous storm near Elisabetpol—Use of Fairlie engines—Glorious views—Vast forests—Mountain plants—Tunnel being built—Dangerous descent—Rion Station—Circassian women—Variety of headgear—Phasis—Large size of fruit—Gori resembling Athens—Meet a Circassian Prince—Croaking of frogs—Fireflies—Poti—Hotel Colchide—A pleasant surprise—Mr. Wilson Sturge—The " Baboshka "—Progress of Batoum—Wooded hills near Batoum—Ruins of Pitzunda—Voyage on the *Juno*—Fellow-travellers—" The captain cannot understand French "—Lifelessness of Black Sea—Anapa—Shipping of Circassian slave-girls—Kertch—Greek influence—Tumuli—Mithridates—Theodosia—Old fortifications—Russian Riviera—Sebastopol . . pp. 292–307

CHAPTER XXII

CONCLUDING REMARKS

Sidelights on Russian Life . . . . . . pp. 308–312

APPENDIX . . . . pp. 313–314

INDEX . . . . pp. 315–319

LIST OF ILLUSTRATIONS

GEORGE HUME	*Frontispiece*
	FACING PAGE
CRIMEA. GENERAL VIEW	32
RUSSIAN PEASANT	48
SCHAMYL AND THE CIRCASSIAN LEADERS, 1858	64
KHARKOV. MONUMENT TO ALEXANDER I	80
KHARKOV. THE RESIDENCE OF MR. G. HUME	96
KHARKOV. MESSRS. HUME AND LISTER'S MILL	112
KHARKOV. MESSRS. HUME AND LISTER'S OFFICES	128
KHARKOV. MR. HUME'S GARDEN	144
KHARKOV. MAIN ALLEY IN MR. HUME'S GARDEN	160
TARTAR CART, CAUCASUS	176
BLIND BEGGAR, TIFLIS	224
A DESCENDANT OF THE CRUSADERS	240
COSSACK FORT, AND ROCK OF TAMARA	256
CAUCASUS MILITARY ROAD AND DARIAL DEFILE	272
MAIDEN'S TOWER, BAKU	288
BALAKHANI. OIL WELL ON FIRE	304
MAP OF SOUTH-WEST RUSSIA	320

INTRODUCTION

At the instigation of relatives and many friends, I have been induced in this, the late autumn of my life, to record some of the reminiscences of my work in Russia. During the whole period of my thirty-five years' connection with the so-called Peasant Empire, I was intimately connected in business and in society with all classes of the community, so that I have had every opportunity of forming an unbiased opinion. It will be seen from the events herein narrated that I have been contemporary with the great evolution that took place immediately after the Crimean War.

The events that happened during the reign of Alexander II have left an indelible imprint upon the country. At the time of my arrival in Russia peace had only been proclaimed in the previous year, 1856, and all the great reforms were still in an embryonic state within the brain of their beneficent author. All the abuses connected with serfdom were still in full swing, the proprietors had still the power to inflict corporal punishment upon an unfortunate moujik at their own discretion, which, although restricted by law in theory to a certain number of strokes with birch or stick, was in practice uncontrolled. Nearly all the large estates were ruled by German stewards, the proprietors not even being cognizant of the oppression which was being practised. It was brought to my notice in five instances that the peasantry, having become exasperated beyond endurance, had hurled their tormentors to the thrashing-floor, and beaten them to death with their flails.

The Crimean War is now generally considered to

have been a great mistake on the part of England. To Russia, however, it was a great boon; it had certainly left her temporarily humiliated, but her unexpectedly gallant defence had gained for her the respect and sympathy, not only of her late enemies, but of all civilized communities. This paved the way for the introduction, step by step, of those great reforms which have raised her in so short a time from a state of semi-barbarism to a co-equal voice with the other Great Powers in the destinies of Europe. It was the boom of the Allies' cannon that aroused her from her long sleep of apathetic indolence and made possible the inception of those great reforms that characterized the reign of Alexander the Liberator.

The time has not yet arrived for a correct judgment to be formed of this monarch, and personally, with many others, I am of opinion that these developments followed too quickly for profitable assimilation, and thus opened the path for the reactionary policy of his successor Alexander III. It is, however, just to observe that the war itself was closely followed by the inauguration of the greatest of all the reforms, the abolition of serfdom; it is equally true that it marked the epoch for the transition of Russia from a period of many abuses to one dominated by lines of thought which are leading her onwards by slow gradations to an advanced state of civilization.

Since 1857 I have had the opportunity of closely studying the sequence of reforms, which followed one another in quick succession. Thus, the great question of the land remained a constant cause of unrest amongst the peasantry, who maintained that at the time of emancipation under the will of the Emperor they were entitled to, and should have received without payment, all the land held by their proprietors. The publication of the Reform took place in the year 1861, but the Emancipation itself was only to be carried out at a two-years' interval in 1863. This the peasantry did not understand, and it gave rise to many incidents of a most regrettable character, so much so that troops were quartered on the villages in order to compel them to go to work.

The Russians are a hospitable people, entertaining their foreign guests with the utmost cordiality and courtesy, laying themselves out to make them feel at home from the date of their arrival to their departure. The educated Russian has a perceptible leaning socially to the French, but politically to the English.

Of course, both Russia and England have separate and often opposing interests, but during the whole time of my residence amongst Russians I seldom heard or saw a single derogatory expression or any sign of national enmity against ourselves, and I feel convinced from conversation with some of the highest in the land that there could be no question, however critical, that could not be adjusted by mutual amicable arrangement and to the satisfaction of the two great nations.

At the time of my arrival in Russia law procedure was carried out by Bureaucratic action, and all the old administrative abuses prevailed; the personal liberty was constantly in danger and dependent upon the uncontrolled will of the Tchinovniks (Men of Rank). It was an Augean stable of abuse, illegality, and extortion, and powers that had accumulated over many generations required to be swept away with firm and remorseless hand.

And yet the officials were not entirely to blame, for they received the meanest of salaries from the State and had to divide their exactions with their immediate superiors. A former Governor of our Province, in talking over his own position as well as that of his subordinates with me, said: "How can you expect men in an official position to live on a salary less than that of the foreman or mechanic of a factory? For myself, I am obliged to keep up a large establishment, receive all visitors of distinction, have a large retinue of servants, keep two carriages, and the whole income that I receive is £500 (5,000 roubles) and the upkeep of my horses." He then added: "I have an estate, that since the Emancipation brings me in a very small revenue in good years, and nothing whatever in bad."

LIST AND DATES OF THE PRINCIPAL EVENTS DURING MY LIFE IN RUSSIA

1861.—Decree for emancipation of twenty-three million serfs on the expiration of two years (March 3rd).
1863.—Confirmation of ditto (March 3rd).
1863.—Polish insurrection.
1864.—Institution of the Zemstvo.
1866.—Inauguration of Kharkov trial by jury.
1870.—Prince Gortschakoff notifies the Powers of the repudiation of the clauses of the Treaty of March 30th, 1856, respecting the Black Sea Fleet.
1870.—Military Reserves established (November 16th).
1871.—Reorganization of the Army (January 12th).
1871.—The Black Sea clauses abrogated by treaty of the Powers (March 13th).
1873.—The inauguration of Universal Military Service.
1874.—The Poll Tax abolished.
1874.—Marriage of the Duke of Edinburgh to the Czar's daughter (January 23rd).
1877.—Russia declares war against Turkey on disputes connected with the Holy Places (April 24th).
1878.—San Stefano Treaty signed (March 3rd).
1881.—Assassination of Alexander II (March 13th).
1884.—Death of General Todleben, the hero of the defence of Sebastopol (July 1st).
1885.—General Komaroff attacks the Afghans at Penjdeh, defeating them with great slaughter, and war nearly precipitated with Great Britain. The dispute, however, was settled by arbitration (by Denmark), and the boundaries between the Afghans and Russians finally fixed (September 10th).
1885.—Celebration of the ninth century of the introduction of Christianity into Russia (July 27th).

INTRODUCTION xix

1888.—Railway accident at Borki on the Kharkov-Azov Railway, the train jumping the rails on a curve owing to excessive speed. The royal family uninjured, but 21 persons killed (October 29th).

1889.—Reactionary policy of Count Tolstoi [1] in forcing Russification on Finland and the German provinces of Russia led to great unrest in those regions.

1890.—The revolt of the students of all the Universities, owing to the stringent rules. Severe punishments inflicted on them by Cossacks, who were ordered to attack and lash them with their heavy whips.

1891.—The year of the great famine throughout the whole of the eastern sections of the Empire, during which all festivities were suspended, and large remittances in money and corn were sent from America, England, and many parts of the Continent.

Not only are the Russians a hospitable people, but they have many philanthropic institutions, excellently organized and supported by voluntary effort. Amongst these the hospitals may be mentioned, for which a very considerable amount is raised by the means of Municipal stamps (of a small amount) which have to be affixed to every ticket that is sold for the theatres, and all places of amusement and recreation where entry money has to be paid.

Again, the institutes for the daughters of noble families are supported by the State, and a large sum of money left by one of the Grand Duchesses; in addition the revenue arising from the monopoly of playing-cards is allotted to them.

The sale of playing-cards is also a source of considerable revenue, they being sold at a high price, in my time at 4s. the pack. It was then the custom to

---

[1] Count Dmitri A. Tolsti, Minister of Education (not to be confused with Count Leo N. Tolstoi, novelist and social reformer).

have a new pack for each separate game as an assurance that they had not been tampered with, so that the income from this source must have been very considerable. The old packs were then sold at second hand, and gradually after the first purchase changed hands at a very cheap rate, the cards being scarcely soiled.

During the winter months, when work was scarce and the destitution in consequence very great, cheap dinners were established in the large Public Hall of the City. Throughout the months of frost and storm the poorer classes could obtain substantial meals at prices varying from 5 to 15 kopecks (one penny to threepence) according to the number of courses required, each course costing one penny. These dinners had in addition a moral value, one of the principal ladies of the City, a member of the Committee for this purpose, presiding each day in rotation during the meal. These ladies included the wives of the Governor and the City Dignitaries, and each voluntarily gave her services for this purpose on an average once a month, sympathy for the poor being thus shown by the more privileged class in a practical form.

Another institution which received large support was that of the Waifs and Strays, who colonized a large freehold estate near the City.

Besides these, there were the deaf and dumb, the blind, and the old men's asylums, the excellent public dispensaries, and the two great orphan asylums, and also many other benefactions which were constantly at work—this surely being great evidence of the charity which exalteth a nation.

The reader must understand that in these records I am writing of a period long since passed away. I do not believe that since that time a new heaven and earth have dawned upon that nation, and I fear lest the new-born activities now prevailing should be drawing hard-earned money from our too-confiding countrymen, which may result in loss and disappointment to many. Russia is not England, and should not be viewed with English eyes; it is a country still in the making, and the sterling principles of honesty and honourable dealing that have been ingrained in our own countrymen from our forefathers have yet to take deep root amongst these Eastern people.

For me Russia has a deep pathos, for during my sojourn in that land it became consecrated to my family as the resting-place of four of our beloved children. One lies in the cemetery of the Mennonites at Berdiansk on the Sea of Azov; a second in Poltava; a third in the village of Sukarabovka, in the churchyard of the estate belonging to a truly noble family, the Karaishes, where my family was passing the summer; and the fourth in the cemetery of Kharkov.

It has also been stated that the Russians are a deeply religious people. That the peasants have a very great religious instinct I quite admit, but theirs is not the religion that we have been taught in Holy Writ as being pure and undefiled. During their long state of serfdom and ignorance they have not had the opportunity of having or being able to read the Holy Scriptures. To them the important features are the forms and ceremonies of the Church, the adoration of the Saints and the Icons, the prostrations, the fastings at stated intervals, the genuflexions, crossing themselves, and pilgrimages—then if that be true religion, the peasants are religious according to their knowledge.

A great work is being carried out by both the Russian and English Bible Societies for the spread of the Word of God among the people, and the State railways have given special facilities by granting free passes on their lines to the colporteurs; but the slightest fringe only has been touched among the millions of the country.

There are two sets of clergy, the black and the white. The black are the monks living in the Monasteries attached to the Cathedrals and Holy Places. These are supposed to be holy men devoted to good works and the due performance of the Church ceremonies. The white clergy are the parish priests, who must be married men, but on the death of a wife are compelled to enter a monastery, following on the Biblical instruction (as they think) of being the husband of one wife.

The services are held in the old Slavonic tongue, a language that is not understood even by the general body of educated Russians; the singing of old Gregorian chants is very attractive, and the Little Russians, many of whom have remarkably fine voices, are educated and engaged as choristers throughout the land.

At the time of my arrival the priests were a hereditary caste, every son of a priest's family being bound to enter the priesthood; eventually, however, the supply grew greater than the demand, and then the compulsion was abrogated. The priests are miserable in their service and in their pay, which averages about £20 a year, together with a piece of glebe land which they plough, sow, and harvest as ordinary peasants. They haggle and bargain over the price to be paid for baptisms, marriages, funerals; they are only half educated, and many are addicted to intemperance.

The religious observances of the higher class, or so-called *intelligencia* of the country, are practically absent, only consisting of such Church ceremonies as the State ordains. I have seldom seen men in the churches except at Easter time, when Confession and Communion are enforced. The ladies, however, are more consistent in their attendance, and after Confession, Communion, and the receipt of absolution, it is customary for them to receive visits of congratulation.

The scope of this work being that of personal narrative, I do not propose to discuss the social and political questions, which have been dealt with by many abler pens than my 'prentice hand can wield.

When compiling these records of my life, I have been greatly aided by having found in a box after my wife's death a complete collection of all the letters I had written to her during the fifty-one years of our married life, which had been particularly numerous owing to our frequent separations during the course of my many journeys and for the education of my sons.

INTRODUCTION xxiii

When bivouacking on the desert, I have often pondered over the mysteries of life and the "divinity that shapes our ends." It seems incontestable that there must be in the case of many of us some plan that fashions our lives. Here in my own case, my birth, training, education, apprenticeship, the study of languages, and subsequent work, all seem to have been chains of evidence leading me onward to be the pioneer of the work destined for me in this country. Thus when hundreds of miles away from any fellow-countryman, and ofttimes a weary traveller, I was led to realize the great mystery of life which comes vividly before us in such solitude, and there are voices in the refrain :

> " Lo, on each seed within its slender rind
> Life's golden threads in endless circle wind,
> Maze within maze the lucid webs are rolled,
> And as they burst the living flame unfold.
> The pulpy acorn ere it swells contains
> The oak's vast branches in its milky veins.
> Each ravell'd bud finds film and fibre line
> Traced with nice pencil on the small design.
> The young narcissus in its bud compressed
> Cradles a second, nestling on its breast,
> In whose fine arms a younger embryon lies,
> Folds in its leaves and shuts its floweret eyes,
> Grain within grain successive harvests swell
> And boundless forests slumber in its shell."

THIRTY-FIVE YEARS IN RUSSIA

CHAPTER I

EARLY LIFE

Parentage—Birth—Christening—St. Giles—Stage-coach travelling—Spartan discipline in childhood—A mother's influence—Cousin Anne—Removal to Feltham—Greenwich Fair and Hospital—Infant-school life—Miss Phillips—Hunting incident—Methods of education—School at Egham House—Incidents of school life—Drilling—A girl's trick—Mr. Tom—Frequent punishments—The German master and gift of snuff—Cricket accident—Close of schooldays—Dates of principal historical events during boyhood—Observations on education.

My earliest recollections are connected with my grandfather, who was the first member of the family to emigrate to England, he having lived up to that time on the borderland, the north side of the Tweed.

The Hume family had formerly occupied a very great position in the districts comprised within Marchment, Greenlaw, Duns, and Kelso, and it is still represented there by the Humes of Wormielaw, who are direct descendants of the old family. Their farm comprises part of the rich pasture-land of the border, and is a very short distance from the bluff upon which stands the grim old ruins of Hume Castle.

My grandfather, by profession a brewer, had been invited to enter the service of one of the most important London breweries in order to superintend the making of Scotch ale, which at that time was in much demand.

I was born in the year 1836 in the neighbourhood of the brewery, and was christened in the Church of St. Giles, Cripplegate, a church which is of such historical interest that in my opinion it compares favourably with any other church in London. Within its crypt lie the remains of John Milton, who, as author of *Paradise Lost* and *Paradise Regained*, is enshrined in the memory of the whole of the English-speaking world. Here also are buried John Fox, the martyrologist, and Sir Martin Frobisher, who in 1588 took a leading part in the defeat of the Spanish Armada. The latter was also one of the first explorers of the Arctic Seas, and died of wounds received in a naval action in 1594. This church is also noted as being the scene of the marriage of Oliver Cromwell on August 29th, 1620.

Long before my grandfather's death, my father had removed from London and started for himself in a brewery in the village of Feltham in Middlesex, but as it was not a success, it passed after some years into other hands. Previous to our removal to Feltham, my father resided at Greenwich in one of my grandfather's houses in Circus Street, going up daily to London to his business. My grandfather on my mother's side was a Scot named Purvis, a man of some substance, having freehold land in the centre of the then rising suburb, which comprised within its bounds Royal Hill, Circus Street, and Prior Street, the latter street bearing my grandmother's maiden name. Greenwich at that time was a fashionable resort, and the Trafalgar, Yacht, and Ship Hotels used to be filled daily in the season with visitors coming for whitebait dinners. Members of the Cabinet also came for the same purpose before the opening of Parliament.

As these hotels were built close to the river and their walls were washed at the flow of the tide, it was a favourite amusement with the visitors to throw coppers from the hotel windows at the ebb tide for the pleasure of seeing the boys, the so-called "mudlarks," scramble for them in the deep mud. Among other great attractions at that time at Greenwich was the fair, which brought thousands once a year to visit the Park, Blackheath, and the Hospital, where the old sailor pensioners, always ready to show visitors over their pretty decorated cubicles, were present in their picturesque garb. The evening generally ended in a visit to Tea-pot Row, which was quite an institution at that time.

One of my childhood's memories is of a long visit by my father and mother to Scotland; and I well remember the day when the stage coach drove up to our home to take them away. At that time, there being no railways, the journey north was a veritable undertaking. On the opening of the railway lines, the picturesqueness of travel ceased, and the horn of the red-coated guard resounded no more through the streets. The stateliness of the coachman seated on his box in all his glory passed away, together with the crowd of small boys, who looked upon him with reverence, and in their place are the shrill notes of the steam whistle, the hoarse puff of the engine, and the whirr of the skidding wheels. During the absence of my parents, my brother and I were placed under the care of my mother's brother, Dr. Purvis, who inaugurated his guardianship by threatening, should we not be good boys, to make us into pills. I am sorely afraid, however, we did not turn out the angelic creatures his threat would achieve, for in after years my aunt used to relate how a stray sofa pillow cleared some valuable ornaments from her drawing-room mantelpiece. Having, however, no personal recollection of the incident, I have systematically regarded this accusation as a myth, or an erroneous effect of the imagination. On the return of our parents we removed to Feltham, which became the centre of our family life over many years.

Our family at this time consisted of three boys and a girl, and also a Scotch cousin Anne, who lived with us up to her marriage. Both my parents being of Scottish origin, the family, as was then the custom, was brought up under Spartan rules, and inured to live a life in which no luxuries were allowed.

I can recall how, at a very early age, we were placed under the too draconian discipline prevalent at that period, consisting in the repression of every childish instinct. This, to my mind, had the effect, instead of fostering the love and confidence which every child should have toward its parents, of leading them to avoid as far as possible any contact with them. Under this system the discipline of the simple life was general in most families. Porridge, dry bread, and milk and water formed our breakfast fare. No condiments of any kind were allowed. Even a piece of cake, except at rare intervals, was forbidden, and the general conduct of the children was regulated by admonitions such as, " Children should be seen and not heard," " Children should only speak when spoken to," or " Children should see, hear, and say nothing."

I was most tenderly attached to my brother, and we resented this treatment, which doubtless made us irritable, as far as children could be. The strict discipline under which we were being brought up had this effect, that our father, instead of being an attracting force, became to us a repelling one, and our intercourse was regulated more by fear of consequences than by filial affection. As a natural result, I was thrown into closer companionship with my brother, who was only fourteen months older than myself, and I can well remember how we used every means of avoiding our father, and were entirely dependent on the moderating influences of our mother, whom we adored. But who can fathom the endurance of a mother's love ? It has been throughout my life an abiding influence. It was at her knees our daily prayers were offered for father mother, sister, and brothers, after which, standing with our hands behind us, we recited Doctor Watts' evening hymn :

" And now another day is gone,
I sing my Maker's praise."

This hymn, which I never have forgotten, has been to me throughout all my wanderings in desert lands a solace and prayer—a solace recalling a mother's tender care, and a prayer that my sins, which were many, might be forgiven, and strength granted for days to come. Yes, I recall how seldom we saw her without her children's socks or other work in her hands, and how, when colds were prevalent, the posset cone full of home-made elderberry wine was embedded in the parlour embers for our later regalement in bed. Also I recall how at stated intervals on coming down in the morning, we found to our horror the cup of senna tea, which at that time was considered indispensable for the young, and which, in spite of protest, we had to drink or have poured ignominiously down our throats in spoonfuls, our mouths being opened by my father pinching our noses.

In our home, notwithstanding the love bestowed upon us by our mother and cousin Anne, stern discipline was enjoined, and it seemed to us that we could do nothing well. Regardless of grammar, the words "don't," "won't," "mustn't," etc., were ever irritating elements in our child life. Through this too constant correction in the past generation, the inevitable reaction has followed, with the effect that the present-day children too often despise parental authority and become aggressively self-assertive and arrogant. Although I cannot recall that we were often chastised by our father, I do know, that instead of hastening joyfully to meet him, taking him into our confidence and asking his advice, we constantly avoided him, and this result was not peculiar to us, but in evidence in most families at that period.

The third member of our family was our Scotch cousin Anne, to whom I have already referred, who, with an occasional helper, served the household, and was the object of our great affection. She it was who tried to save us, by timely warning, from many a well-deserved punishment, and on baking days made us many little delicacies from sweetened pieces of dough, formed to represent rabbits, dogs, or pigs, with currants for eyes. At this distance of time, I can still recall how they were to us the very perfection of art, and also our grief when told she was leaving us to be married, and the intense indignation we felt when her husband carried her away a few months later.

I must not forget to record our love for our dog "Spot." He was a large spotted carriage dog of Danish breed, far from good-looking, with bleary albino eyes, and was to us children the most affectionate of animals. He could be trusted to allow no stranger to approach us. He was faithful, loving, and true, the confidant of our grief, the partaker of our joys. No one would admire him on his points, but he was beautiful to us, and we deeply sorrowed when, owing to a carriage accident, he had to be destroyed, and died licking my father's hand. We buried him in our garden, mourning with many tears the loss of our dear old friend and playmate.

It was at the early age of about five years that my school life began, when my brother and I first entered the village infant school, which was kept by a Miss Phillips, who was quite a character.

This school was typical of those existing in the earlier half of the last century, in which most of the children of the middle class received their elementary education. The school was a mixed one, consisting of the sons and daughters of the farmers who formed the bulk of the important element of the village community. As nearly as I can recollect, there were from twenty to thirty pupils, well known to each other, who occupied the large front room of the house. Miss Phillips instructed the higher class, while the elementary pupils were under the care of one of the seniors. Poor Miss Phillips, upon whose features generations of wayward pupils had left a forbidding impress, grimly presided in a high upholstered, straight-backed chair. Nature had not been very gracious to the poor woman, for one of her legs was so much shorter than the other that it had to be supplemented by an iron patten, which, having failed to grow with her growth, produced a movement when she walked which earned for her in the village the sobriquet of "Hop and go one." This custom had become so general that I am convinced it was very often used inadvertently in her presence. Owing to the position of her chair, backing the corner, the children could not be supervised when, on opening the school with prayer, she knelt facing the back, thus giving them a splendid opportunity for the interchange of grimaces and other amenities.

Before my cousin Anne left us, we had outgrown the necessity for her leadership through the village, and trudged alone along the road leading to the school. Midway between it and our house was a sheet of water, the overflow of a ditch which crossed the road. This sheet of water was known as the Watersplash, and to cross it a slightly raised wooden footpath had been erected for pedestrians; but what boy could resist the challenge of another's "I'll do your dags," without making an attempt to jump the stream! Often a small boy landed in the middle and the soaking entailed punishment. This punishment generally consisted of his having to stand with naked feet on a stool, with his face to the wall, a conical dunce's cap on his head, and a placard on his back marked "Dunce," and he had to stand thus until his socks and boots were dried.

The village was in a hunting district, and as the meet was held not far from it, during the season gay cavalcades of fair women and red-coated men, together with the hounds, often passed our school windows. Miss Phillips, who had a great dislike to the hunt, on such occasions as these generally gave the order for prayer, quite oblivious of the fact that while she, with her face to the corner, might be calling down fire from heaven on the devoted hunt, the children, with their noses flattened on the windows, were silently revelling in the unholy pageant.

At the New Year it was usually the custom to supplement the fees payable to the teacher by gifts in kind, which in my father's case invariably took the form of coal. Memory recalls how on one occasion I had to accompany her, laden with a big basket of bits of slate, which she wished my father to exchange for coal, but I believe she was referred to the merchant from whom the coal was bought.

In those days in the majority of elementary schools the system of education was by "rote"—that is to say, the lesson had to be learnt word for word by heart without regard to its signification, simply as an effort of memory, and the least failure in word was usually followed by punishment or by moving down places in the class. The school hours commenced at nine o'clock in the morning, lasting until twelve, and from two to four in the afternoon. For the seniors, the morning lessons comprised reading, writing, grammar, and spelling, and in the afternoon arithmetic, dictation, and needlework for the girls, the last being replaced by geography for the boys. In the junior class, the order in the morning was the alphabet, pot-hooks and hangers, and simple spelling, while the multiplication table and sampler work in cross-stitch occupied the afternoon. Specimens of this so-called art-work are doubtless still to be found in middle-class houses. It consisted in working figures of animals, houses, and trees, regardless of perspective and all being about the same size, with worsted in cross-stitch on a square of canvas, and underneath were the numerals and alphabet. These squares, when finished and lined, were generally used for kettle-holders, and were presented to our parents on their birthdays.

I fear, as I was high-spirited and rebellious of control, I must often have proved a sore trial to the poor woman, and the punishments that ensued were not conducive to my self-respect. For instance, on one occasion I remember when I was adorned with the dunce's cap and with a placard with "Liar" in large letters hanging on my back, she tried her best, but failed, to make me go into the street to fetch her loaf of bread from the baker's cart. On another occasion she tied me to the banisters with thread. So long as punishments were restricted to the house I had no strong objection, but I rebelled when ordered to make a public exhibition of myself.

With the lapse of time our elementary education finished, and before the age of seven years my brother and I entered a boarding school, the " Egham House Academy," under the headmastership of a Dr. Bailey. He was a pedagogue of the old school, who believed that human nature in boys had to be licked into shape with a cane. For seven long years I had to undergo a discipline of cruelty and neglect; being subjected to a system which tended to intensify all that was evil and to destroy, instead of fostering, all that was good in my nature.

The school was a large one, there being well over a hundred boys when we entered. It was extensively advertised for the sons of gentlemen who were supposed to be destined for the army or the professions. I well recollect when my father first drove us to the school, and left us in the playground, how we were surrounded by junior boys and jeered at because our dress was not the orthodox Eton style. The school house was a large Elizabethan mansion standing in extensive grounds, enclosed on three sides by high, heavily buttressed walls, with a forbidding-looking moat at the back. Adjacent to the house, but separated from it for some distance by a large quadrangle, was the large school-room built over arcades, where in wet weather the boys used to play. In the main building the rooms were large and commodious, especially the dining-room, which had two long tables accommodating all the boarders and presided over by the doctor and the chief usher. The dormitories, as I recollect them, were rooms bearing the names of ancient statesmen which I have forgotten. The lower range was allotted to juniors, the middle to seniors, and the highest of all, called the double room, was assigned to the pupils of the most advanced class and contained also the cubicles of the ushers.

Many of the pupils were day boarders, but several others were of a most objectionable class called "parlour boarders," practically young men who were being coached for the examinations for entry into the army. These youths were, almost without exception, cruel bullies who domineered over the younger boys and made them fag for them, using language brutalizing to themselves and demoralizing to all those who were subject to their influence. Needless to say, I deeply resented the brutality of these boarders, not so much on my own account as for my elder brother, who, being of a much milder disposition than myself, came in for an unfairly large dose of kicks. The reader of to-day will doubtless wonder why the junior boys made no complaint of the treatment they received, either to the teachers or the parents, but under the strict and unwritten code of schoolboy honour the worst possible sin was to deserve the epithet "sneak."

The curriculum of the school work followed that of Eton in almost every detail, and the Eton Latin Grammar was the basis of our studies. So far as I am personally concerned, I have found that the classical knowledge gained during the seven years spent in that seminary has been of the greatest assistance to me in the study of other languages. At this school Latin was obligatory, but French and German could be taken instead of Greek. I have no complaint to make of the general course of instruction given, but to all education there are two sides, the moral and the intellectual. Not only in this school, however, but in the great majority of those at that period, the moral side was practically ignored, and the intellectual training was accompanied by excessive physical punishment. In fact, Dickens in his description of "Dotheboys Hall" only put into an exaggerated form the system prevalent in schools of this class during the first half of the last century, and if any of my fellow-pupils at that school should read these pages, they will easily recall the old Elizabethan house with its cricket ground and the copse of trees near the entry, the scene of many a fight where our schoolboy differences were settled.

At that time the Napoleonic wars were not yet forgotten and almost every school was placed under discipline and taught military exercises. I well recollect how the old serjeant, decorated with many medals, used to come from Windsor every Wednesday and Saturday morning to drill us. The guns used were old flint-locks which had seen service, and the sword-sticks had basket hilts. As I write these lines I see the old serjeant looking down the line and hear him calling in his gruff voice, "Chests out, gentlemen; stomachs in. Your lines are like a dog's hind leg," etc. I believe these drills were of immense service in the physical development of the boys, and I regret that, owing to the general apathy which has overtaken our nation, drilling in board schools has not been made obligatory.

In the springtime it was the custom for the boys to be dosed with brimstone and treacle, very much in the same way that Dickens has described it—the same spoon being used for each of the recipients, who were drawn up in single file to receive the dose. I recollect on one occasion having an attack of scarlatina, which caused me to be confined in the so-called Infirmary (situated in the attic) and being dosed with the most horrid medicines, very fashionable at that time, viz. the black draught and the blue pill. In this connection I may mention the following incident: Our nearest neighbour at home was a gentleman farmer named Harris, who had two daughters about the same age as ourselves. We had all attended Miss Phillips' school, so it was perfectly natural that we should pair off, my brother with Elizabeth the elder girl, and I with Annie the younger. On our going to Dr. Bailey's, their two brothers also became students, and the two girls were entered at a boarding school in the same town. As our schools constantly met in our walks, or in going to and coming from church, an opportunity was given us of surreptitiously passing small notes which we at that age considered love letters. At the girls' boarding school it was usual to celebrate the breaking up for the holidays by a party and dance, to which their brothers and ourselves had always been invited. On the above-named occasion, however, as I was ill, I could not go, and remained in the school infirmary, bemoaning my sad fate.

The next morning, however, nurse brought me a dainty little packet which contained a piece of cake with a paper attached, on which was written " A Gift from Annie." Reader, what would you have done in the circumstances? I feel sure that the most loving of your thoughts would have gone out to the centre of your heart's affection, and you would have done what I did, *i.e.* proceeded to demolish the cake. Doubtless, too, there would have been a similar sequel, for inserted insidiously in that piece of cake were three pills neither silvered nor sugared, one of which I had chewed. I can assure you it was in every respect the most bitter pill of my boyhood, spoiling as it did my earliest idea of womanhood and depriving me for a long period of the anticipatory pleasure usually connected with the thought of cake.

I can most confidently assert that the seven long years I spent at that school were years of endurance. The food was often tainted and was quite insufficient for the needs of growing boys, who were thus compelled to spend their pocket money, generally from twopence to threepence a week, on the most solid food that amount of money could procure, which in the case of my brother and myself frequently took the form of a penny loaf and a saveloy.

To my mind, punishment inflicted was not in any way proportionate to the offence committed. The custom prevailing was that in serious cases the janitor of the school was sent to invite the culprit to attend in the doctor's study. It often happened in my own case that I went there without the slightest knowledge of having committed an offence, so that on the receipt of an invitation I generally provided against eventualities by casemating my more vulnerable parts with copybooks, which, together with loud, tearful vociferations, seemed to me to be the most efficacious way of meeting the situation and rendering the punishment less painful. For a long time these frequent visitations continued, and at last I discovered the source of the persistent persecution under which I suffered. In accordance with a schoolboy's code of honour, however, I could not refer the matter to parental consideration.

It appeared that the doctor's son Tom, who was about four years my senior, had made up his mind that I should fag for him, and I had equally made up mine that I would have nothing to do with him. Our dislike of each other was intense. He was arrogance personified, and it was a common belief in the school that he sneaked to his father of those pupils to whom he owed a grudge. I was fully convinced that he alone could have been the inventor of my many offences, or else I suffered for actions so remote that they must surely have happened under a previous incarnation.

One morning, after the usual prayer, the doctor solemnly announced to the assembled school that his son had been advanced to the dignity of junior teacher, and that henceforth he expected him to be spoken of, and addressed by the pupils, as Mr. Thomas (later on this was graciously permitted to be shortened to Mr. Tom). Of course it was too good an opportunity to be missed by the boys, and poor Tom's life was made intolerable by persistent inquiries on the most trivial questions, which were addressed to him as *Mr.* Tom, with a most pronounced emphasis on the Mr.

A further cause of personal spite arose from the following circumstances: *Mr.* Tom, as junior teacher, had a special cubicle assigned to him in the double room allotted to the ushers and the pupils of the advanced class, of which I was then a member. He was reading for "Holy Orders," and often retired earlier than the senior boys, presumably to study. One evening on going up to bed I saw that Mr. Tom's door was slightly ajar, and caught a sight that induced me to hastily summon some of my fellow-students. There we saw the curate *in posse*, wearing a black petticoat as a cassock, with his nightgown as a surplice over his clothes, gesticulating in various postures before the mirror. A few days later, a band of six of us, with our nightgowns over our clothes, serenaded our friend, paraphrasing from the Litany. We asked that we might be delivered from all the subtleties of the devil and from our enemies, persecutors, and slanderers, to which the boys answered " Amen." This of course put Mr. Tom into a frightful passion, but he dared not give vent to it owing to the ridicule which would be aroused throughout the school. Eventually, however, as the sequel will show, he had his revenge.

In addition to Mr. Tom, the German master, Herr Koenig, and the French master, M. Nolong, had their cubicles in this dormitory. The former was an inordinate taker of snuff, and on all possible occasions used to work on the feelings of the dormitory boys by telling us of the great poverty he endured, of his poor salary, and of the general distress in his family; stating also that he was under notice to leave at the end of the term and did not know what would become of him. Being at a very impressionable age, we felt keenly sorry for him, and a subscription in the school having realised fifteen shillings, it was left to us to choose the form our gift should take. Of course, various secret conferences were held and many suggestions were made, with the result that I and two others were told off to carry the business through. We felt it would be derogatory to him to offer him the money, and knowing his predilection for snuff it was decided to present him with as much of it as the sum collected would purchase. The special brand he favoured having been ascertained from the packets in his cubicle, we proceeded to the tobacconist with whom we were told he traded, and duly ordered the supply. On its arrival we found that the parcel, instead of being addressed as directed, had been left, with the invoice, at the doctor's, and to our surprise, we three, on being summoned to the doctor, found him, his son Tom, and Mr. Koenig together.

It appeared that Tom had been cognisant of the transaction from its commencement, one of the boys in our room having doubtless kept him informed. We were closely questioned by the doctor regarding the whole of the circumstances, with the result (doubtless an entirely satisfactory one to our embryonic curate) that the snuff was returned forthwith to the tobacconist and the money subscribed was confiscated to the uses of the cricket club; we three members of the committee were ordered to write out five hundred lines of "Virgil," while poor Koenig had to pack his box and leave the school immediately. This happened at the close of my brother's last quarter at the school, he having in 1849 reached the assigned limit of his schooldays. Arrangements had already been made for him to enter the nursery of Messrs. Turner (of Slough) as an apprentice to that business at the New Year, and as this was our first separation since my earliest infancy, the grief I felt at returning to the Academy without him will readily be understood. We were the very antithesis of each other in character. He was slow and reflective, I was quick and impulsive; and while his mind required a stimulus, mine needed a curb, and the deficiencies of each were thus mutually supplied. It was all the harder to part, seeing that our many years' intercourse had made us interdependent.

In reviewing the schoolboy period of my life, I am of opinion that, so far as the curriculum was concerned, it was efficient for preparing the pupils either for practical or professional life. In our own case, the practical side was followed, and the elementary knowledge of French and German proved of infinite value in my own future career. The harsh system, however, under which the teaching was given had, I am sure, a most humiliating influence on our characters, causing us to seek refuge in subterfuge and evasion. Punishment for the most trivial offence, by cane and writing of lines during play hours, was constantly inflicted, almost justifying the solution given by a boy when asked to give a definition of a lie—that it was " an abomination to the Lord, but a very present help in time of trouble."

The last year of my school life came to an abrupt end, owing to an accident which happened to me in the cricket field during the first game of the season. Being rather an adept at round-hand bowling, which was then the vogue, I took point duty, when, owing to my inattention, the ball struck me full in the side and broke two of my ribs, necessitating my removal home. The case became complicated. An operation had to be performed, the result being a long period of convalescence and a deep indent in my side, which still remains to remind me to pay strict and watchful attention to the immediate duties in hand.

The years of my boyhood had been epoch-making years; the Napoleonic wars were not yet forgotten, and nurse-girls still tried to calm recalcitrant children with the threat that " Bony " was coming and would have them.

From 1837, when Queen Victoria ascended the throne, to 1851, the year of the Great Exhibition, there ensued a long series of events, political and social, which left an indelible impress on the political, intellectual, and scientific history of our country, and gave to the reign of our great Queen the title of " The Victorian Era." Thus from 1837 to 1851, to illustrate my point, a few salient examples may be quoted:

1837.—The Queen ascended the throne.

1840.—Marriage of the Queen.

1841.—Opening of the first Ragged School in Field Lane.

1843.—O'Connell's agitation for the repeal of the Union in Ireland.

1844.—Bread riots in north of England, Ireland, and Scotland—the Chartist propaganda started.

1845.—The potato disease virulent; a Commission of Inquiry appointed.

1846.—Potato famine in Ireland: starvation spreading—the Anti-Corn Law agitation begun.

1847.—Starvation in Ireland increasing; March 24th fixed as a Day of Humiliation.

1848.—A year in which the spirit of revolution and unrest pervaded every continental country. Italy, Austria, Prussia, and Belgium were all under martial law, and in a state of semi-revolution; while in France the monarchy collapsed, and the King and royal family took refuge in England, which did not escape the general unrest. Great Chartist riots in Trafalgar Square, accompanied by loss of life. On April 10th, the monster petition in favour of the Five Points of the Charter presented to Parliament by the Chartists. Numbers of private persons sworn in, for the protection of life and property, as special constables. (My father, who was a member of the Barber-Surgeons Company, was enrolled and turned out on that occasion as one of the patrols.)

1849.—Cholera, which had been spasmodic, became epidemic, and the mortality increased to so alarming an extent that on Sunday, September 18th, special prayers for deliverance were offered in all the churches.

1850.—The "No Popery" Riots, arising from the Pope's action after the passing by the House of Commons of the Disabilities Bill, which gave religious freedom to all sections of the various churches. The Pope immediately issued a Bull appointing arbitrarily, and contrary to law, two Archbishops and twelve Bishops over England, and dividing England into Roman Catholic dioceses. This unfortunately led to the establishment here of monasteries and convents, whose members, expelled by their own countries, have found in ours a refuge and a privileged position.

1851.—On May 1st the Great Exhibition was opened by the Queen and Prince Albert, with much pomp and ceremony. A further notable event was the passing of the Ecclesiastical Titles Bill, a measure which was brought in to maintain the rights of the Crown against the Papal aggression. At a later period, however, this act was repealed, a piece of unnecessary legislation.

Appendix to Schooldays

It will be seen from many of my foregoing observations, that I am not sure that the present educational system is proving the success the large expenditure incurred would lead us to expect. On my return home after an absence of thirty-three years I must confess I did not find any material difference between the men and women of the present generation and those of the past one. From the discipline of the schools, rightly enforced, I expected to find superior refinement, but I heard in the street the same old expletives in an even more exaggerated form. I saw gangs of young, strong men standing at the corners of the streets; I saw no greater sobriety among the working-classes, and was forced to ask myself, " In what direction has our system failed, and in what lies the remedy ? "

It would be presumption on my part to dogmatize or lay down any fixed rules which would meet the case of every boy and girl, but there are certain principles, dictated by common sense, which, to my mind, might alter the situation.

First: feeling from my own personal experience that the strict military discipline of my schooldays had a good effect on the whole conduct of my life, I would enforce physical and manual education from a very early age in every school, and engage a retired army drill-serjeant to serve a series of schools.

Second : I would take the parent into my confidence, after the infant has passed his first childhood, with a view to ascertaining whether he had observed any bent in the child's character—my own opinion being that the characteristics of the future man are noticeable even at the very early age of five or six years.

Third: I am very strongly of opinion that education should be more practical, the classes smaller, and that attendance at evening continuation schools should be compulsory until eighteen years of age.

Fourth: in my opinion, children should be taught that skilled labour is far more essential to their own and the general welfare of the country than unskilled labour, and, given a certain amount of ambition in the individual, there is an incomparably greater chance of success in life.

Fifth: the training should follow the lines of the dominant industries of the localities where the schools are situated.

Sixth: very special attention should be given to the training of the farm labourer, the cultivating of the land being our greatest industry, and facilities should be given, by means of scholarships, for successful students to obtain for themselves a start in life on farms formed for cultivation on the intensive principle prevalent in France.

CHAPTER II

APPRENTICE DAYS

Apprenticed at Ipswich — Unhappy experiences — Evening studies — Charles Freeman — Typhus fever — Colchester — Brewery incident—Effects of lack of ambition in workmen—Close of apprenticeship—Enter Penn's—Examination for Naval Engineers—Narrow escape from death—Work on men-of-war—*Warrior*, the first ironclad—Narrow escape on *Duke of Wellington*—The *Mithridates*—Severe tempest in Bay of Biscay—Failure of superheating apparatus—Arrival at Odessa—Transferred to Russian Steam Navigation Company—Formation of Steam Navigation Company—Object of same—Repudiation of clause of Treaty of Paris *re* Black Sea.

ON convalescence I found that my father had made arrangements for me to become the indentured apprentice of Mr. W. of Ipswich, in order to learn the whole art and mystery of mechanical engineering, which was then in its infancy. Owing to there being at that time no labour-saving machines and no division of labour, the apprentices of that day were far more highly skilled than those of later times. For instance, on entering I was put into the blacksmith's shop, and from thence by gradation to the fitting, turnery, foundry, pattern-making, erecting-shop, and drawing-office.

As an indoor apprentice, I was to receive no wages, but pocket-money of one shilling per week was to be paid me at my father's expense, and during the whole time of my apprenticeship I received only one penny per hour for overtime. I little thought when I entered on my duties that I should be expected as indoor apprentice to black the boots of the family and do other menial work, but I found that I was to be so employed half an hour before the factory work commenced. Altogether I had a most miserable time and experience, not only on this account, against which I rebelled, but also because of the relationship between husband and wife, which was of a most distressing character. I admit that the husband, who was naturally of a very cynical disposition, was often exasperating, but the wife was a veritable virago, who expended the vials of her wrath on my devoted head.

My life at that period would have been unbearable had it not been for the affection shown me by the members of a family whose love I have retained throughout my life, and whose ready sympathy and advice was always a solace in my troubles. The father of the family, through whose influence I had come to Ipswich, had been a schoolfellow of my own father, since which time constant correspondence and intercourse had sealed their friendship and had also incited his dear wife to take me, a friendless lad, to their hearts, and almost incorporate me as one of their family. With them I regularly spent every Sunday, and was invited to be present at every family or social gathering. It is no wonder, therefore, that they became enshrined in my heart as few others have been, and their beneficent influence in my life was a great consolation in the trials of my otherwise miserable surroundings. My working hours in the shops were from six to six, after which I betook myself to the Mechanics' Institute, where, under a well-known and highly respected teacher, Dr. Christian, I studied to perfect myself in the French and German languages, which subsequently became indispensable to me.

About that time, there came to the town a lecturer, the representative of the Anti-Slavery Society, who had upon the platform a young man named "Charles," a runaway slave, with an unprecedented natural talent for mathematics. The lecturer was taken ill, and died leaving poor Charles stranded, but his case was taken up by influential men in the town; sufficient work was found to keep him, and he supplemented this by holding an evening class of mathematics for young men. This class I joined, and I can say with truth, that under his tuition I made more progress than during the whole of my schooldays. Charles had no surname, and therefore received from his protectors that of Freeman ; his subsequent career was cut short by sickness, culminating in consumption. Sir George Williams, the founder of the Young Men's Christian Association, became interested in him, and took him to London in his employ, where he died.

Of course with every successive year my services were becoming more valuable to my master. The original bad feeling which had existed between us, on account of my refusal to do menial service, became a thing of the past, when I was stricken down with typhus fever of the most virulent type and for days hung between life and death. The doctor who attended me considered the case so critical that he advised that my uncle, Dr. Purvis, should be summoned from London in consultation. When he arrived I was unconscious, and he took back so unfavourable a report that my mother immediately came down, finding on her arrival that on that very day the crisis had passed favourably. The nurse who had attended me took the disease and died, and had the family not been removed temporarily, others might have taken it also.

This illness brought about a great change in my circumstances. My master one day informed me that, as my room was required, he had decided to board me out, and that he had made arrangements accordingly. To this I had not the slightest objection, and in fact rejoiced at the announcement. The lodging provided for me was with a widow, who, besides two other boarders, had an old sea captain living in the house. I had to share my room with a workman, whom I found to be a very intelligent man, a great politician and an exponent, in his nightly visits to the public-house parlour, of the Five Points of the Charter. He never failed to return soon enough to give the captain a game of cribbage before retiring for the night, which allowed me longer time for my studies at the Institute. One thing, however, at this time marred my life's enjoyment, and it arose from the fact that my master only allowed my landlady nine shillings a week for my board and lodging, an amount to my mind quite inadequate to pay for the upkeep of a growing lad. I thus felt that I was sponging upon her resources, which I knew to be meagre.

In the works we had for a long time been engaged on machinery for a brewery in Colchester, consisting of engine, boiler, mash tun, and all other apparatus and accessories. With three others I was told off to erect it, and was forced to solve the problem how to make both ends meet on an income of nine shillings per week with one shilling extra for pocket-money. The matter was all the more complicated because my landlady wanted two shillings weekly to keep my room, but ultimately consented to accept eighteenpence, thus leaving me the sum of eight and sixpence for board and lodging in Colchester. As there were four of us, we took a lodging in a large loft over a coach-painter's shop, and the smell of the paint and varnish which came up through the half-inch interstices of the floor clung to me afterwards for months. For this accommodation we paid altogether six shillings per week, which left me seven shillings for my board, or one shilling per day.

We each had a corner of our loft, and lay on mattresses without bedsteads, owing to the roof sloping upwards abruptly two feet from the floor. The problem of living on one shilling a day I not only solved, but had sixpence over wherewith to buy a *Chambers's Journal* at the end of each month.

It was at this time the custom of the trade to pay the workman a shilling a day outing money, but during the whole of my apprenticeship this was withheld. I am quite aware that there may be many who are reading this who will declare that they could have lived on less than this, but I do not think that, even amongst the strictest adherents to the simple life, there are many who would care to prolong the experience over any lengthy period.

On a recent visit to the town after an interval of close upon sixty years, I have been greatly impressed with the improvements that have been carried out during that period. Remembering as I do the old-fashioned town of the past, with its narrow and squalid streets, it seemed to me as if the " Spirit of Progress " had found a resting-place there, and under its ægis the past linked with the present had during my absence almost transformed the town. The old castle (sadly neglected, as I remember it) now forms the entry to a noble park, and its museum is rich in the treasures of the antiquities of the district. Knowing the landmarks of the neighbourhood in which the brewery where I had worked was situated, I had no difficulty in locating the position, as it was in close proximity to the Abbey Gate. I found, however, that the spot was occupied by a clothing factory, and on making inquiry discovered that the old brewery of my time had been merged into a large concern of the same character on the other side of the river.

On the completion of our work in the brewery, I returned to Ipswich to resume my duties in the factory, but there is one episode which occurred when I had reached nineteen years of age which causes me to look back upon it with very mingled feelings. I believe that I may say truly that, under the most adverse circumstances, I had fulfilled the duties of my apprenticeship to the best of my ability, so much so, that having to transform the machinery in another brewery in a country village, I was put in charge of the work, with five men under me. This job was at a distance of three miles from the railway station, and the only lodging to be had was in the public-house belonging to the brewery. Being only nineteen years of age and an apprentice, my authority over the men was slight, and I found the greatest difficulty in keeping them to their working hours, so that it was not progressing as it should have been.

One day when I was in the bar of the house, begging the men (who as usual had extended their meal-time) to return to their work, the door opened and my master entered, and immediately peremptorily ordered me into the brewery. I stood at the mash tun as he came in, when he swore at me, saying that I was drinking with the men, and finished by ordering me to go home and not let him see me any more. Thereupon I returned to Ipswich, packed up my belongings and went home; but within three days he wrote my father to send me back to fulfil the obligations of my indenture, and, after an acknowledgment of hastiness of temper on both sides, I returned, receiving most kindly greeting from all my fellow-workmen, especially from those who had been the cause of the trouble. I felt most deeply the accusation of drinking with the men, seeing that I was almost, if not quite, a total abstainer.

I have often been greatly surprised to meet, during my working days, men of good education and with almost every quality to make for themselves a successful career, but who, for want of ambition, have allowed themselves to fall into a groove and be content with the weekly pittance of an ordinary workman. As an example, I may mention the case of a young man named Reginald Borrowdale, who worked year after year at the next vice to myself in the fitting-shop. He was the son of a clergyman, and although a good workman, with great abilities, was willing to work for a weekly wage of twenty-eight shillings. I felt a great interest in him, tried my best to arouse in him some ambition; but all in vain, for when my apprenticeship ceased I left him still in his groove.

Young man, you who may be reading this and just starting in life, take my well-considered advice and avoid falling into a groove, till the mind becomes warped, energy stagnates, and you are devoid of all initiative; as year follows year you settle down into the state of a monotonous drudge, with your views of life circumscribed to the narrowest point. Take **my** earnest advice, be not tempted by a black coat; the humblest skilled mechanic having ambition and initiative has the world for his workshop and independence for his crown. The greatest mistake made by the working-class Trade Unions has been, to my mind, circumscribing the indenture system, under the mistaken notion that it gave rise to competition which lowered wages. This, however, has not that effect. The workman, instead of being competent in all branches, has become a specialist in one only, and the employer has gained considerably through this division of labour, whilst the abolition of the indenture has greatly benefited free labour and given rise to more serious competition among those who have risen from the ranks.

The finish of my apprenticeship coincided with the close of the Crimean War, and through the interests of Mr. Wigzall, the manager of the great engineering works of John Penn & Son of Greenwich, I obtained work there, commencing as an improver at twenty-four shillings per week. It was the proudest day of my life when I poured my first week's wages into my mother's lap. At that time, having only received a shilling a week pocket-money and a penny an hour overtime, my first week's wages loomed large in my estimation.

Penn's

Shortly after starting in the erecting-shop, the foreman, Mr. Stone, sent for me to his box, and informed me that inspectors were to be sent down from London to test the efficiency of any of our young men who wished to enter the Navy as engineers. He said that fifteen names had already been inscribed, and he wished to know if I were willing to have my name added to the list. He spoke very kindly, stating that he had been watching my work, had no fault to find with me, and he had already given orders to raise my wages two shillings per week. The result of the examination was that I came out first on the list, principally, I think, because I had good marks for languages. However, owing to peace having been proclaimed we were not required, receiving instead a letter of thanks.

At that time Penn had in hand a large order from the Government for gun-boat engines, which had to be completed by a certain date. In the erecting-shop each engine was put in charge of a skilled operator, who had three men assistants allotted him. One of these engines was put into my charge, and I had a most marvellous escape from death. Along the sides of the erecting-shop there were travelling cranes for removing heavy parts from place to place. I had already got my bedding blocks fixed, and the engine frame, which weighed about four tons, suspended ready for lowering, when, owing to a flaw in the hook of the crane, it suddenly collapsed. Had it fallen in any other direction, or the blocks given way, I, being in the centre ready to guide it, must have been crushed. Upon these engines I worked for six days and three alternate nights each week until the work, which lasted some weeks, was completed.

I well recollect how, on my return home on the nights I had for rest, I was so worn out that I fell asleep before my supper could be placed before me. This was the last of my work in the erecting-shop, for I afterwards joined the staff of Mr. Parker, our outside foreman, and under him was engaged erecting the engines in several of our men-of-war, the *Conqueror*, the *Meanee* (the first frigate presented to the British Government by India), and the *Duke of Wellington*, all of which were of the wooden-wall type.

Just before leaving the erecting-shop, the men of the works, including myself, followed to the grave our foreman, Mr. Stone, who was drowned on his holidays whilst bathing. He was a man of great merit in his profession, and strictly impartial in his dealings with the men. Personally I may say that it was with a feeling of deep sadness that I followed him to his last resting-place.

In connection with the warship, the *Duke of Wellington*, which had been cut in two and lengthened to take the engines, I had another escape from death. The vessel was in Sheerness dockyard, and was placed alongside the dockyard wall for the screw propeller in its frame to be lowered down the screw well. The crane being posted, and my duty being that of signalman acting under Mr. Parker's instructions, by flags, the order was given to the driver of the large crane on the dock side to commence lifting. I was stationed on the poop, holding the flags which gave the signals for lowering or raising to the foreman of the crane. The screw, in its frame, was gradually raised and swung over the ship, and when the workmen had just entered it into the well, the brake on the crane snapped, and the screw crashed from the top to the bottom, making fire fly owing to the friction of the chains. On the release of the brake power the main cog-wheel was wrenched from its boss, and a piece of the wheel, weighing about a hundredweight, flew apart and embedded itself in the building near the Admiral's house. Another piece of about the same weight fell within a foot of me and embedded itself in the deck. The frightened workmen on the poop immediately jumped to the main deck, two of them having each a leg broken and several others sustaining contusions. I think it was only Mr. Parker and myself who remained uninjured.

The last vessel I worked on was at the Plymouth Keyham Dockyard, this being the *Warrior*, the first engined ironclad. To me this always remains a pleasant memory, owing to the friendly relations between Mr. Parker and myself. Distinguished visitors were frequent, and on one occasion we received notice from the Admiralty that the ship would be visited on a certain day by the Prince Regent of Prussia (afterwards the Emperor William I) together with his son Frederick, who had come over for his marriage with our Princess Royal, and I had the honour of accompanying him with the foreman over the vessel.

At this time I was often employed on boats for the speed trials of their engines, both round the Eddystone and on the measured mile. The last vessel upon which I was engaged was one named the *Mithridates*, which was built for the Russian Government in Samuda's Yard. It was upon this vessel I was destined to make my first acquaintance with Russia, having been specially appointed from Penn's Works to accompany it as a supernumerary engineer, in order to watch and report upon the new apparatus for super-heating the steam by the smoke-box gases. These gave, however, most deplorable results. While working on this boat fixing the engines, preparatory to starting for Odessa, it was found that various parts were required for completing the work; these Mr. Penn, who was on board, sent me to the City to obtain. On my return I had to report that I was unsuccessful, as the factory was closed, owing to its being one of the great Jewish holidays. I was about to speak in an uncomplimentary manner of the Jewish firm, when Mr. Penn, glancing at Samuda, who was a Jew, stopped me by putting his foot on mine.

The boat was a paddle steamer built for river work. It was flat bottomed, but too lightly ballasted for the time of year. It had every possible convenience for passengers, besides being lavishly decorated; and as it was only intended to take the ship to Odessa to deliver it to the Company, the crew was a scratch one. The captain was an old pensioned commander of the Royal Navy; the chief engineer, a Mr. Scott, and the other officers and men were only engaged for the voyage. Almost immediately after starting, and even before we entered the Bay of Biscay, the most severe tempest I have ever experienced, during my many passages across the Bay, broke over the vessel, and for at least three days we were in the gravest peril of being engulfed. The vessel was like a cockle shell; the ocean waves dashed over her from stem to stern, clearing before them everything not lashed. The whole ship's company, from the captain downwards, was sick, and as for myself, perhaps the less said the better. To turn the vessel was impossible, for had we fallen into a trough of the sea the vessel was doomed, so that we had to face the storm head-on. About the fourth day the sea began to moderate, and we arrived safely at Gibraltar without any great dilapidations. That which added greatly to the danger of this passage was that the apparatus with which I was more specially concerned, viz. the super-heater, was a failure, and on arrival at the Rock it had to be removed and the engines refitted.

For the purpose of explaining to the non-technical reader the economic results to be obtained by super-heating, it may be stated that if it could be sufficiently introduced, it would in all cases make for great economy in coal and water. It will be readily understood that steam under any pressure when leaving a boiler is saturated with moisture, but should it be subjected to a further heating of say, 200–250 degrees Fahrenheit, the greater part of this moisture would form a larger volume of steam with a decreased volume of water. In our case, had we been able to stop the engines in mid-ocean, we might have detached the apparatus, but the combined forces of wind and waves rendered such action impossible. Both Mr. Scott and myself were constantly at work lubricating the working parts, but it was an utter failure and we were powerless to remedy it. It was only by constant drenching with oil and cooling the trunnions with water that we were able to reach port. Many a time man lives a lifetime in an hour, and I am confident not one on board ever forgot that passage through the Bay.

The main cause of the failure arose from the fact that super-heating the steam heated it to such an extent that the oil dried up and was burned to a leathery skin. No lubrication could stand it, and on opening up the slides we found their faces, instead of being steam-tight, deeply grooved. On telegraphing to the factory, the repairs were left to our discretion, and it took us about eight days' hard work before we could restart. This was my first visit to the Rock, and it interested me greatly, standing as it does, like an inverted ship, abruptly rising from the sea to a height of 1,439 feet. In spite of sieges and bombardments, since 1704 it has remained in the possession of the English. It took them four years' siege to gain it, but it was well worth the cost, seeing that this pillar of " Hercules " stands a safe guardian station of our fleet and affords shelter for the biggest vessels in its new harbour.

On leaving we steamed for Malta, and during the voyage, owing to an accident, I nearly lost my left hand in the machinery. Again we had to stop some days to refit the engines before we could proceed. Nothing further of any moment occurred until our arrival at Odessa, which had been eagerly expected, as we were more than a fortnight over our time. It would appear that the vessel had to be given over to the authorities after trial, and, owing to the fore-mentioned accidents, a thorough examination showed a very considerable amount of work was necessary before they would accept it. In the meantime the scratch crew, captain, officers, and men returned home overland, except Scott and myself, who remained to carry out the work. This was eventually accomplished to the satisfaction of the authorities, and, after trial trips round the coast of the Black Sea and up the River Dnieper, the vessel was taken over, and I was invited to become its chief engineer. Mr. Scott remained also in the service of the Company, and was transferred to a larger vessel.

When I received notice that the Company had taken over the vessel, I telegraphed to Mr. Penn for instructions, and he replied, "Study your own interests in the matter, as work in England is very slack, and we are discharging hands." Under these circumstances, I thought my best policy was to accept the offer made to remain in the service of the Company, as engineer on the *Mithridates*.

The Russian Steam Navigation Company, which is

CRIMEA. GENERAL VIEW.

still existing, was formed immediately after the Crimean War, having for its object the training and employment of the officers and sailors that had formed the crews of the Russian warships sunk at the mouth of the harbour of Sebastopol for its defence. According to the Treaty of Paris, the Russians were not permitted to have a fleet in the Black Sea, but from a very early date they entertained the idea of abrogating that clause of the treaty. This they carried out at the close of the Franco-German War by formal notice of repudiation, which was confirmed by the Powers on March 13th, 1871.

Although nominally a company with a large share-capital, its existence depended almost entirely (during many years after its inception) on a subsidy from the Government of so liberal a character that it was commonly reported that the vessels could sail backwards and forwards to and from the various ports, and still pay a reasonable dividend to the shareholders. The subsidy, however, was gradually diminished as the vessels became self-supporting. During my connection with the Company, an Admiral of the Russian fleet was chairman, he being a talented and courteous gentleman.

CHAPTER III

ODESSA AND SEBASTOPOL

Refit of vessel—Odessa and its history—Mr. Melville—Purchase of socks—Learning Russian—Introduction to Mr. Wagner—State of Odessa streets—Easter Sunday festival—My first visit to Sebastopol—Journey of Grand Duke Constantine—Description of Sebastopol Harbour—Colonel Gowen—Visits to battlefields—Accident on Plains of Inkerman—The cemetery and Balaclava.

As I have already said, it was necessary upon our arrival at Odessa to thoroughly refit the vessel, and Scott and myself were placed in charge of the repairs. The boat was brought into the Quarantine Harbour close to the Company's workshops, and on examination we found the machinery in such a state of dilapidation that, owing to the absence both of skilled labour and the necessary machines, it took us two months to complete the repairs. During that time I had every opportunity to make myself acquainted with the city and its environs.

Odessa, as viewed from the sea, is of imposing appearance, being built on a terrace 150 feet above sea level, and connected with the harbour by a flight of 200 granite steps. Originally a fishing village, it had in the year 1795 only 2,250 inhabitants, whereas to-day it has over 630,000, one-third of whom are Jews, and about 30,000 are foreigners of all nationalities. It is now the chief centre for the export of all agricultural produce of the southern provinces of the Empire, the value of its exports in 1912 amounted to £8,000,000, and among the cities of the Empire it ranks fourth. Besieged and taken from the Turks in 1789 by the French Captain de Ribas, whose name is perpetuated in that of one of its principal streets, it was finally ceded to Russia in 1794, and in 1803 became the chief town of a new district under Armand, Duc de Richelieu. The monument of this governor surmounts the granite steps above-mentioned on the Nikolai Boulevard, which forms the main promenade of the city. Its cathedral, which can hold 5,000 worshippers, was founded in 1795. All the main buildings are constructed of soft shell lime-stone, a peculiarity in this connection being that all shaping of the stone was done with the axe. The underground quarries, from which this material was derived in former times, now form extensive catacombs under part of the town.

During this time I made the acquaintance of Mr. Melville, a very remarkable Scot, tall and gaunt in his appearance, and truly British in thought and feeling. He was the Agent for the British and Foreign Bible Society, and had remained in Odessa throughout the Crimean War, during the whole of which time he had devoted himself entirely to the work of distributing the Scriptures among the Russian soldiers. It was through my attending the English church that I owed my introduction to him by the clergyman, and we soon became on a very friendly footing. I related to him one day the dilemma in which I had found myself, through not being able to speak the Russian language. The adventure was as follows:

Not having been provided with underclothing sufficiently warm for spending the whole winter in Russia, I needed certain garments, especially socks; and as advised, proceeded to the Palais Royal, being assured that everything wanted could be found there. But to get the goods was not so easy. The windows of the shops in this quadrangle seemed entirely devoted to goods for ladies' wear, but at last I discovered one for men's wear, with socks in the window.

Entering and removing my cap (as is usual in Russia when entering a shop), and at that time not being acquainted with the Russian language, I asked the young damsel in both French and German to show me the goods I required, but she could not understand me. My opinion was that, as it was the dinner hour, they had left her as the *locum tenens*, it not being possible, I thought, that a shop especially devoted to these commodities should lack a stock of them.

Seeing therefore the boxes on the shelves with the toes hanging out, I pointed to them, and she soon littered the whole of the counter with boxes; but in vain—all were cotton goods. Noticing that, like myself, the girl was evidently confused, a happy inspiration occurred to me, which cleared the situation, for putting my foot upon the counter I showed her my cotton sock, at the same time, with a laugh, uttering the bleat of a sheep, "Ba-a, ba-a," which immediately brought me the goods I required.

The tale spread into the papers, and on one occasion it was told me as the exploit of a mad Englishman. As I myself was the hero, I must leave my readers to judge whether the adjective applied was the correct one. This greatly amused my friend, who at once offered to teach me Russian, which offer I gratefully accepted.

In accordance with this arrangement I had to be at his lodging three times weekly, precisely at six o'clock a.m., when the lesson lasted exactly one hour, following which the samovar was brought in and he made tea. In this case, as in all his actions, precision was the key-note. The tea put into the pot each day seemed the same in quantity to a single grain, and the brew both in quality and quantity was uniformly correct. The rising foam on the tumbler was carefully skimmed and deposited in the slop-basin; the lemon cut exactly the right thickness, and the sugar added to a specified lump; then, after the required amber colour had been duly attained, the tea was handed over to me with an urbane dignity and grace that completed this work of perfection.

Through the influence of this good man I became acquainted with most of the members of the British

Colony, all of whom held him in the very highest respect. More especially I was presented to his great friend Mr. Wagner, who was the wealthy proprietor of the old Lyceum Buildings, containing a large number of shops, in addition to his own stores, the English Magazine and church. Mr. Wagner was a generous coadjutor with Mr. Melville in every good work, and I may here mention that the two friends were deeply interested in the Mennonite section of the German Colonies. It was at Mr. Melville's instigation that I became filled with enthusiasm at the idea of going into the interior to investigate the situation, which on its fruition was destined to effect a complete economic transformation in the whole of the farming industry in South Russia.

At the time of my arrival in Odessa and for many a subsequent year, it may rightly have been termed, during the spring and autumn rains, a veritable Augean mud-stable. Many of its streets were simply impassable for foot passengers, and I have often paid a droshky-man from fourpence to sixpence just to put me across the road. Any one attempting to cross in goloshes invariably stuck, and was glad to leave them in the mud and pass over only in his boots. It is related on good authority that a Cossack and his horse had been lost in the mud, and even so late as 1858 a woman sank in it and was suffocated. The Countess Kapnist also tells me that she drove with a friend from Astafia over the spot where a Jew, with his horse and cart, had sunk in the mud only two weeks previously. This state of things proved almost insufferable for the inhabitants; the death-rate was enormous, and it could not be otherwise: the miasmatic vapours arising from the mud mixed with manure and churned in the roads made family life, more especially for the young, almost impossible. Odessa bore the reputation of being an "ink-bottle" one half the year, and a "sand-duster" the other. The significance of this latter title arises from the fact that, in common with most Eastern nations, blotting paper is not used, the writing being dried by dusting with sand, often coloured.

Since George Furness, however, who was very badly treated by the Town Council, commenced the work of paving Odessa, the old conditions have passed away, and on my last visit I was greatly impressed with the creditable condition of the streets.

In accordance with the custom in the Eastern Church on the eve of its greatest festival, Easter Sunday, food of all kinds is brought into the churches to be blessed; the day is passed in fasting till midnight, but immediately after the cry is raised " Christ is risen." Congratulations are interchanged on every side, the answer being given " Truly Christ is risen," and kissing becomes general. I would, however, advise any young man, who may feel inclined to test his right to a kiss at Easter-tide from any maiden whom he may meet, to take warning from my own example. For coming down the High Street with two friends on my first Easter night, I personally tried it, and received instead of the conventional kiss a smart slap in the face, to the intense delight of my two companions. Having, however, found later in a general way that the Russian girl, like her sister of other nations, is not always adverse to this custom, I have come to the conclusion that in this special instance the young woman was either a heretic or belonged to the order of flagellants. It may be taken, therefore, as a general rule that in all countries " kissing goes by favour."

Sebastopol

My first visit to Sebastopol (the formidable fortress which was the main object of attack during the Crimean War) took place in 1858, scarcely two years after the treaty of peace which had been signed on March 30th, 1856. The fall of the fortress had been virtually assured in September 1855, when the Russians abandoned the south side of the town, crossing over to the north. It was with no small interest that I had looked forward to my visit, consecrated as the place was to the memory of 45,000 of our gallant countrymen who, either as killed or wounded, fell victims in that war.

Our boat, the *Mithridates,* which was on its first journey, after having been taken over by the Company, had been appointed to carry the Grand Duke Constantine and his suite from Odessa to inspect the naval station, he being Lord High Admiral of Russia at the time. Before leaving the ship, his aide-de-camp presented me with a small case containing a scarf-pin, it being the usual custom for members of the Imperial family to give such tokens of satisfaction to the chief officers of the boats on which they travelled. The weather was very stormy, even in the harbour, and when descending the companion ladder to get into the boat, which was rising and falling with the waves, my watch-chain caught in the rail and the case flew out of my waistcoat pocket.

The harbour is of great extent, capable of accommodating the largest European fleets. It is well sheltered by a range of high hills a few miles distant to the north, the Yaila Dagh, of which the Tchatuir Dagh (in Tartar, " the tent ") is the highest summit. The towns of Theodosia, Yalta, etc., are on the south coast under its protecting screen and form the Riviera of the Russian Empire.

The harbour has a narrow entry, less than 3,000 feet wide, well guarded by two strong forts, and at the time of my visit was still blocked by the sinking of the Russian naval fleets across it for protective purposes, the masts of which were still standing out of the water. Colonel Gowen, representing an American company, which had undertaken to clear away the obstructing vessels, was engaged in this work, assisted by a number of trained divers. It was commonly known, however, that the contract did not prove a very great financial success.

I have had opportunities, on the various occasions

when I have visited Sebastopol, to note the gradual restoration which was being effected. It took, however, several years before the results of the bombardment were even partially obliterated. The population of the place, which before the war had numbered 40,000, had been reduced to a few hundreds, living in temporary shelters built of materials obtained from the ruins due to the bombardment. Only fourteen houses had remained intact. The barracks, a very extended and prominent building on the north side of the harbour, were entirely roofless, and the great docks, (one of which contained a vessel) long remained as they were, blown up by the Allies on leaving.

Viewed from the narrower standpoint of our national interest, there is little doubt that on the whole the Crimean War was a mistake. The Russians indeed hold that the English, who formed the smaller portion of the allied forces, were actually beaten, and that the honours of the war were gained by the French. To themselves, however, it was the commencement of a new era of freedom and progress. The boom of the Allies' cannon awakened Russia from her long sleep of apathetic indolence, and the British and French shot burst asunder the shackles of thirty millions of serfs. From this date commenced the long series of reforms on Western lines, which will always be the crowning glory of the reign of Alexander II, surnamed the Liberator.

In visiting the battlefield, which extended from Kamisch Bay (the French camp with St. George's Monastery as their head-quarters) to the small gulf of Balaclava (celebrated as the head-quarters of the English Army and of the ever-memorable charge of the Light Brigade), and thence to Inkerman, an excellent bird's-eye view is obtained of the whole scene of the operations. A non-military visitor cannot but ask himself the question why the complex siege of Sebastopol was planned without closing the narrow isthmus of Perekop, three miles broad, through which Russia obtained all her supplies. Also why it was that thousands of British lives were lost attempting to storm the Redan, an earthwork thrown up in a few days by the Russians, whereas the Malakoff was the key to the whole position, and once captured could have enfiladed the whole of the two Redans lying on either side.

An incident occurred when visiting the heights of Inkerman with the captain of our vessel, for on going up we met a party of men bearing the bodies of two British sailors. It appeared they had gone up to visit the battlefield, over which were scattered large numbers of shot and shell, some of the latter being still alive. Apparently one of them must have knocked his pipe on a fuse, which, exploding the shell, led to the death of himself and his companion. These proved to be sailors from a vessel that was loading bones for the British market, a proceeding which, when it became known, caused a painful sensation at home, although attempts were made to prove that they were bones of horses, oxen, etc., and not of human origin.

The scene of the British occupation was clearly marked by the large number of bottles forming mounds, which, however, on a later occasion I found had been turfed over, and probably, like the tumuli at Kertch, will bear evidence to future generations of a past foreign occupation. These immense heaps spoke volumes to my mind of my native country. A place that will undoubtedly be visited by every Briton coming to this land is the English cemetery, the last resting-place of thousands of our bravest and our best. To me it brought sadness to see the deplorable condition that it was in, when compared with those of the Russian and the French. Overgrown with grass and weeds, with but few memorial stones to mark the resting-place of departed heroes, it was a scene arousing deep pathos, knowing that there was scarcely a home throughout our island that had not to mourn the loss of some near and dear to them. Amongst the few memorials I found one with the name of Hedley Vicars, whose life-story by Miss Marsh was widely read throughout the British Isles. It is gratifying to know that deep interest was aroused in England on this scene of desolation being made known, and, a Consul being appointed at Sebastopol, the cemetery was restored, and a yearly subsidy given for it to be kept in order.

CHAPTER IV

FURTHER SEA EXPERIENCES

Transfer to *Gounib*—Meaning of the name—Transport of pilgrims to Jerusalem and Mecca—Exciting incident at sea—Fight between pilgrims—Storm at Jaffa—Imminent destruction of ship—Algiers and Lisbon—Discharge cargo at Waterford—Arrival at Odessa—Appointed superintendent of Company's repairing shops—Supersession and disagreement with a Colonel—Interview with Admiral—Offer of resignation refused—Unpleasant position and final resignation—Voyage to Constantinople in s.s. *Alexander II*—Storm in Black Sea—Meeting Mr. Graham in Constantinople—Decision to introduce steam thrashers and reaping machines into Russia.

ON the *Mithridates* I made voyages also to Trebizond, Salonica, and Kherson, on my return finding that I had been transferred to the *Gounib*. The name given to the boat, *Gounib*, was derived from the rock-fastness which was the scene of the final stand made by the great Circassian leader, Schamyl, the grim old warrior who held the Russians at bay for many years. Owing to his brilliant defence, he gained and retained the respect of his captors, who endowed him with a liberal allowance for the remainder of his life. On taking up my post, I was surprised to see, when passing through the saloon, that there had been fixed to the mast, gun-racks provided with weapons, and all the men on board were told off in squads, including myself and my stokers. The reason for our being placed under military discipline was as follows :

The vessel had been chartered for the purpose of taking pilgrims from Odessa and Constantinople to Jaffa and Alexandria. Of these, half were Russians bound for Jerusalem (mostly of apparently the very lowest class), who were taken on board in Odessa, and on arrival in Constantinople the remainder of our passengers came on board, being Mohammedans on the road to Mecca. These latter were all armed (more or less) with yataghans, daggers, or pistols, whilst the Christians of the Greek Church were unarmed. The deadly hatred existing between these two religious bodies had been aggravated by the recent Crimean War, and this, combined with the experience on previous voyages, necessitated precautionary measures being taken, and, as the sequel proved, very necessary.

The pilgrims were placed in the hold of the vessel, with only a low match-board partition dividing those of the Greek Church from the Mohammedans. One night, however, the ship's bell sounded the tocsin. and all who could be spared hastened to their posts Arms were distributed, the hold was surrounded, and the storming party quickly descended. The din was deafening. The partition had been destroyed, and we were just in time to prevent an onslaught by the Turks upon the Russians. We soon separated them, and one by one the Turks had to ascend to the deck and deposit their arms with the purser, the riot thus being quelled.

Arriving at Jaffa, the Russian contingent went on shore and we anchored in the Bay, intending to take coal on board and blow out our boilers, which had become incrusted with salt. The morning was lovely, and as we intended staying for three days, plans were made by some of the officers to visit Jerusalem, and we all went to our breakfast in the saloon. As we sat chatting, the noise of a mighty wind arose, and rushing on deck we were enveloped in a sea of spray, a fearful tornado having suddenly come upon us, lifting the sea bodily as it were into an immense wave. This striking our vessel heeled it over, snapped the chain cable from the anchor and drove us out to sea. What saved the vessel from destruction was, that I deferred blowing out the boilers until after the meal-time, and we had just steam enough by the aid of the engines to round the rocks which formed the Bay. So great was the terror amongst the stokers that, with only a few exceptions, I could not get them to serve the fires, and I was obliged to strip and with the aid of three or four others do the stoking.

The men were lying all over the place terror-stricken, crossing and prostrating themselves, and calling upon their saints to save them. Afterwards it appeared that the Consul at Jaffa, not seeing the vessel after the storm had passed, had telegraphed to Lloyd's in London the total loss of the *Gounib* with all hands. My father saw the account in the papers in London, but fortunately did not tell my mother. He saw the announcement of our arrival at Alexandria, however, which relieved his anxiety.

On a second voyage, we loaded a cargo of maize bound for Waterford, the captain being a man of high position in the Navy and a perfect gentleman, both in bearing and conduct to the men. The sailing master, and the real but not the nominal captain of the boat, was a Slavonian, an old salt who spoke English fluently, and had sailed all seas. We arrived at Malta in fairly good time, but on leaving met with very heavy seas which caused the cargo to shift and our vessel to heel. This delayed the boat considerably, so that we had to make for Algiers to take in coal and refit. In order to carry out the work, we had to remain five days, and those of the officers on board who were not required on service, including myself, took the opportunity of visiting Constantine. Algiers had not long been taken over by the French, and an English company was constructing large store-houses along the quay.

Leaving this port, we made for our destination, but again met with a very heavy ground-swell, obliging us to steam up the Tagus to Oporto, where we were further delayed three days. It will be seen by this account that bulk-heads had not yet been made compulsory in grain boats, and the lives of sailors in such vessels were often subject to exceedingly great risks. Before we got to Algiers, the boat had gathered such a list, that in order to cross from one side to another we had to cling to the upper side and watch our opportunity to cross as the vessel came over. After discharging the cargo, we went to London for orders, and taking in ballast, after a slight refit, returned to Odessa, when I found that I had been transferred to the superintendent's office in the repairing-shop.

The director was a newly appointed military engineer colonel, who knew nothing about naval machinery, and had never been a voyage. He was really of no use whatever in the matter of directing, but had the power to order the men about at his will. The workmen, who had had considerable experience with me during the repairs to the *Mithridates*, were always ready to assist me, but of course could not resist superior authority. This condition of affairs interfered greatly with the course of business, and sooner or later it was evident it must come to an end; and this it did, as usually happens under such circumstances, abruptly.

The colonel, on taking up his duties, had given orders for various pieces of furniture to be made in the shops, which were put down in the books against various ships, whereas the goods had been delivered at his own house. I felt exceedingly worried that this state of affairs should go on, because it was not only against common honesty, but when discovered I might myself be accused of being an accessory to the deed. I therefore kept, for future use, a private account of the delivery of all goods to his house, at the same time being fully determined that a stop should be put to it.

One Friday morning a thrust-block to the engine of the mail boat (which was to start at four o'clock that afternoon with the mails, and could not be delayed for a single minute) was brought in for repairs, with scarcely time enough to carry out the work. I put two men at once on the job, and on going to lunch the work was so far advanced that I could leave it for a short time, giving them strict orders not to drop tools until my return. Judge of my surprise when on coming

IN RUSSIA 47

back I found that the colonel had taken the men from this important and indispensable work, and put them on the construction of a paper-weight for his own use! Thereupon I took a hammer from the bench, smashed the thing into a hundred pieces, and sent a lad to fetch the colonel. However, there was not a moment to lose, and by strenuous effort we got the work done and fixed just in time.

The paper-weight in question was being formed from the electric cable which at that time had just been laid between England and America, and was the first of its kind. The shore-end section was thicker than the deep-sea cable, being subject to the friction of the rocks and shingle of the coast. For the purpose of making the paper-weight, use had been made of a marble slab which served as the base of the column, to which a short piece of the shore end was fixed: Upon the latter was a much longer one of the deep-sea section, both together forming a column on the slab.

On quitting the ship after seeing that the work was completed, I again sent for the colonel, and, pointing to the débris of the column, explained to him that I would not and could not put up with his interference any longer, and that I was resolved to see the admiral and ask him to accept my resignation. The colonel attempted to ride his high horse, but I told him his first duty, like mine, was the interest of the Company, and that I had been brought up under the deepest conviction that "honesty was the best policy," also, that as long as I had anything to do with Russia or anywhere else, this should be my leading principle. I thereupon sought an interview with the admiral, a fine old gentleman who spoke English almost without an accent. The interview was granted, and a time appointed for some days later.

During the interval I heard that the colonel had been summoned to the office. At the time appointed for the interview, I placed before the admiral the whole of the circumstances connected with the case, giving him a written statement; on leaving he cordially shook hands with me, and asked me to continue in the service. I never heard any result from the office, but shortly after the colonel was recalled to St. Petersburg.¹ I understood that my resignation was not accepted, and during the further time I remained no other chief was appointed.

It was at this time that a new era was dawning on Russia. Alexander II, surnamed, and rightly so, the "Liberator," had commenced his beneficent reign; and nepotism, which had for some years ruled over all appointments, was in a certain measure being replaced by efficiency, and privilege was becoming a less-dominant characteristic of appointments. In my own case, although I cannot clearly define the form of the solidarity of the various officials and commanders connected with the fleet, it became evident to me, from the many trivial complaints constantly arising, that there was a dead set against me, doubtless on account of my having exposed the colonel: I therefore, acting on the opinion of my advisers and friends, in due course resigned my appointment into other hands.

On leaving the Russian Steam Navigation Company, I almost immediately received an invitation from a very large firm of timber merchants, requesting me to go to Constantinople to inspect for them a large tug-boat named *Napoleon III*. They had been in treaty for this boat some time, intending to purchase it on a favourable report, for the purpose of towing the immense rafts of timber which during the spring descend the River Dnieper from the forest regions in the north. The agreement having been signed, I proceeded to the *Golden Horn*, accompanied by the captain that they had appointed, and after visiting the vessel we arranged for the vendors to have her dry-docked for thorough inspection. Following on our report, the vessel was purchased and thoroughly overhauled, the various necessary repairs occupying about six weeks.

When she was ballasted and provided with a scratch

¹ Now Petrograd.

RUSSIAN PEASANT.

crew, we made ready to sail. A long time previous to this I had been increasingly anxious as to the sobriety of our captain. On several occasions he had seemed to me to be subject to hallucinations and fits of depression, but I was not prepared for the events which ensued during our voyage to Odessa. On leaving the Bosphorus, we met with one of those sudden storms which so often arise in the Black Sea, and for a whole week we were being buffeted and tossed about by the waves, in perfect ignorance of our position, with a coal supply gradually diminishing; but worst of all, the captain was lying drunk in his cabin nearly the whole time. At last the men came to me and asked me to take charge of the vessel; but being ignorant of our position, and no sun appearing by which to take our bearings, we drifted on.

I had both the cabins and bunks searched for alcohol, and found in a locker a small barrelful, which I ordered to be carried up and thrown overboard. Thereupon he recovered more or less, and on the day after we sighted land, which he declared to be Odessa, but seeing a Turkish flag flying I knew it must be in Turkey. On arrival it turned out to be Kustendji, which we had reached with the greatest difficulty, after having exhausted every vestige of coal and also most of the wooden fittings from the deck. From this port, after taking in coal, etc., we followed the coast-line to Odessa, where we were received with acclamation by the owners. They had feared that the vessel had gone down in the severest storm experienced during that season, but they never knew the anxiety that I had undergone during that voyage.

In the course of my lengthened stay in Constantinople, superintending the repairs to the tug-boat, I stayed at the Pera Hotel, kept by a Greek named Spiro. This man had obtained a great notoriety during the Crimean War for his eccentricities. For instance, when dinner was announced, a procession of cooks and waiters marched round the table, headed by the host bearing the soup ladle, and, like Hobson's choice, you had no other selection of rooms except the one he decided to allot.

One day going up the long steps to the hotel, I heard my name called, and looking round, saw the figure of a man, wearing a red fez, gesticulating and running towards me. To my utter astonishment, he proved to be a fellow-apprentice of mine when at Ipswich, of the name of Graham, neither of us being aware of our common presence in Constantinople.

I learnt from him that he was very dissatisfied with the conditions under which he was working at the arsenal, his principal grievance being that the stipulated salary was not paid him, and he asked me if I could assist him to obtain a place in the Russian Steam Navigation Company. This I ultimately arranged for him temporarily.

In furtherance of my conversation with Messrs. Melville and Wagner respecting the introduction of labour-saving machines into the Mennonite colonies, I laid a scheme before them regarding the purchase of certain machines for reaping and thrashing, at the same time introducing Mr. Graham to them, as he desired to be associated with me in the enterprise. I gave them fully to understand that the money required was far beyond the means I had at my disposal, and asked them if they approved the plan how far they would be prepared to help. On this Mr. Wagner stated that he was willing to back the scheme, and would advance any sum that was necessary without any binding documents whatever. This was the commencement of the joint activities of Mr. Graham and myself in the southern provinces of Russia.

CHAPTER V

INTRODUCTION OF REAPING MACHINE INTO RUSSIA

Arrival at Berdiansk—Desiccation of Sea of Azov—Phenomenon illustrating drying of Red Sea before Moses—Shooting excursions—A narrow escape—Mr. Hahn—Meeting after many years—A wedding trip—Terrific storm and cloud burst—Mennonite worship—First visit to German colonies—Their origin—Settlement by Catherine II—Windmills of mediæval type—Great hospitality—" Bees "—Introduction of reaping machine—Mr. Dick—Opinion of village blacksmith—" The Grasshopper and the Locust "—Stampede of horses—Success of machine—Amazement of peasants—Desire to see demon in reaper—The Mennonites—Their origin—Main tenets—Opposition to military service—Comparison with Quakers and Plymouth Brethren—Emigration to America—Arrangement with General Todleben—Their present number—The Stundists—The unrighteousness of Mammon—Compulsory baptism.

ON arrival at Berdiansk with letters of introduction from Mr. Melville to the British and German Consuls respectively, Messrs. Cumberbatch and Jansen, I found that they had already been apprised of my coming, and had provided comfortable quarters for me. The town is situated on the Sea of Azov, a shallow sea lying in a saucer-like depression, said to be gradually drying up, and united with the Black Sea by the Straits of Kertch. This desiccation seems certain, as within my own experience vessels which in 1860 could be loaded at six miles from the shore, before my departure in 1890 were forced to load at a distance of sixteen miles. On its northern apex is situated the town of Taganrog, once a flourishing seaport and noted as the place where the Emperor Alexander I died. It is at the mouth of the River Don, one of the largest streams in Europe.

I have twice seen a curious phenomenon, illustrating

the waters of the Red Sea being held up for the passage of the Israelites. Under the continuous strong action of the south-west wind, the river is driven back for several miles, leaving the bed bare and exposed, with several vessels lying stranded on the mud. The whole district is noted for its hard wheat (the Arnaoutki), which is in great demand in Italy, France, and the south of Europe generally for the manufacture of macaroni. It is also used for strengthening the softer cereals.

While awaiting the arrival of our machines, I frequently accompanied Mr. Cumberbatch on his shooting excursions. On one occasion he had caused to be prepared for us cunningly devised pits covered with straw on the borders of some large lakes, which pits we had to enter at three o'clock in the morning of a cold autumn day, to await the rising of the migrating wild geese. The birds were there all right, but their scouts had seen us, and when they rose they were out of gunshot on the farther bank, so we drew blank. Returning, we met the proprietor of the land and lake, who told us that geese were not ducks, and invited us to come to his house the next morning, at the same time promising us some game.

Accordingly we arrived as appointed, when we found him equipped and ready to accompany us. On approaching the lake, he instructed us to place ourselves amongst a herd of cattle which was being slowly driven towards the birds. In this manner we arrived within good range, both my shots telling, and between us we bagged seven.

On another occasion, having been introduced to the steward of Count Orloff, I was invited to accompany Mr. Cumberbatch to a snipe shoot amongst the cane-brakes; this bird is a difficult one to shoot and requires a steady hand and quick eye. Mr. Hahn, the steward, rode on horseback to the proposed position, whilst I was seated on a spring cart with the Consul. Scarcely had we arrived, when a bird must have flown low, for a shot was fired, and the back part of my straw hat was shot through, without a single pellet touching my head. It was a marvellous escape, like so many I have had; but in God's providence I am still left to tell the tale, of which there is a sequel.

Some years afterwards I had been to Vienna, and returning to Russia by train entered a first-class compartment, and sitting opposite me was a white-haired old gentleman, with a ruddy face, who seemed strangely familiar to me. Like a flash it came upon me that it must be Hahn, so, determining to find out, I addressed him in German, excusing myself for intrusion, and asking him if I were correct in thinking his name was Hahn. He started momentarily, and then said, "Your face is remarkably familiar, and I have been wondering where I had seen you." Instead of telling him outright, I recalled the episode on the banks of the Ushan Lee, the name of the river. "My name is Hume." Then came tears into the old man's eyes, and getting up he threw his arms around my neck, gave me three kisses, and sat down overcome with emotion. He told me he had often recalled the incident when out shooting, and thanked God that I had so providentially escaped.

An incident which might have had a dramatic ending followed close on the above. I had been invited to a wedding which was to be celebrated at the homestead of a well-to-do family, living about forty miles away, this necessitating my riding to the place of meeting to attend the ceremony. By starting early I hoped to arrive in time for the afternoon coffee and meet the other guests prior to the wedding next day. The morning was fine, and the weather seemed settled fair; but on reaching a wide and steep ravine, black clouds came galloping up with all the portents of a storm. On they came with ever-increasing velocity, and, foreseeing danger from the cloud burst which in these parts always accompanies storms, I pressed my horse to cross before it began. We got to the bottom of the dip, when that terrible wind preceding the freshets began to blow, the lightning flashed around, and—the one and only time I have so heard it—the thunder seemed to roll along the ground. The horse turned tail and would not budge, so I hastily ungirthed him and took my clothes, together with the saddle and bridle, and rushed up the slope on to the ridge, only just in time to see and hear the rush of the water, which came down the valley in a furious torrent, carrying my horse away like a wisp before the wind.

Well, there I stood fifteen miles from any shelter or human being, wet to the skin, and I should think even a Mark Tapley would have felt some misgivings as to being jolly under such circumstances. What I decided was to go forward carrying with me my best clothes, soaked as they were, and to leave the saddle and bridle to their fate. My road lay along the crest of the ravine ridge, when, looking ahead, I descried a dark object evidently coming towards me, which, at first doubtful, turned out to be my horse. He had evidently been able to land after the freshet had exhausted itself. Fancy my feelings and my appearance!—looking a mud-soaked, straight-haired, brigand-like loafer, whom no lady would have trusted to show her through a wood.

However, arriving at my destination, we were all equal to the occasion, the girls more so. After a bath, my clothes having been taken away to be dried, the door was slightly opened and a bundle thrust in. I then understood the giggling which had been going on outside, for the bundle consisted of a complete set, I suppose, of women's clothes, which I duly donned; and having fined the girls a kiss all round, I proceeded with much merriment to exact the fine.

The next day the simple ceremony of the wedding took place, and all ended happily. I have often attended their Sunday services in the chapel, generally a large square room with a reading-desk where the preacher holds forth in good high-class German, although their usual dialect is a jargon of Dutch origin, which is really better defined as being Low German. The custom of separating the sexes prevails as a fully-recognized institution, both socially and in the chapel, the women on the left side and the men on the right, being face to face. The service is generally long drawn out, the hymns especially so, and I often wondered when the last syllable of the last line would end. I soon, however, got accustomed to them, and much admired their sterling honesty; in business transactions their word alone was their bond.

THE MENNONITE COLONIES

The harvest of 1861 had been so superabundant that a considerable portion of the crop remained unharvested, through scarcity of labour, until very late in the autumn, and then much of it rotted in the fields. With the breaking up of the ice and the opening of navigation in that year, we received our machines from England; and, introduced by Mr. Jansen, I started on a journey through the Mennonite colonies with a view to introducing the reaping and thrashing machinery, which had not hitherto been seen there. On my preliminary journey, I found that the colonies consisted of a large number of villages inhabited by the followers of Menno, a sect of Bible Christians who had emigrated from Prussia on the introduction of obligatory military service in that country. The bearing of arms was contrary to their religion, and, under special Charter, exemption from military service had been granted them by the Empress Catherine of Russia.

The villages of this section of the colonies, with a population of 60,000 inhabitants, embraced the whole district from Berdiansk to the River Malotchnaya, and certain colonies beyond the Dnieper. They are models of arrangement and construction, and were planned under the supervision of a special Government inspector. Each farmstead is provided with barn and stables attached at right angles to the dwelling-houses, all being substantially built and tiled with Dutch tiles. Their gable ends are whitewashed and face the street, presenting a very neat appearance, and this with the trim fences and gates gives one a justifiable impression of industrial prosperity. Another pleasant feature is the large number of storks, whose nests are perched upon the ridges of the houses. I consider this bird one of the most chivalrous of his kind, seeing that the male always arrives first and prepares the home nest for his mate.

At the time of my arrival, a conspicuous feature of each village throughout the colonies was the number of windmills used for grinding corn. These followed the mediæval practice of turning the sails (which were covered with sail-cloth) to the wind by a pole. The grain was thrashed out by being trodden under foot by oxen or horses, though I noticed, among the larger landowners, a large granite stone cut into wide teeth was also used. The winnowing was done by throwing the corn into the air. In fact, the whole operation was biblical and primitive, and of course under such conditions the quantity of land sown was very small. The only attempt at mechanical working I found to be grinding the corn by treadmill worked by the weight of the horses on a plane table.

The principal village, or town as they call it, was Halbstadt, which contains the municipal buildings, educational high schools, etc. It is with a deep sense of gratitude that I record the fact that I received the ungrudging hospitality of these good people and was invited to all their social gatherings, more especially to those called in America "Bees," which are organized in every village. In the autumn the pigs, which form the chief meat food during the winter months, are killed and dressed. Sometimes, however, it is proposed to kill an ox or a calf, but this is only done when the principal joints thereof are previously ordered. I have been present at festivals where sixteen pigs have been killed and dressed in one day, the hams being put into brine, and all other joints made ready for curing or prepared for sausages of various kinds, besides which a dinner has been provided and cooked for the occasion.

In my time it was always roast goose stuffed with chestnuts.

The division of the sexes prevails at the festivals, the women sitting at one side of the table and the men at the other. From place to place, in due course, the "Bees" fly; the same ceremonies are performed, until the last village in the circuit has stored its winter provisions.

The inhabitants of these villages are farmers possessing about 120 acres of land, and in the larger ones there are so-called "Beisitzers," who have no land, but are the artisans of the districts, such as blacksmiths, carpenters, etc. It was in such a village as this that I first tried the mower. When the machines arrived in the spring, I had visited on introduction a very large estate belonging to a rich German proprietor, and had asked him to allow me to give the machines a trial on a field of corn, and also whether, seeing that he was often sending corn to Berdiansk, he would allow two reapers to be brought thence in the returning empty wagons to his yard, to remain until July for inspection by the colonists. His decision was that he had heard that such machines were very good at thrashing out the corn, but never that any one in the colonies had used one. He had already engaged a sufficient number of men for cutting his corn, and could not therefore give the trial, but would willingly order the reapers to be brought from the town on the wagons, and they could then stand in one of his barns for inspection.

It had, however, got noised abroad that a young Englishman had arrived in the district, bringing with him a newly-invented wonderful machine, which was erroneously said to be capable of cutting three acres in one day, and this had excited much curiosity. On the arrival of the machines at Steinbach, I again proceeded thither to erect them, and met a Mr. Dick, a preacher, who was much respected throughout the colonies. After examining the machine when I had fully explained it to him, he said that he began to see that there was a possibility of its doing the work I predicted. The only thing he feared was that the beater apparatus which brought the corn on to the knives might thrash a considerable quantity of grain out of the ears. Mr. Dick had seen something of the world beyond the village, having been to Moscow and St. Petersburg, and had inspected mechanical contrivances used by manufacturers which had astounded him. He was a man of considerable culture and natural ability, and became much interested, ultimately asking me to go to the village of Podonau, his dwelling-place, where he would show me a field of rye on which the machine might be tried.

Of course I pointed out to him that the horses had not been trained, and that the noise of the machine usually affected them before they had become accustomed to the working. We arranged that on a certain Friday morning a preliminary trial should be carried out apart from the reaping, and, if satisfactory, the cutting should take place on the ensuing Monday.

On bringing the machines to Podonau, the blacksmith of the village, called locally " The Mechanic," was specially invited to inspect them and give his decision upon them. He was a veritable type of a Dutch burgher of mediæval times—broad in the beam, with his unstockinged feet thrust into slippers much trodden down at the heels, and smoking a cherry-wood pipe at least four feet long. Such was the umpire who was to give his verdict upon these unfamiliar machines. It was only necessary to look at the man's face to see that he had decided on his verdict. After going round and examining the reaper, refusing any information I was ready to give, he turned to the villagers, who were standing by open-mouthed, and sententiously gave his opinion. " That is no machine ; that is a grasshopper." To this I replied, " No, no ! it is no grasshopper, but a locust, and you will see it clear the corn to the ground cleaner than the work of locusts." The ultimate result proved my locust to be nearer the truth than his grasshopper.

The machine was American, Wood's patent, consisting of a cutting bar with dog-tooth knives, a plane table with a seated back for raking off the sheaves, and a revolving beater for bringing the corn on to the knives. When all was ready, Mr. Dick ordered the horses to be harnessed to the machine. They were a beautiful carriage pair, evidently very fresh, and not recently in harness. I took my place on the very small seat provided, and lifting the reins prepared to guide the horses; but they suddenly took the bits in their teeth, and well it was that the men had stood off, for they began kicking and plunging so that it was a marvel how I escaped being thrown under their heels. Then the unwonted rattle of the gearing at the rear caused them to stampede, and mad with terror they rushed through the village to the open steppe. I feel sure that Mazeppa tied to the wild horse was child's play to this. With the machine leaping and shaking with the irregularities of the ground, it was with the greatest difficulty I kept my seat; there was no question of using the reins, for I was forced to let the horses go their own sweet way, and it was only when, in a white foam, they gradually became exhausted that I was at last able to conquer them.

When I found that I could control and guide them with the machinery in full work, I dismounted, soothed and pacified them, and wiped them down with dry steppe grass, leading them gently towards the village. Half-way I was met by a large number of the villagers on horseback, who expressed their surprise at finding me safe and sound. One of them, a young man, gave me his horse, and assured Mr. Dick on his arrival that they were so thoroughly broken in that he could go anywhere with them, which was confirmed practically the next day, Saturday. The bridles of Russian horses are without blinkers, and this fact was probably the cause of a great part of the mishap. In subsequent trials with fresh horses, I always had the training done with their eyes bandaged.

Mr. Dick, uninfluenced by the entreaties of the women folk, decided that cutting should be tried on the Monday as arranged. When the great day arrived, people from the neighbouring villages flocked in on horseback, or in buggies, to see the wonderful sight of a modern harvester; and as I drove it, I was followed by a crowd critically examining the ground to see how much corn had been thrashed out, and their verdict was " Not half so much as by hand work." When the trial of the Burgess & Key machine (which gained the first prize of £500 for reapers at the Great Exhibition of 1851) was carried out, the Russian peasants following it were simply astounded at seeing the corn come rolling off in a long continuous swathe ready for the binder. At last they took off their caps and crossed themselves, devoutly praying that they might not have been present at an invention of the devil.

On another occasion when the steam thrasher was at work, a deputation from a neighbouring village came begging our man in charge to call out the unclean spirit that was doing the work, so that they might see it. He, instead of explaining to them the working of it, told them that he could not do that, because he would have to work the machine himself, besides which there would be the devil to pay amongst the villagers. I admonished him, and explained to him that in introducing these machines we looked upon ourselves not merely as the pioneers of a great industry, but also as emissaries of civilization, and, seeing that superstition and ignorance go hand in hand, our duty lay through enlightenment to destroy the source and power of it.

The Russian peasant, owing to the state of ignorance in which serfdom has kept him, is naturally most superstitious. A woman will not cross the road before a man, fearing she might bring him misfortune; also should a priest or cat cross before him when first driving out in the morning, the driver will return and begin his journey afresh.

A series of bad harvests ensuing, it was long before any extended use was made of the machines, so that we earned little or nothing from our first venture.

Subsequently, however, the use of them extended. Our business in the steam machinery increased, and the manufacture of reapers and such small machinery was eventually taken up by others, thousands being made yearly in factories in Chortitz, Alexandroff, and Berdiansk. It was interesting to me, the pioneer, on visiting the colonies in 1891, to be shown the machine which I had introduced into Russia in 1861. This Wood's machine, being light and suitable for their horses, now finds a home in almost every peasant's cottage or colonist's homestead in South Russia.

The Mennonites

To the general reader it may be of interest to give a short description of the origin and experiences of this people, all the more that it seemed extremely strange that for conscience' sake they should have found in Russia, the most despotic of all countries and known for its intolerance, a refuge and asylum. All the more extraordinary was the fact that, at the time of their immigration, the Holy Synod of Russia was using every means in its power to bring the adherents of all other communities under the priestly domination of the Greek Church. Yet here I found them, in a corner of the Empire, enjoying the full rights and freedom of citizens, and practising their religious tenets without let or hindrance from the Russian hierarchy.

This remarkable community dates its origin from the time of Luther, and is considered to be the first dissenting section of that period. Its original founder was one Obbo Phillipoz in 1523, who, however, left the community early, in disagreement on the point of church fellowship. The name Mennonite is derived from Menno Simens (1492–1559), who became in 1537 the missioner of that body, which had separated itself from Luther owing to being in disagreement with his tenets. This formed a new community, and ultimately took the name and leadership of Menno.

The main tenets of this new sect were first, that, discarding all priestly domination outside the Bible and the believer's conscience, no forms or ceremonies should be tolerated in the Christian Church. Secondly, that neither baptism nor the Lord's Supper conferred grace, and that it was only those of the New Birth that formed the true body. Baptism is performed by pouring water on the head, and formerly, or it may still perhaps be, there was the custom of feet-washing with the Lord's Supper. Further, amongst their tenets, marriage out of the community is forbidden, or only sanctioned after profession of faith.

They deny all right of the civil authority to bind their conscience under any circumstances whatever. This excludes the taking of oaths and the acceptance of any office under Government, even to the extent of refusing magisterial duties. Whilst they inculcate obedience to all laws which do not bind their conscience and are rightly enforced by the civil authority, they repudiate under any circumstance the taking of human life. As a consequence, they refuse all enactments forcing them into obligatory military service, and stand fast on the charter given them by the Empress Catherine, which conceded to them full freedom for ever from conscription, and granted to each family an allotment of land for their support. The date on which the sect was founded was 1523, in the town of Zurich.

In their church government they have no settled ministry; their leaders, who preach without text, are chosen from the community. This is considered a great honour; and owing to the sermons being in High German, instead of the German which is the common speech of the people, the preachers chosen must of necessity be men of fair education. The women take no part whatever in the church government, and in their simple chapels are seated separately, the men to the right and the women to the left of the preacher. Instrumental music in worship is prohibited, and to an unaccustomed ear the long-drawn-out ending to each line of their hymns sounds very monotonous.

In their services they have been compared to the Quakers, being much addicted to silent prayer; they also agree in their opposition to military service. On more than one occasion the members of the British Quaker sect have visited the colonies and preached in their chapels, which, they pointed out to me, they had considered to be a great honour conferred upon them by the English community, and consequently much appreciated.

Again, they have been compared to the Plymouth Brethren, with whom, certainly, they have much affinity. They differ from them, however, in church government and practice, one special point being that they do not require for church fellowship strict uniformity in their religious opinions, a tenet which has caused so many doctrinal differences and splits amongst the Plymouth Brethren, otherwise a most estimable class of Christians.

As a community, the Mennonites are highly esteemed by all classes in Russia, being strictly honest in all their dealings, and reliable in all their undertakings. Instances have personally come under my notice when (as very seldom occurs, however) a member of their community being unable to meet his liabilities, the colony has subscribed the amount due and satisfied the debt.

During my frequent visits to the villages, I used, together with my host and his family, to attend their services. At that time Spurgeon was greatly esteemed; his sermons were translated into German and Dutch, and very often formed the subject of the discourse, being much prized.

From the above it will be seen that in the eyes of the Church of Rome a community of this description would be considered not only subversive of all religion, but a danger to civil authority. Hence much persecution ensued; members of the sect were tortured and drowned, and, as was usual in those times with those who only wished to live their religious life quietly and apart from the world, the blood of the martyrs led to the teaching and spread of the new religion to Germany, Holland, and France. It was mainly, however, the introduction of universal obligatory military service that sent them farther afield; and as each country in turn adopted conscription, they have fled from its enactment.

When in 1870 universal military service became law, the Mennonites, having in mind the charter which specially exempted them from it, were much agitated, and on the Government insisting, a large number left for Canada and the States. In order to stay the exodus of so laborious and God-fearing a community, the leaders (including among them our dear friends the family of the German Consul, the Jansens, with whom we have kept in touch ever since) were forced to leave, and probably the majority would have followed. This drastic action, however, did not avail to stay the exodus, so General Todleben, the hero of the defence at Sebastopol, was sent down armed with full powers to settle matters. This ended in a compromise arrangement, under which they could not be called to the fighting ranks, but must serve three years in the Forestry Department, and be trained as bearers of the wounded and in the art of giving first aid.

The present adherents of the sect number about 250,000, of which 80,000 are in the United States, 75,000 in Russia, 60,000 in Holland and 25,000 in Canada, the remainder being spread in small communities in Germany, Poland, Switzerland, Galicia, and France.

Shortly after the Crimean War, an agitation took place among the more earnest Christians of the denomination, in consequence of their opinion that there had been a serious backsliding of the community, as a whole, from the principles for which they stood. This movement led to the formation of a brotherhood among them, which eventually attracted the attention of the priestly authorities. Year by year, during the

SCHAMYL AND THE CIRCASSIAN LEADERS, 1858.

time of harvest, there was a great immigration of Russian labourers from the villages of the interior for the ingathering. These usually returned annually to the same Mennonite household, and joined with them in their evening meditations, known as the Gebetstunde, or hour of prayer. From this name eventually arose that of the Stundists. These labourers, with the well-known impressibility of the Russian peasant in religious matters, became missioners of the new doctrines in their various villages, and to so great an extent that the priesthood were greatly affected in their material interests through losing their fees for marriages, christenings, burials, etc. On this the ecclesiastical authorities took action, and sent round commissioners, comprising priests, deacons, and superior members of the clergy, to report as to the number of Stundists in the various villages of their districts.

A German Mennonite friend related to me the following incident. He was at the time the mayor of the village, when he received notice from the ecclesiastical authorities of Ekaterinoslav that a commission was visiting the district, and amongst others his own village. He was to prepare them lodgings and all due hospitality, as well as fresh horses for their next journey. Having found necessary lodging for the others in the village, he himself hospitably entertained the leaders, and in course of conversation inquired whether they had found many Stundists in that locality. To this they cheerfully replied that, thanks to God, there were not many in that neighbourhood.

Knowing of the widespread character of Stundism in his own district, he felt much surprise, and took an early opportunity of interviewing the coachman who had been driving them, the latter himself a Stundist. To the queries put the Russian replied that they had only found one, an old woman, who unlike the others, declined to pay the sum (perhaps two roubles) demanded in order to place them in the ranks of the orthodox. My friend thereupon objected that purchasing exemption in such a manner was not consistent with the principles held by the Stundist community, and was answered, " Brother, I fear that you have not studied your Bible to profit, for have you not read the words in the Gospel (Luke xvi. 9), ' Make to yourselves friends of the mammon of unrighteousness ' ? ''—which, if stretching a doctrinal point, certainly brought immediate relief to a harassed community.

The outcome of this visit, however, was that the children of Russians who had not been baptized into the Orthodox Church were to be so compulsorily, and throughout the whole district most scandalous scenes took place : the baptism according to the Orthodox Church being by immersion, the young people were chased throughout the villages, stripped naked, and plunged into water, hundreds of girls up to the age of fourteen being thus treated.

CHAPTER VI

INTRODUCTION OF STEAM THRASHER

First hire of thrashing machine—The police inspector—Nature of contract—Transport of machines—Work begun on old corn—Infringement of agreement—Peasants fascinated by the machines—M. Popoff—His hospitality—Granaries for storing corn—Sleeping under tarpaulins—Watch for robbers of stored wheat—The thieves trapped—M. Popoff's help—Interview with and assault on inspector—Work for M. Popoff—Reconciliation with the inspector—Our subsequent meeting.

HAVING finished reaping, the thrashing season commenced, and an episode occurred which might have ended with most serious consequences to ourselves and our incipient industry. The first inquirer that we had for the hire of our thrashing machine was a police inspector (stanavoy), who was at the head of one of the Melitopol districts. He told us that he had heard that we had brought into the country a machine worked by steam, suitable for thrashing and grading the corn. He stated to us that he had 450 acres of corn, consisting of 200 under wheat and the remainder under barley and rye. He was a man of commanding presence and, clothed in the uniform of his class, impressed us at the time very favourably. He was very urgent that the machines should be sent off forthwith, as within a fortnight the reaping would be finished, and it would be much to his advantage if the corn could be carted direct to the machine without the extra labour of making it into ricks. He also informed us that he had commenced carting the rye to the thrashing-floor, and this could be done first, the machines afterwards being removed to the fields.

On this we asked for references, but he, not being known in Berdiansk, was not in a position to give them. After consultation with our friends, we thought it advisable to close with his offer, more especially as there was no difficulty about the price to be charged. The district was a large agricultural one and the centre of a number of rich proprietors living in the immediate neighbourhood. This was a great attraction to us, as we never had any intention of working the machines for a living, the main object being to introduce them for sale. On this a contract was drawn up, the principal stipulations being that, in addition to the payment of a fixed amount per pood of grain delivered, the cartage of the machines, fuel, and all the etceteras should be at his expense, as also the necessary number of workmen to be employed on the machines; failing which he was to pay a certain amount per hour of standing, and at the end of the work the machines were to be returned to Berdiansk or be delivered elsewhere to our order. We on our part found the machines and driver and all other mechanical appliances necessary for carrying on the work.

In due course the bullocks arrived, and their departure from the town with the machines made a goodly show for a large number of the inhabitants, who had become interested both in us and our work. The machines required sixteen pairs of oxen, and a further twenty pairs for coal and impedimenta. Our man Charles was put in charge of the convoy with instructions to advise us when he commenced working, so that I might follow. On receipt of the notice that work had begun I at once started. The place was distant eighty-five miles (English), and on my arrival, to my great astonishment, I found Charles had already been at work a fortnight on corn that had been stacked two years, and was honeycombed with dilapidation caused by rats, mice, and cattle. Of course it was self-evident that, we being paid under our contract by the weight of corn delivered, the machines under these circumstances had not only been yielding no profit, but the amount earned was far from covering the outlay we had incurred for coal and current expenses.

I thereupon immediately stopped work, went to the house of the police inspector and explained to him that I could not and should not resume, until a reasonable agreement with regard to payment for the time lost and expenditure incurred on the work already done had been come to. We having received 500 roubles in advance on signing the contract had him well in hand, and I was therefore enabled to make an equitable arrangement, after a good deal of haggling, for the balance of the fortnight's work that had been done outside our agreement.

The next day the machines were moved to the estate, which was twelve miles from the village and upon the very verge of the steppe. We at once got them into work, with most excellent results which drew the attention not only of the adjacent proprietors, but also of those whose estates were at a distance.

Shortly afterwards I was informed by the steward of the estate on which we were working that the harvest and land were not the property of the police inspector, but belonged to a non-resident owner to whom our contract had been sublet at a greatly enhanced price. Although in reality, however, this might be termed an infringement of our agreement (the contract having been completed under the assumption that he himself was owner), seeing that the work was proceeding very satisfactorily I determined to proceed without making objections. Many of the landowners of the district visited me, owing to it having been noised abroad that two Englishmen had brought into the district some wonderful labour-saving machines, which not only thrashed the corn from the ear, but also delivered it clean and assorted into the sacks.

It must be remembered that this class of machine was a very recent invention, and that we were exhibiting the first of its kind that had ever been imported into that part of Russia. It was therefore not only interesting to the proprietors, to whom it was quite a revelation, but more than all it fascinated the peasantry, who had not only never seen a steam engine, but had never heard of one. Therefore on the great holidays large numbers arrived to inspect them, and kept my man Charles busy in explaining their action to them. On one occasion I recollect, in talking about it amongst themselves, they ascribed it to Satanic power.

About this time I made the acquaintance of the son of the late General Popoff, who had inherited from his father 7,000 serfs, together with a large inventory of sheep, cattle, and land. These formed together an inheritance of great intrinsic value, second to none throughout the whole district, and gave the young man an immense influence. It being in those days the custom for the parents of an only son to adopt temporarily an English lad of the same age to be his companion and fellow-student (mainly with a view to perfecting the boy in the English language), this had been done in the present case, and M. Popoff not only spoke English perfectly, but was well versed in its literature. He thus had much in common with myself, and we became on exceedingly friendly terms. During the many weeks that I lived with him in his princely house, I felt perfectly at home, and he did everything possible to make my stay in his village pleasurable. His father had been one of the Russian heroes of the Crimean defence, and had from his own resources supplied a regiment to the State, mostly from his own serfs. It was quite open house for the neighbouring proprietors, which led to my having a large number of introductions. On my first acquaintance he had warned me that I had fallen into bad hands, and that at some time or another I should require assistance, in which case he authorized me to send for him, day or night.

The reader will recollect that under our agreement with the police inspector we were to be paid by the pood weight of corn delivered. This, however, owing to there being no scales available, could not be done, so I had the number of full sacks counted and checked by his foreman in order that no discrepancy could possibly arise. These were then removed and emptied on to the floor of a large sunken shed, whose thatched roof sprang direct from the ground. This kind of granary is common on all estates at a distance from the home farm, and generally marks the spot where the *tok*, or thrashing-floor, is placed. The entry to them is gained along a path gradually descending from the surface of the ground to the level of the door of the granary, which, situated below the soil level, is fastened by a large padlock.

In or about the second week of working, Charles was warned by one of the men that at night a portion of the corn thrashed out during the day was being removed, and his informant advised him to set a watch. We were sleeping, like the peasants engaged in the work, on the bare ground in the open, only Charles had rigged up for himself and me a roof out of the tarpaulin of the machines, the one from the engine being spread upon the ground, and that of the machine forming the roof. In this way we had contrived not only a resting-place for the nights, protected from possible rain or dew, but it constituted also our storehouse, being sufficiently spacious to accommodate all our stores, food, oil for lubrication, yarn for wiping down the engine, and all the spare parts for the machines. Charles having told me of the warning he had received, I organized a watch for that night. Armed with a stout stick, I took upon myself the first part until midnight, at which time he succeeded me.

Everything being now prepared, even to having ropes provided for binding any possible prisoners, I took up my position, lying low in the shadow of the roof, but nothing occurred during my watch, when I gave place to my assistant. About two hours afterwards, and before the first streaks of the dawn were visible, I was suddenly awakened by Charles, who told me he had heard in the distance a creaking sound of wheels on the wooden axles of a peasant's cart, which appeared to be advancing towards us. Continuing our watch, we soon heard distinctly the sound of the bullock carts slowly nearing the shed. *Two* vehicles having entered the long pathway, the outlines were now fully visible, and their descent commenced quietly and cautiously. They then stopped, unyoked the oxen, and turned each cart with the pole in front, so that it could be pushed back into the shed and be ready for the subsequent ascent. Two men were employed, and it became an absolute certainty that it was a plot to rob us of our stipulated quota of the corn delivered. This action was not only robbing us, but at the same time depriving the real proprietor of a portion of his harvest for the benefit of the police inspector, who I have never doubted was the instigator of the robbery. After satisfying myself that the two men and vehicles were inside the shed, we descended the incline, armed with our sticks and carrying the ropes. On entering, I called upon them to surrender, when one of them, evading Charles, rushed out and got clear off. The other, however, essaying to do the same, I floored, when we bound him with ropes, fastened him to the cart wheel, and locked him in. On seeing all safe, I mounted my horse, which had been allotted to me under the agreement, and rode over at a gallop the ten versts (about seven miles) that separated me from M. Popoff's domain, and arrived there just before breakfast.

After listening to my story, this kind host told me he had been afraid that I should have difficulties with the inspector, " but," he added, " when he knows that I am protecting you, he will not dare to molest you." He then sent for his steward and ordered him immediately to send off fourteen pairs of bullocks, and gave him strict orders to personally attend the removal of the machines from the estate to his own ground.

It so happened that within two miles of the boundary of the two estates, the steward had several teams of oxen ploughing, so we rode over together, and by midday the machines, together with their accessories, were successfully removed from the estate. After interviewing my prisoner, and becoming assured he was acting under orders, I released him from his bonds, ordered food to be given him, and placed him under Charles until the arrival of the police inspector.

My prisoner also fully convinced me that what he had told me was correct, and that it was the third time he had been engaged in removing the corn under his master's orders. At about two o'clock in the afternoon the inspector arrived on horseback, and was greatly surprised to find the machines gone and the workpeople idle. I then told him I was only awaiting his arrival to demand a final settlement, being fully persuaded from his action at the commencement of the work, and again by the surreptitious removal of the corn, that no confidence whatever could be placed in his honest fulfilment of the contract he had made, and for these reasons I would do no more work, and asked him to settle.

On this he called upon God and all the saints to witness that he was innocent of any abstraction from the shed, and began, in all the foulest language with which the Russian is so abundantly endowed, to revile the prisoner, who he then ordered to be arrested and taken to the village to await his arrival. Hereupon, my righteous indignation being aroused, I went up to him and, taking his horse by the bridle, shouted, "That poor man is not the thief and vagabond,—it is yourself; he only acted under your orders." On this he struck me over the head with his riding whip, when with one bound I dragged him from his horse, and snatching his whip belaboured him before all the men, not one of whom stirred to help his master in spite of his orders to arrest me.

I then mounted his horse, and, together with Charles on the other, rode off the field to the machines. On arriving we found that the steward was there yoking up for the homestead, where we arrived safe and sound, to the great delight of M. Popoff that we should have been able to get away so readily. We returned the horses to the inspector, together with a letter stating that we were ready to make a final settlement, as the contract had been broken and I refused to work any further for him. Next day I started work for my kind host, and during the next ten weeks was engaged in thrashing at his home and various outlying farmsteads, enjoying his hospitality and doing mutually profitable work.

He was a true gentleman of a refined type, and a good musician. He had a band in uniform, led by a German conductor, a doctor in charge of a hospital, certificated nurses and schools, all composed of men, women, and boys from his own serfs. He treated me as one of his family or as an honoured guest, and I always look back upon that period of my life with the liveliest satisfaction.

It would be about six weeks after I had been engaged upon the home farm, when M. Popoff entered the barn, accompanied by the police inspector, who coming up to me offered me his hand, whereupon I turned my back and walked away. Coming up to me M. Popoff said: " I want you to make it up with this man. You punished him well, but seeing that I am protecting you, and could get him dismissed at any moment, he is desirous of making it up. You must remember also that you are in Russia, and not in England. Here, beating an official in the Emperor's uniform is a great offence, however great the provocation, so come with us and settle up amicably. He says also that you have some of the 500 roubles hand money to return, and this we will arrange at the same time."

The advice was so convincing that it broke down my wounded pride, and I accompanied them home, when after a good dinner we buried the hatchet with champagne honours, and I had no difficulty with the balancing of our accounts. Years passed, no thought of him ever crossed my mind, when the inspector entered our office in Kharkov, and coming up to me embraced me. He had greatly altered in appearance, being in civilian clothes and very white. He told me our mutual friend was dead, and that he had married a French lady by whom he had two sons, who were being educated in Paris. Thus ended an episode which, with my after experiences in Russia, impressed upon me their oft-quoted aphorism, " God is high and the Czar is far," as governing the autocratic actions of the officials.

On one of the farmsteads of M. Popoff's estates, I had noticed a number of hillocks, which, owing to the regularity of their position, aroused my curiosity, from their great resemblance to the ancient kurgans or tumuli which, scattered over the Steppes, mark the last resting-places of many of the great leaders of the nomadic tribes. He then told me that these mounds covered the deep pits in which the manure was deposited for the extraction of the nitrate.

Prior to the introduction of nitrates from Chili, the method adopted was as follows: The whole of the manure collected during the year was deposited in these pits and covered in. During a period of five years, a chemical change took place, by which the nitrates in the straw became separated, and after extraction were sold to the Government for use in the manufacture of gunpowder. Nearly every large estate owner had nitrate pits, and the output was so arranged that each year one could be opened and worked for the benefit of the estate.

It seemed to me an anomaly that every landowner with whom I conversed contended that manuring the land was detrimental under their climate, owing to its overheating the soil.

CHAPTER VII

LIFE ON THE OPEN STEPPE, 1861

Successful year closed—New machines ordered—Disastrous harvest in 1862—Drought—Absence of means of irrigation—M. Popoff—Proclamation of freedom of serfs—Their disappointment—Emperor's tea—Charles Pope—Life on Steppe near Wassilefka—Deportation of Crimean Tartars—Shooting on Steppe—Bustard hunting—Opinion of Russian peasant—Migration of peasantry during harvests—Amusing racial quarrels—Bargaining—Picnics on Steppe—Beautiful nights—Steppe cooking—Tartar servant—Religious instincts of peasants—Superstitions—Financial difficulty—Unexpected settlement—Journey to Ekaterinoslav—Snowstorm—Hospitality of great Russian landowner.

THE year just closed had been a remarkable one. We had, after the first trial of the reaping machines and thrasher, not only been able to do a very profitable business by working for the proprietors at a very remunerative price, but had also been able to introduce them to a very large circle who fully appreciated that we were presenting to them a most valuable resource against future scarcity of labour.

After the reaping comes the thrashing, and this we did on the spot, without carting or binding, at so much per pood (a Russian weight equalling thirty-six pounds English). As a result we had earned so much that not only had we been able to pay Mr. Wagner the amount he had advanced together with the interest, but also had made sufficient to pay in England half the value of another set. In doing this, although we were leaving ourselves without a great margin for eventualities, we thought that we had good prospects for future work in the ensuing season.

Under these circumstances we wrote to the agricultural firm from whom we had made our previous purchases, proposing to pay them half the money down for a new set, and the balance to become payable after the harvest of 1862. We hoped that, working with the two machines, we should not only be able to meet the half then due, but probably to order a third. The firm with whom we were in communication were Quakers, who, although in their prayers may have been moved by the Spirit of God, in their practice and their dealings with us appear to have been regulated by the spirit of greed. We only required the machines to be sent off in May, and, seeing that they had already received in advance half the price, we thought it rather harsh dealing that we should be compelled to pay 5 per cent. interest, not from the date of delivery, but from the date of order; but from further letters our offer of paying from June 1st, 1862, was agreed to.

The first machine was still at work when the order for the second was given, and in fact its earnings during the autumn were the only means that we had to rely upon for our commissariat during the coming winter, and we had in view a further great expense, seeing that my partner, in view of our present success, had arranged for his fiancée to come over to be married at the Consulate. In so far as our prospects were concerned, we felt that our budget was in order, but the year 1862 opened disastrously. The winter itself was almost without snow, and this was followed by the failure of both the earlier and the latter rains. Day by day we anxiously scanned the heavens to see for any signs of rain clouds; but all in vain—the sky was as brass. And as April was fast approaching, after which there could be no prospect for harvest, our spirits sank, and we felt that we had embarked needlessly upon an expenditure which was only justifiable under better circumstances. So complete was the failure that the barley when fully ripe had only ears an inch long, containing a few dried-up grains. With straws and ears together it did not exceed six inches, and it was cut down and used as fodder. Similar results followed with all other cereals, and there was no demand either for the reapers or thrasher that we had in hand.

It is in Russia as in India: give mother earth good food and plenty to drink, she will willingly give her increase and produce bountifully and sumptuously for the support of man and beast. Failing this, as it was this year in Russia, she will yield no increase, and it often happens (as is usual in life, that misfortunes come not alone) that the land will sometimes give only one good year out of three. And yet I can scarcely conceive any country more favourably provided, if it were only in the possession of a people with initiative and enterprise.

When I think of the vast mass of snow that falls in winter, being allowed, on melting in the spring, to swell the torrents that hasten to the rivers, and hence to the sea, bearing with them vast deposits of the black earth that otherwise would give food to the people and wealth to the nation, the thought has often occurred to me how under similar circumstances in India our people have dealt with this problem,—by the construction of a vast network of irrigation canals, so that the famines which were so prevalent in the past have become year by year more and more a memory. The example thus set, if followed, would give in Russia, in like measure at a far less outlay, similar results, and thereby lessen the ever-recurring famine years.

It was from the balcony of M. Popoff's house that I heard him, surrounded by all the proprietors of the district, read out to his seven thousand serfs, drawn up before his house according to their village, the Emperor's Ukase granting them their freedom. There they stood in serried rank, a picture of varied manhood in every stage of its development, from grey old age to early adolescence, as fine a body of men as you might wish to see. Standing without a smile, bareheaded, they listened with reverence to their Emperor's message, each mayor of the villages wearing his badge, and several the Emperor's coat that had been bestowed upon them for special service rendered to the State. Yet on the close of the ceremony there was no responsive cheer, and not the slightest enthusiasm on so momentous an occasion. It was evident from their silence that they felt keen disappointment at no mention having been made that, together with their freedom, the whole land of the proprietors was to become the property of the late serfs. These representatives of the peasantry dispersed to their own villages evidently deeply depressed, and throughout all the years that have passed since then they have been and are still fully convinced that the proprietors had not fulfilled their Emperor's commands.

I remember this day so distinctly owing to a solecism that I had innocently performed after the great dinner which was given, a mistake which caused a smile amongst the guests. Quite unknown to me, but evidently not so with some of the guests, instead of coffee as usual, Emperor's tea was given in its place, and was handed round with cream and sugar on the tray. Never having tasted this superlative tea (each pound of which costs between two and three pounds sterling), I innocently, thinking it was coffee, put into it cream and sugar; but afterwards I was told that the tea only should have been drunk, without any addition. I tried some afterwards on another occasion, but greatly preferred my cup of coffee.

My manner of life at this time was as follows: My assistant with the machine was Charles Pope, a sailor boy who had been shipwrecked in the Sea of Azov, but rescued by Mr. Hahn, of Orlofka, who received a silver medal from the British Government in commemoration. In the short time he had been with us, he had become sufficiently proficient to keep the machine going when I was absent, which left me a considerable vacant time during the day, my principal work being to do the necessary repairs in the evening. The place where the thrashing was to be carried out was twenty miles from Wassilefka where M. Popoff lived, and from the Monday to the

Saturday we lived in the open on the field. The work required seventy men, who were brought back also to the village on the Saturday, returning on the Sunday evening.

During the interval from Saturday to Monday Charles and three other men remained with the machinery, but I returned to the house. It will be seen from the number of men required that their daily maintenance of food, which had to be supplied, kept up almost daily communication with the village. The machines were placed in a convenient centre to which the corn, cut but not bound, was brought from all points. After it passed through the drum it became separated from the ears, passing out of one end of the machine through a sieve, dividing it into various grades, while from the other end the straw and cavings poured out in an unceasing stream.

Under the system that I had adopted the proprietor could afford to pay me well, seeing that he was saved the whole expense of caving, separating, and binding. For myself personally, to keep up the means of communication, M. Popoff—who was continually inviting me to come over to the house, especially at meal-times—had selected for me an Arab horse from his stud, together with his Tartar groom in whose family it had been bred. At that time the forcible deportation of the Crimean Tartars was in full swing; and being unable to carry their cherished steeds with them on board ship, they were being disposed of for a trifling sum. The one chosen for me was a grey mare with dark hairs sprinkled as it were over her coat. She was indeed an animal to be loved, and I became much attached to it. My Tartar servant watched over her with the tenderest care, which she reciprocated with a whinny. In her movements she was an ambler, and to ride her was a pleasure, she being equal to the very best lady's horse.

Although we had every provision that was possible sent with us for the week, this did not include meat, for which I was dependent on my gun. This seldom

KHARKOV. MONUMENT TO ALEXANDER I.

failed, for partridges were fairly abundant, and occasionally I went for bigger game. We were here in the country of the big bustard, and when it was announced that a tarda, or school, was near, I together with my Tartar would arm ourselves with our Cossack whips (one of which I still possess) ready for the hunt. Leaving all dogs and guns behind, we brace up the girths and set out, keeping well against the wind. The birds have a sharp eye and scent, and throw out sentinels wherever they settle. The approach to them must be cautiously carried out, and immediately there is the first sign of movement, go for them all your horse can do, and you get a run that throws the finest fox-hunting into the shade.

The bustard is not only the largest European bird, but is the most wary; its great weight, however, requires the impetus of a long run, and then a momentary pause, before it can rise. The aim of the hunt is to ride it down before the impetus is exhausted and the pause occurs which allows the bird time to start a new flight. The object, of course, of the rider is to prevent the flight and kill the bird with the leaden end of the whip. As for eating, I do not care for it, but both the peasants and Cossacks are fond of it after they have buried it three days in the ground.

Peasant Life in South Russia

Under the new system established by us of carting the corn from the field direct to the thrashing machine, a great saving of labour was accomplished. In South Russia during normal years, harvesting commences in July, and thrashing, which began before August 1st, 1861, was in full swing by that date. Very often the so-called fields are probably fifteen to twenty miles away from the villages, and the peasants bivouac on the Steppe during the week, returning home on Saturday and going out again on Sunday night. As the season lasts for about seven weeks, during that period my life was passed amongst the workmen in the open air. As a class, I found the Russian peasant to be eminently amenable to good treatment, but very sullen and obstinate when crossed. Our machines required, for carting and working, about seventy men, and, being always with the men, I learned to know them thoroughly and to respect them. I found many of them to be endowed with a very fair amount of common sense, who, had they been educated, would have made for themselves careers in life. As an evidence of this, many of the proprietors of villages had selected, from among their serfs, youths to be educated as doctors, or trained to give efficient first-aid in cases requiring immediate attention before summoning the doctor of the district, who, in this land of vast distances, often live many miles away.

To me, the peasantry as a class became very attractive, and when, as sometimes happened, I would join them around their camp fire, I have told them tales of my own land and of our own peasantry, which tales always greatly interested them, more especially the fact that education with us was obligatory and all could read and write. It was always interesting to me to hear them interject remarks, or ask questions, as they often showed a shrewdness little short of marvellous.

It was, and probably is still, the custom for large numbers of them to leave their villages in the far-away interior and come south, to be hired for the harvesting. The then prevailing custom caused them to congregate in the larger villages having hiring bazaars, where the price was fixed according to the result of the harvest. These men trudged on foot, some of them two or three hundred miles, and after finishing their work returned in the early part of October with the money they had earned. They moved more or less in gangs, each belonging to their own village, and some of their wives accompanied them to do the cooking. On the road you may meet them trudging along and carrying their belongings, with the women of the party riding in a horse-drawn vehicle of the commonest description.

By nature, these uneducated men are, with very few exceptions, polite yet not subservient. They uncover their heads in speaking to their superiors and are hospitable to a degree unknown to any workmen of our own land. It has often happened that I have been asked to accept some of their cabbage soup (an offer which I have occasionally accepted when it was not fasting soup) which is made with oil. On my consenting they would pour some into my own dish, wish me God's help, stand and bow low at the honour that I had done them, and not resume their sitting position round the common pot until I had finished.

Russia is not only a country of many climates, but it is also one of many peoples. The Crimean district in which I was living was "Little Russia," whereas the migrating peasantry came from Russia proper. It was very amusing to see and hear a disagreement between members of the two nationalities. One would think that the enmity between the two individuals was deadly. The epithets bestowed upon relatives and parents were terrible and disgusting, yet after a time it would end by the Little Russian, as the last superlative sign of contempt, placing his thumb between his two forefingers and pointing it energetically three times towards the face of the Russian peasant, who in retort would scornfully call the Little Russian "Mazeppa," both then spitting on the ground and walking away. Still more exciting is it to see a quarrel between a Russian and a Jew. When calling each other the conventional names out of their vocabulary, the Russian will hold up the edge of his coat, forming a pig's ear, and shake it in the Jew's face, whilst the latter on his part would perform the action of the Little Russian.

The peasants are very fond of attending their bazaars weekly, and it is a very instructive sight to see the bargaining between them for the sale or purchase of a cow, calf, or any other animal. Such bargaining between themselves will last a considerable time, during which much vodka will be consumed, at the same time the price gradually varying until a deadlock is reached between buyer and seller. At this point a third party often intervenes, makes them join hands, and placing his across theirs, so as to form the sign of the cross, says " Pa-polam "—that is, "Halve the difference"—and the bargain is closed.

It has been said that the true character of a people is revealed by the men in their cups. Judged by this standard, we certainly cannot consider our nation to be anything but morose and quarrelsome; the Russian, on the contrary, is surely a descendant of Mark Tapley. To them, the rolling down the street, holding each other up by crossing arms over the shoulder and singing their loudest, is a sign of good fellowship to the utmost degree. The passers-by, well accustomed to such sights, may smilingly make some remark to them, when they will be forthwith pressed, not to fight, but to have a drink at their expense; the danger is lest they become quarrelsome on a refusal.

During the time that I was in the country, no man was ever brought up before a magistrate for being drunk. Should such a one be found in the gutter, as very often happened, the policeman would call a "droshky," lift him in with the help of the coachman, and deposit him in the police station, and on his becoming sober he would send him home. The Tartars, being Mohammedans, are, as a rule, not drunkards, strong drinks being against the precepts of the Koran; and my servant never touched them. He was not above missing his five prayers daily to Allah, which the Prophet of his religion enjoined, but I think that when he did pray he made up for this by an extra number of prostrations towards the East.

In our morning rides to get something for dinner, we would generally start with our guns soon after breakfast, accompanied by two or more of the mongrels that always infest the camps, and it seldom happened that we returned without some game, usually partridges, larks, or, in the season, snipe and woodcock from amongst the canebrakes of the river. In addition to this, our proprietor had supplied us with quite a farmyard, consisting of a cow and chickens, and had also sent me supplies of bread, etc., from his own table.

Occasionally, M. Popoff, having sent provisions in advance, would improvise a picnic, bringing with him some of his friends and neighbours who were desirous of seeing this wonderful machine, and they would enjoy an al-fresco repast prepared by my Tartar, accompanied by the whirr of the drum and the buzz of the corn passing through the machine.

But, watchman, what of the night? Those glorious summer nights, when, stretched upon my tarpaulin, with my saddle for a pillow, I could gaze upwards upon the stars of the firmament, standing out in all their brilliancy against a deep, dark, velvety background. I have often felt on these occasions that the stars do really rule the night. But I would warn the weary traveller of the moonlight, for it behoves him to be careful, and envelop his head in a bashlick or other covering; for being moonstruck is no myth, and the word lunacy expresses no fiction.

My servant was really an excellent cook, and, no matter how poor the commissariat, could place before me a good dinner. As cooks, the Tartars are well renowned throughout the whole of Russia, where, as a general rule, they serve in that capacity in the railway stations. On our first arrival he prepared his oven, which consisted of a large square hole dug in the ground, to which was attached a horizontal chimney, formed by a long trench covered in with mould beaten hard, on the top of hurdles, and this chimney was cleverly arranged so that the draught could be regulated as desired. After having heated the oven with straw from the machine, he would prepare the bird by covering it with wet clay, feathers and all included. He then deposited it in the glowing embers of his oven, when all would be closed down. In the fulness of time the bird would be taken out like a red-hot brick, which on being pulled apart left all the feathers in the clay, and when cleaned a very appetizing repast would be placed before me.

The traveller who writes the experiences of his travels in Russia has usually come to the country with introductions either from official quarters or influential friends. After five or six weeks' residence amongst this hospitable people, he will have seen one side of their character, and that their most attractive. I would not detract in the slightest degree from their possessing qualities of a most agreeable social nature, but, at the same time, there is another side, which, from my long residence and association with every class from peer to peasant, I think I may, without undue self-laudation, claim to be more intimately acquainted with than even the generality of their own people.

I feel, however, in writing these reminiscences it is not my duty to moralize, but simply to relate the facts as they have come under my own observation; and I think the reader will recognize that I am more than superficially acquainted with both sides. The Russians themselves acknowledge that they are Eastern in origin, and certainly in many respects they are Eastern in their practices—that is to say, they are consummate diplomats, and, generally speaking, it may be said that language was given to them to hide their thoughts. It behoves people of our own nation to be specially careful in all their joint dealings, and to be well-advised in any agreements or contracts they may have to make with them.

It has been said by our visiting bishops, journalists, etc., that the peasantry and the people generally are deeply religious, and, on their return home, they express views that are not in accordance with the true facts. If true religion consists in prostration, presentation of candles, and in adoration of saints, then certainly, so far as form is concerned, they fulfil the description presented. But this to my mind is not religion. They are but actions inculcated in them from their very birth. I have more than once asked pilgrims who have been unusually diligent in their adoration, what prayer they offer at the time of their prostration, and the answer I have invariably received is "God, have mercy." The number of times this is said constitutes the number of prayers offered; the more efficacious being those accompanied by the forehead knocking the floor.

Religion, as we understand it, has many adherents amongst the dissenting sections, but these are never presented to the visitors as representative of the piety of the nation. Until quite recently they have been persecuted, banished and banned by the action of the Holy Synod.

From many of my foregoing notes, the reader will have gathered that the peasantry are superstitious, and, more or less, this prevails throughout the various classes. For instance, if a man on issuing from the gate of the house meet a woman, she will, fearing to bring him misfortune, return to her home until he has restarted again; should the coachman on issuing from the gate of the house meet a priest or a cat, he will return until they have passed and only then renew his journey.

I was once talking to an elderly gentleman upon his religion. He so continually mentioned his good angel, that my curiosity was aroused, and I asked him to explain why he did so. He said: "You know, sir, that it would be only under the most pressing circumstances that we would wake a man out of his sleep, the reason being that two angels are assigned to accompany him from the cradle to the grave—one the Spirit of Evil, and the other the Beneficent Spirit of all Good. The former inspires our wicked thoughts with evil dreams and actions, and these too often predominate in our waking hours; whereas the good angel combats the machinations of the evil one, and when human nature is tired out with the daily conflict, he folds his wings over the weary soul, soothing it with sleep and pleasant dreams."

On leaving Wassilefka, I left behind me the most pleasant of experiences. M. Popoff had not only behaved most generously, but had also agreed to take charge of the machinery during the winter, and made me understand that if the next year's harvest turned out favourably he would certainly purchase it. Owing, however, to the drought and the consequent failure of the harvest through the whole district, this hope was not realized at that time, once more illustrating the adage that " Man proposes and God disposes."

As already seen, we had given bills for the balance of the cost of another machine to become payable at a certain date in November of that year, and on reaching home I found that the machine had arrived, but no prospect whatever lay before us for the payment of the obligations as they became due. Under these circumstances, we wrote to the manufacturers, fully explaining our position, and asking them to prolong payment over another season. From early spring to late September no rain had fallen and the harvest was an utter failure. We ourselves had only sufficient for our winter's sustenance, and there was no prospect of anything more accruing. We offered to pay them 5 per cent. interest at the term and renew the bills at short dates; but when the answer came, it was something in this style. I recollect that it was addressed to me personally, because I had made their acquaintance when ordering the first machine, and it was written in the Quaker tongue, in this wise, " Friend, thou hast given thy bond; it is out of our hands, and thou must meet it when it becomes due."

At the moment I felt so exasperated that I tore it in pieces and stamped upon it; all the more so that we had dealt with them for one machine and paid for it, and also half the value of the other now received. We had also paid the freight and duties, so that they must have known that the circumstances were of such a nature that we were not really in a position to carry out the agreement, but at the same time there was plenty of security.

Our friend, the English Consul, advised us to take no notice of it whatever, and we knew well that the

Queen's writ could not run in Russia, so there was nothing to fear. At the same time we tried to raise means to meet the claim. In the town there was a firm of merchants of the name of Poro & Pertika, who claimed English nationality from having been born in the Ionian Islands, and with whom I was on terms of friendship. Having mentioned to Mr. Poro the circumstances, he said that they had received a letter from a client who had a large estate in the Don Cossack country, where the harvest was a good medium one, and who stated that he had heard that steam thrashing machines were to be had in Odessa, and he proposed going there to see them. He said then, " If he intends to purchase one, I think he could not do better than come here, where he could see the machine and have it sent forward without delay."

The upshot of the whole affair was that we received the money for the machine the day before that bill became due, when it was paid, and it was the last business we ever did with a Quaker firm. As a result of the manner in which we had been treated by this firm, they lost a future business connection which in subsequent years averaged from £50,000 to £75,000 per annum.

BERDIANSK TO EKATERINOSLAV

Following on the successful construction of a steam corn-mill at Einlager, we had been requested to visit the firm of Thiesen & Heese, of Ekaterinoslav, with the view to the erection of a similar one for them. With this object, it being the late autumn, I hired a German fourgon (a covered vehicle on springs with four wheels) drawn by two horses, for the journey of approximately one hundred and forty-five miles. It was at the very treacherous time of the year when snowstorms might possibly be expected, and I took every precaution against any accident that might arise. With this view I laid in a plentiful supply of provisions for myself and driver, a sack of corn for the horses, and also a good supply of hay fastened in a net behind the wagon.

The itinerary of the journey was so arranged that we might spend each night at a German village, but even the very best plans are unavailing when the whole country-side is covered with a coating of snow four or five inches thick. There are on the Steppes no roads of any kind. Across these vast plains when covered with snow all tracks are hidden, and along these the Tchumaks, or in other words, Steppe Riders, when the storms arise, put up long sticks with a wisp of straw bound at the top to mark the direction.

It was on the third day when the storm began, and we had left our shelter about five hours. We had already crossed the River Malotchnaya, when the soughing of the wind began, and the ominous appearance of the clouds presaged the advent of one of those storms called Metels, or sweepers; these come down suddenly and with such relentless fury that the snow, falling at first in soft flakes, is soon hardened by the frost and becomes like dust. This, driven by the wind in horizontal lines, no man or horse can withstand, the former taking refuge in the wagon and the latter turning tail against the wind.

In our case, we at all events were supplied with provisions both for man and beast, and had no fear that, though lost on the Steppe, we should be in danger. Under such circumstances it is always better to have something upon which one can rely as a last resource, and I have always had with me a little instrument to point my road—my compass that hangs on my watch-chain at the present moment, which informed me silently of the direction in which we should steer.

Following on this course, and guided by the barking of dogs and the smell of fuel, or, as it is called, "the smell of the villages," we reached a village, which we found to be Gregorefka, owned by Count Cancrine. To go farther that night was impossible; the horses were thoroughly done up, and we too were almost frozen. Under these circumstances, I drove direct to the Palace, and ringing the bell, asked the footman who answered it whether the Count was in. On being informed that he and his family were spending the winter there, I asked him to tell his master than an Englishman who had lost his way on the Steppe begged an interview. He thereupon came down, and I found myself face to face with (as he eventually informed me) the eldest son of the Count Cancrine, who was the great financier of the reign of the Emperor Nicholas.

I must have looked the picture of an Esquimaux, dripping with wet snow, unwashed and unkempt; but my nationality was my passport, and with that virtue of hospitality which I think more than in all other nationalities is ingrafted in the Russian nature, he gave orders for my luggage to be brought in and my horses to be sent to the stables. Very soon after a nice guest-chamber was placed at my disposal. After having a good wash and attiring myself in becoming garments, I was ushered into his cabinet, and he must have thought I was a very different personage from the one he had greeted in the hall, for he received me in the most friendly manner, and presently introduced me to his wife and three daughters, with whom I soon became on very friendly terms. It seemed to me a most extraordinary thing that neither of the girls could speak Russian at all fluently. They had been brought up in Paris, and as this was the first winter of their return, they were very desirous to go back.

In the cabinet where I was received, in glass cases around the room were the uniforms and orders which had been presented to his father by various crowned heads. The large estate owned by his father consisted of sixty thousand acres, through the centre of which flowed the river. This estate, together with the inventory, on his father's death had been divided between himself and his brother Victor, each of whom had inherited, together with land, thirty thousand sheep.

The storm which had caused me to seek shelter lasted a whole week, but when the blizzard ceased I told the Count that I must hasten my departure. It was, however, with great difficulty that I got his consent, and I can quite understand that a family living in the isolation of a country house on the Russian Steppe must find it extremely dull and uninteresting in winter, and be ready to receive and entertain any one with whom they can associate. At last there could be no excuse for my staying longer, and the morning for my departure arrived. After having received very friendly wishes for my successful journey, the Count escorted me to the hall. On opening the door, I was surprised to see, instead of my own horses, his four-horse covered sledge; and upon inquiry it appeared that in order that I should have my own horses fresh, he had sent my man with them, thirty miles in advance, two days before.

I had afterwards the pleasure of meeting both the brothers at Kiev, and always received the same friendly hospitality. All my intercourse with this family made me realize to its full extent the value of the knowledge that I gained in my earlier youth. I found that a knowledge of French was indispensable in the family and society, at that time Russian only being spoken to dependents and servants.

With reference to the expression "the smell of the villages," used above, the traveller when passing through them in the summer will observe in every yard of the cottages the women engaged in treading out the manure. This they form into briquettes, which on being dried in the sun constitute their only fuel during the winter months. Some of the peasants have so keen a scent that they are able to name the village they are approaching by the smell, the reason being that they discern whether the manure used contains a larger amount of sheep droppings, which give a different odour to the ordinary manure. The pungent smell of the smoke borne by the wind can be recognized miles away, before the barking of the dogs is heard; and this I can testify, as it has often occurred to me during my travels, that the driver has informed me, long before I was aware of it, of our approach to some village as we were travelling against the wind.

CHAPTER VIII

THE STEPPE : ITS POPULATION, CHARACTER, AND FAUNA

Extent of Crimean Steppe—Nomad tribes—Herds of horses—Black-earth soil—Underground water supply—Ravines and hills due to water action—Kurgans, or Scythian burial-places—Comparison of climates in South Russia and England—Good effects from rain—Sheep pasturage—Sheep dogs—Abundance of wild flowers—Cloud effects—Enemies of agriculture—Hessian fly and Hungarian beetle—Marmot (Souslik)—Jerboa—Bird life—The mirage—History of Steppe—Locusts—Tarantula—Serpents.

THE so-called Steppe of Crimean Tartary is a vast extent of country, extending from a fringe of cultivated land, bordering on the River Dnieper, to within a few miles of the Sea of Azov, and embraces an area of 300 by 200 miles. Although this vast land is uncultivated as regards its major portion, it varies greatly in its conditions, many of its districts being quite capable of cultivation, having been colonized and containing settled communities of German Mennonites, Lutherans, Bulgarians, Tartars, etc.

Beyond the Sea of Azov to the east, the Steppe forms the pasture ground of various Oriental tribes, such as the Kirghizes, Kalmucks, Bashkirs, Tartars, etc., who occupy themselves with pasture and possess extensive flocks and herds.

These tribes are supposed to be the remnants of the Mongol invaders who, under the great leader Genghis Khan, ravished the whole of Asia and the Northern Hemisphere from Cathay to the Carpathians. These nomads follow up the pasture zones with their flocks and herds, moving their tents according to the season. Most of these tribes have very strong features, and are far from being prepossessing in their appearance, having high cheek-bones, narrow slits of eyes, and flat faces. Those who occupy themselves with the breeding of cattle and horses are very often rich, as they always have a ready market for these animals, not only in Russia, but also in Austria and Prussia, it being from this source that the military authorities in these lands obtain their mounts.

I have often met with herds (or so-called Taboons) of these wild, unshod animals being driven across the Steppe to the port of embarkation. On one occasion being out shooting with a German friend, we came upon one of these droves, and getting into conversation with the driver, and seeing the lasso cord hanging to his saddle, we asked him to give us an example of its working; upon this he asked my friend to point out which horse he would like, and, thinking to puzzle him, one quite in the centre was pointed out. Having set them all on a gallop, he threw the rope and caught the horse indicated by the neck.

The Steppe inhabited by these Eastern tribes is far more of the desert type than the one with which I am more particularly acquainted, and to which I am chiefly directing my remarks—having traversed it repeatedly in all directions and in all seasons. It must not be supposed that these vast plains of Crimean Tartary, over which you may travel for days without meeting a single traveller, are composed of desert sands or rock boulders and the stone debris of a disintegrated past formation. It is true that occasionally there are tracks of sand, but for the most part, and that the vastly predominating one, the surface soil is composed of a rich black earth, varying in depth from a few inches to several feet, undoubtedly a vegetable mould, whose origin and deposition have puzzled many geologists. Throughout the whole of the black-earth region, no stone or pebble of the size of a thumb-nail is to be found. It is only owing to the aridity of the climate, the lack of water, and still more the lack of initiative on the part of the Government (the owner of the soil) that this Steppe has not been developed into fertile regions.

The existence of a good underground water supply has been abundantly proved, mainly at depths from 70 to 200 feet. From this source every colonist is supplied with water from wells which are scattered in various parts for the use of the flocks of sheep that in spring move northward following the pasture; more notable still is the fact that a Scottish firm of wellborers in putting down a bore in the town of Melitopol, an oasis in the centre of the Steppe, obtained artesian water which was flowing for some years before I left Russia. Mr. Winning, the well-borer, told me he was convinced that an underground current must exist which forced the water to the surface, and that the outflow itself in his opinion was the overflow of the River Dnieper during the spring thaw.

The Steppes are not uniformly flat plains, but in a general way may be described as undulating, many parts having been cut into deep ravines by the action of the water, which at some parts are so pronounced as to give it the appearance of hill formation. This I have observed particularly in one district, where the melting of the snows in the spring-time had given rise to torrents which, cutting into the tablelands, had produced a miniature Switzerland.

It has often been remarked to me that travelling over the Steppe must be of an extremely monotonous character. On entering it there lies before the traveller a vast expanse circumscribed only by the horizon, and without any variety of scenery to break the dull monotony of the view. But to a contemplative mind it possesses ever-varying features of abounding interest. To me it has ever appealed as replete with historical memories of a past civilization. Across these plains successive tribes of Phœnicians, Scythians, Greeks, and Tartars have fought and conquered in their day, and travellers passing over them cannot but notice the many hillocks (so-called Mohuls or Kurgans) which have been the burial-places of the great chieftains of the past. Many of these have been opened, and in them have been found relics of the bygone ages, in the shape of the rich treasures which are now preserved in the Hermitage of St. Petersburg and the local museum at Kertch.

When passing through the water-worn ravines (often rich in vegetation), my indignation has been aroused that the negligence of man should allow the winter snows and the spring rains to run to waste, carrying with them in each succeeding year large deposits of the rich black earth. This can never be replaced, and is being deposited in the sand-logged deltas of the rivers. As I have already said, the greatest drawback in the cultivation of these so-called waste lands is undoubtedly drought, and this fact I have always tried to impress upon the authorities with whom I have come in contact.

In my opinion the two nations who are most ready to decry their country are Russia and England, and I am fully of opinion that, country for country, we in England are hard to beat. Our climate has none of those great extremes to be found in Russia or even in Canada, and whilst it may not be all that could be desired, it certainly lacks most of what is undesirable. For instance, with regard to the drought, it may be said that in one year out of three some parts of Russia are in a state of semi-starvation owing to the lack of rain, and during the heat of summer the Continental conditions of high temperature are extremely wearing to the body.

Under these drawbacks it is not to be wondered at that the land is barren and waste. It is true that the Government, in the neighbourhood of towns and colonies, let out plots of about 10 desiatines (25 acres) which are eagerly taken up by the peasantry and the dwellers in the immediate villages and towns. Should abundant rains fall on the soil during the autumn and spring, together with one good one during May, the land which has merely been tickled with the plough will laugh with a copious harvest. This, however, is

KHARKOV. THE RESIDENCE OF MR. G. HUME.

quite a speculation ; for though it is reckoned that there should be one fairly good year in three, and a bumper one in seven, yet the seasons are so irregular that only after long periods of years a fair average can be determined.

In the year 1862, we ourselves took up one of these plots with the view of growing corn, for the purpose of exhibiting to the peasants and colonists the working of our machines. The result was that the yield was nothing, the sparse corn that did come up being only six inches high, including the ear, so that we let it off to be grazed by sheep, and this indeed finished our farming experiment.

Again a certain amount of revenue is gained by the Government letting out the land as pasturage for sheep, in my day one rouble (two shillings) per head being charged. The shepherds are to be met with now and again moving in front of the flocks, and leading them on from south to north, following up the pasturage. If when travelling the unusual barking of dogs is heard, it is a sure sign that a flock of sheep is on the move. It is, however, advisable to keep a fair distance from them, as the dogs are savage as wolves, and respect not the stranger, neither man nor beast.

On leaving civilization behind and entering the solitude of the Steppe, it is well to remember that one should be supplied with provisions for several days' journey. Personally I have found that cold weak tea with lemon and sugar is a most acceptable reviver during the heat of the day. No one who has not experienced it can have the slightest idea of what excessive thirst means. It affects the body in such a manner that you can feel every vestige of moisture being extracted, also the tongue becomes dried, swells and fills the throat, rendering articulation and swallowing difficult. The worst thing to be done under the circumstances is to drink water inordinately, but to rinse the mouth and gargle the throat is the best sedative.

In the early spring after the melting of the snow,

the most striking evidence of the potentialities of the soil for cultivation is the large assortment of wild flowers that carpet it. Having been personally astonished at their profusion, I asked the daughters of a colonist friend, who had received an advanced course of education, if they would make me a collection from the open Steppe of the most common of the species within a reasonable radius of their village. They took up the idea with enthusiasm, with the result that I received from them an album containing 167 different species and an intimation that, these being from the Steppe, doubtless others could be found in the sheltered spots and ravines.

The air in the open is so pure and fresh that one enjoys its invigorating effect and experiences a veritable joy in living. When the traveller, wearied with a long morning in the saddle, or long seated in a covered cart (fourgon), unsaddles and unharnesses for the midday meal and siesta, he enjoys with real delight lying on his back and dozing off to the music of his grazing cattle. The darkened room, with its stifling atmosphere and its household pests, the flies, fleas, mosquitoes, cockroaches, and many others, are all absent; and as there is always in the open air a little air movement, on the hottest day, the sweet breath of heaven soothes the tired brain and gives strength for renewed exertion.

During my many traversings of these regions I have found that they have grown in attractiveness and have become increasingly interesting. The Steppe is the centre of a deep silence, only broken by the ever-changing voices of Nature in her varying moods. The cloud effects are very beautiful, owing to the pure, clear atmosphere through which they are seen. For instance, there is the " mare's tail " cloud, the cirrus blown by the wind in the upper strata into long, feathery sprays. Again, there are beautiful displays of cirro-cumulus, the cloud appearing like a flock of sheep or the markings of a mackerel, whence comes the sailor's name of a " mackerel " sky. At other times there is a fine-weather type appearing mornings and evenings, and ushering in the brightest days. This type would probably on Howard's definition be "stratus." When the weather is more disturbed, grand masses of cumulo-stratus, spreading wide at their base, appear as mountains crowned with snow. In the later autumn oncoming dark and heavy nimbus clouds mark the advance of heavy thunderstorms, which in such cases are very severe.

At eventide the summer and autumn sunsets make the clouds glow with a golden fringe, or the fitful gleams of sunlight line them with a silver border. The after-glow from the great orb just sunk below the horizon seems as it were fain to depart, and returns to kiss a fond good-night to the ever weary and restless world.

There is also something attractive to the eye, for instance, on an absolutely calm day when there suddenly arise columns of dust, ofttimes many of them tiny spirals of whirlwinds careering along at full speed, racing each other along the plains, impelled by some zephyr until, exhausted, they collapse. In the autumn also the big burian bushes broken off are formed into great balls, which, driven by the wind, leaping and bounding in headlong flight, gradually, on being broken up, spread the fertilizing element of nitrate on the soil. A professor of botany informed me that this was a nitraceous plant, so endowed by nature that when broken up it is quite indispensable to vegetation.

The agriculturist in Russia has many enemies to contend with; besides those of the climate, with its fickle character. However excellent and genial may have been the seeding and growing time, and however high his hopes may have been raised for an abundant crop, yet there is no certainty of a remunerative return for his hard work and long waiting until he can celebrate his " Harvest Home."

When one considers that in a vast empire like Russia, 90 per cent. of its population are dependent for their living on the soil, and that throughout a whole year all their hopes, all their capital, and all their energies are centred in an abundant yield, it is a pathetic thought that a single hailstorm or even the winds of heaven may destroy in one short hour the arduous labours of a whole year.

Not only are these dangers ever imminent, but other enemies not less fatal are ever on the watch, and one of them in particular gathers its deadly phalanx in far-distant lands. Amongst these we have the Hessian fly, the larvæ of which settle in the joints of the cornstalk and gradually destroy its fibre, so that its undeveloped head, including the ear, falls to the ground. By it I have seen the most promising crops devastated, the fields having the appearance of littered stubble.

Another most destructive creature is a beetle known in Russia as the Hungarian or Austrian beetle. It first made its appearance in an epidemic form in the sixties, when it commenced its ravages in the southern districts of the corn-growing zones, and caused widespread destruction. Being a life member of the Agricultural Society of Poltava, I was requested to obtain from the Agricultural Society of England, on their behalf, information how to deal with it, and for that purpose its whole life's history was forwarded to the society. If I rightly remember, the answer received principally advised deep ploughing, but this was considered impracticable at that time.

This beetle, that had made its appearance so suddenly in the southern provinces, spread with great rapidity throughout the corn-growing districts of the so called garden of Russia. The pest makes its appearance at the blossoming stage of the grain upon which it lives, having a great predilection for the summer wheat. It not only sucks the grain in its milky form, but scrabbles the hardening grain from the more advanced ears. This beetle is not a long liver, and when it has finished destroying the harvest it returns to the earth, where it lays its eggs and dies. An interval of from two to three years now occurs;

In the spring-time of the next year the eggs hatch out, and the larva or grub, passing through various stages, takes the above-named time before the next generation arrives at maturity.

Amongst other animal scourges of the agriculturist and possibly one of the most destructive that infest the Steppe is the marmot (the so-called souslik) a species of rat, but very much larger and with a short tail. It is very pretty, and seems endowed with a large amount of intelligence. These settle in colonies near the growing crops, and being very prolific they increase with surprising rapidity, and I have seen large tracks of cultivated land that have been devastated by them. I have often in my travels come across their colonies and noticed their action on the approach of man: they throw out their sentinels, who, seated on their haunches, announce the approach of danger by a whistle, when the whole place becomes alive, and they can be seen disappearing into their holes; these holes lead into chambers where they hibernate, and, owing to their custom of making several outlets, they are very difficult to catch.

So destructive had they become, that the Government set a price upon their tails, and each peasant landowner had to send in a certain number of these under penalty. A wonderful discovery was soon made, for in some districts the marmot must have grown two tails, as the reward claimed was far in excess of the number estimated by the Government. It was, however, afterwards discovered that through the medium of the usual exchange those that had been presented by "A" and had received the reward were re-presented by "B," who in his turn again claimed a recompense. The Government then, finding how it was being defrauded, fell back on a chemical solution, which they pumped into the holes (after, as they believed, all of them were stopped), but finding this also a failure they tried drowning the marmots. When I left Russia in 1893 the exchange for the tails was in full swing, so that they were at a premium.

A further rodent is the jerboa, the prettiest of its tribe, whose lightning springs almost deceive the eye; but it is not at all destructive, being numerically rare.

Bird life is also abundant, but the only prominent songster is the lark, which is seen everywhere. I used to watch it with great interest, it being very amusing to see its efforts to deceive; for instance, it never descends directly to its nest, stops all song a long distance before it descends, and then proceeds homewards through the grass without a sound. Its note can be heard from heaven's gate, a sound extremely grateful to the ear, more especially when no other bird can be seen.

Most of the others belong to the predatory class. Eagles, hawks of all kinds, and carrion crows are very abundant; these are frequently met with feeding upon horses and cattle that have fallen upon the track and been abandoned. As the traveller approaches they rise from their ghastly meal with a great flapping of wings, but only to return when the danger is past.

The Mirage

The most puzzling of the phenomena that meet the eye of the traveller is the mirage. Suddenly in the distance will appear the vision of a great lake, with ships apparently sailing on its surface, or a delightful landscape with houses, trees, and shrubs reflected in it—the whole so vivid in every detail that it produces an extraordinary impression of reality upon the spectator's mind. On one occasion, when travelling with my son, the vision of a large lake appeared, in the middle of which was a conical-shaped hill or highland upon whose summit was perched an enormous eagle. The apparition was so clear that even the horses were deceived, and hastened their paces in anticipation of the cool and refreshing drink which they thought so near.

This optical delusion is due to the rarefaction of the air at rest in contact with the sand or soil which has become abnormally heated by the sun's rays. In consequence, the density of the surface air is diminished for some distance upward from the ground. This gives rise to successive bending of the rays of light in their passage through the atmosphere. Thus rays passing from more dense to less dense strata are bent upwards by total reflection from the lower less dense layers ; the image so produced when viewed horizontally gives rise to the illusion, which is usually in reality a reflection from the clouds or sky.

The history of the Steppe commences with the conquest of the Celtic Cimerians by the Scythians in 712 B.C., and also during that same period Greek colonists began to settle along the coast, who, becoming hard pressed, placed themselves under the protection of Mithridates VI, King of Pontus, 114 B.C. Following on, the Romans took possession, and for services rendered restored the Pontian Kingdom as a vassal of Rome and a tributary state. Since those early days the Crimea and its territories have been the battle-ground of many tribes and nations. They were overrun by the Goths in A.D. 250, and then successively by the Huns, the Khazara, the Byzantine Greeks, the Kipchaks, and the Mongols (1237). Again, in the thirteenth century the Genoese seized the settlements from the Venetians, holding them till 1745, when the all-conquering Ottoman captured them.

Later the Tartars, who were already firmly seated in the north, after the destruction of the great Golden Horde by Tamerlane, founded an independent kingdom, and ultimately established their seat of government at Baktchi-Serai. From the year 1748 to 1777 the Tartars were tributary to Turkey ; but after the victory by Russia under Suvórov, which resulted in the downfall of the Turks, the Tartars became the dependents of Russia and were finally absorbed in 1783.

Of these various tribes that have ebbed and flowed throughout the ages over these Steppe lands, it is surprising that so few remains of any importance are to be found. In addition to the Kurgans, or burial-places of the Scythians, already mentioned, which are scattered over the whole area, there are the immense mounds, almost completely composed of pottery, in the near neighbourhood of Kertch, and the old picturesque ruins of forts of Grecian invaders, that dot the coast of the Russian Riviera from Theodosia to Cape Saria. This embraces the sea-bathing resorts of Alupka, Yalta, Alushta, Sudak, Theodosia, together with the Emperor's Palace and Park at Livadia. Protected from the north and east by the abruptly rising mountain range of Yaila-Dagh, they enjoy an almost Italian climate, and the semi-tropical plants and flowers flourish in the open. Within this area the vines from whence is produced the full-bodied wine of the district, and all other fruit of the ordinary kind, such as apples, pears, etc., grow luxuriantly. These are of the finest quality and supply the internal markets of Russia.

The Locusts

The worst enemy of the insect tribe that the agriculturist dreads is the locust, which fortunately, however, is not a very frequent visitor, but which when it comes, should it settle near a village under cultivation, destroys every vestige of vegetation throughout the whole radius of its place of settlement. On the approach of locusts, under Government regulations all villagers and colonists within twenty miles are bound to turn out and hasten to the spot with their families and horses to take part in their extirpation; this, however, is no easy task, especially if they may have been hatched in some unknown and inaccessible part of the country.

During my stay in Russia I had been five times an eye witness of the extraordinary density of the mass, and of the destructive effects that follow. The first time, when serving as engineer on board the *Mithridates*, we were coasting along Circassia, when a cloud of them passed over the vessel. Thousands, doubtless wearied with their flight, fell into the sea, but large numbers kept the sailors busy clearing the deck; the stokers in the engine and boiler rooms had still more trouble, owing to the locusts becoming frizzled with the heat; and the atmosphere was polluted with the stench. One large specimen that I preserved measured two and a half inches in length. In my opinion, in view of the very large number that fell on board and over an extensive area of the sea, the main body must have reached the Crimea, for which they were steering, in a very attenuated condition.

The second time was in 1864, when a cloud coming from the east, having from a distance all the appearance of a rising storm, flew in the afternoon over Berdiansk, where I was residing, and they were in such numbers that the sky was darkened by their passage. The height of their flight was from three to four hundred feet from the earth, and the noise was like the suppressed whirr of an aeroplane. This particular body devastated the country thirty miles distant from the town, eating to their very roots the whole of the standing crops, and all the vegetable products to such an extent that even the leaves of the trees were devoured.

There are several species of these insects, of which the most destructive is the migratory locust, or *Acrydium migratorium*. They are of a greenish colour, with strongly-developed muscular legs well adapted for jumping; they are migratory, and the largest specimens reach a length of from $2\frac{1}{2}$ to 3 inches. The leaping and flying being their only means of progression, it is curious to see the constant springing when large numbers are in motion.

It might be thought that many accounts of these destructive creatures are exaggerations; but from what I have personally seen of the havoc and destruction caused by them, over extensive tracts of country, I can fully confirm the Biblical record that they are indeed "very grievous, for they covered the face of the whole earth so that the land was darkened, and did eat every herb of the land, and all the fruit of the trees."

In another of my journeys, I passed for over an hour through a cloud of these insects that had settled on the ground. The noise of their feeding could be heard for a considerable time before reaching them; from the whirring sound of their movements, they must have been millions in number, and before we got clear of them the wheels of our carriage were clogged with their bodies.

On another occasion during the early summer I passed over a district which had been devastated the previous autumn and in which the female had deposited her eggs. Those I have seen seemed to be in a kind of sack and numbered from sixty to seventy, but there being no membrane, these must have been held together by some glutinous matter. In the spring-time the eggs are hatched by the sun, and the larvæ have all the appearance of silkworm grubs. They grow rapidly, and, increasing in size day by day, soon cover a very extensive area of land; when sufficiently strong (in about six weeks' time), having exhausted all their food supply, they commence their onward march, not yet having developed their wings. In this nothing stops them: they climb every obstacle, trees and houses are scaled, and should the windows be open they invade the rooms. In their path all vegetation disappears, and even the most favoured lands are turned into an arid desert. The wings, which have hitherto been confined in sheaths, having become developed for flight, they rise and fly before the wind to new pastures, carrying on their work of devastation throughout the whole district traversed.

On the fifth occasion, when travelling to Baku on the Caspian, the train ran into a cloud of these insects at a station about ten miles from the city. The sky became darkened and the windows rattled, as if we were passing through a hailstorm, instead of which, however, it was an immense body of locusts which were rattling on the glass. So numerous were they, that the train began to lose its grip and decrease in speed, ultimately coming to a standstill. It appears that on every train bags of sand are carried in view of such a necessity, but the crushing of the bodies clogs

IN RUSSIA

the wheels; and until the cloud passed nothing could be done, after which we proceeded at a snail's pace, arriving in the city over three hours late.

In order to combat the plague, under the Regulations of the Government all inhabitants, as previously stated, have, under requisition of the authorities, to hasten to the region affected and use their best endeavours to destroy the insects. On such occasions a busy scene is presented. Men, women, and children arrive in all kinds of vehicles and cut deep trenches along the whole line of the advancing host. Within these trenches fires are laid, fed by Steppe grass, and are constantly renewed, into these being swept thousands upon thousands of the dreaded enemy.

The German colonist on his part is far more practical than the peasant, and has invented a machine which is effective in crushing many thousands a day. Horses in single or double span are harnessed by whipple trees to a frame upon which is placed a seat for the driver, and to which a bar of wood of a suitable length is attached. On this bar are fixed loose fingers of wood which give to the inequalities of the ground, and when loaded with bags of sand crush the insects in their path. This has certainly proved the most efficient means that have been employed hitherto; but at this time of the year every hour of the day is of great value to the farmer, and should the insects not be moving in the direction of his farmstead he stays away, and the enemy moves out of the twenty-mile radius. In the meantime the insects take their flight, the vanguard only having been destroyed, and the serried legions follow on.

Fortunately, the invasions of locusts are of rare occurrence; and from the measures that are being employed for their destruction when in the egg stage, the quantities to be dealt with are becoming more manageable.

Up to the period of which I am writing, the attention of the peasant was directed not to their destruction, but to their removal from his own land to a barren uncultivated district. For this purpose a man mounted on a white horse would ride up to the leaders of the host, and turning them off the whole body attained the purpose to a certain degree. In addition all the other inhabitants of the village turned out and received them with yells, shrieks, and the din of metal pots and pans, hoping to drive them away, but with little success.

One of the most dangerous of the invertebrates here is the tarantula spider, whose bite is extremely venomous. Our housekeeper on one occasion had a very narrow escape from death through the bite of one of these Arachnids causing blood poisoning; her arm was swollen to double its size. Their nesting-place is indicated by small deep holes in the Steppe, and some places are infested by them to a considerable extent. In bivouacking for the night on the Steppe, care must therefore be taken to examine round the camping-place for some considerable distance. In addition to the holes formed by these spiders, there are others of a larger size due to the field crickets; these are much more numerous, and I have often fallen asleep to the music of their chirp.

In the ravines, and more especially in the damp places near the river, a large number of snakes is to be found; and on one occasion walking near the River Dnieper I stooped down to pick up a stone, when I heard a hiss, and starting back saw a long black serpent of the most venomous character on its tail ready to strike. Not having any weapon or stick with me, it escaped.

I was once walking down the garden with a military friend of mine; he was dressed in full uniform with sword, being a captain in the guards. All of a sudden he rushed away at full speed down the garden path without any intimation of his intention, and when I reached him exclaimed, " Did you see that snake? it was on your side and ready to strike." I certainly had not seen it, but think if I had had a sword I might have used it with effect. He stated that he dreaded these reptiles more than anything else, and would rather face the cannon's mouth.

CHAPTER IX

LIFE IN POLTAVA AND KHARKOV

Marriage—Third failure of harvest—Removal from Berdiansk to Poltava—Visit to German colonies—Incident of river crossing—Establishment at Poltava—Steppe journey to Novo-Moskovsk from Keitchkass—Perilous position in snowstorm—Kharkov—Distillery contract difficulty—Country tracks in winter—Inability to obtain workmen—Friendships formed in Poltava—Establishment of mill at Kharkov—Mill burnt down—Agency for Messrs. Marshall, Sons & Co. arranged—Partnership with Mr. Lister—Improvements in machines—Prosperous times—The Baron incident—The carriage incident.

BERDIANSK, POLTAVA

OWING to a two-years' succession of bad harvests, it became evident that Berdiansk did not offer sufficient prospects for expansion that could yield permanent support for two families. In the year 1863, on January 20th, I had married, and therefore taken upon myself great responsibilities.

Looking back upon close on fifty years of happy married life, I cannot but express my thankfulness to my dear wife for the devotion with which she accompanied me through all the vicissitudes and trials herein recorded, she retaining throughout the long years we shared together the love and affection of her family and a very large circle of friends.

Having taken the above resolution, Mr. Graham and I resolved to dissolve our partnership, he remaining in Berdiansk, while I went forth to seek new fields. Previous to our final departure, I had visited, together with my wife, a number of the German colonies, and, armed with an introduction from Mr. Jansen, the

German Consul, we made the acquaintance of the leading members, who heartily invited us to stay with them during our inland journey. After long deliberation with our friends, the city of Poltava was considered to offer the best prospects for a settlement, it being the centre of Russia's finest agricultural districts. This town is well known also from a historical standpoint, as being the scene of a crushing defeat of Charles XII of Sweden by Peter the Great.

On our first journey, the following incident occurred. It had been arranged that we should stop at the house of a Mr. Reimer, who at that time was the mayor of the village of Orloffka. To reach this place we had to cross the River Malotchnaya, where our coachman, having misjudged the ford, drove us into the middle of the stream, when we immediately sank to the axles of the carriage. The position became a very difficult one, as it would have been impossible for the driver to descend without himself becoming embedded, and water began to invade the carriage itself.

At this juncture we heard in the distance the voices of men approaching the ford, who soon appeared accompanying their teams of bullocks. We therefore hailed them, and they commenced bargaining as to the amount to be paid them for rendering assistance, the sum finally settled being 25 roubles (£2 10s.). The coachman could by leaning over unhook the traces, thus freeing the horses; the bullocks being attached to the carriage in a few minutes landed us on the bank, and the horses were then also extricated, the whole operation taking nearly half an hour.

Soon after we arrived at our host's house, when I related the whole circumstances. On hearing this, Mr. Reimer became extremely angry, and at once sent a man on horseback to bring back the men who had helped us. On their arrival, after being bitterly upbraided for breaking the accepted law of the Steppe, which enjoined mutual aid to be given in case of necessity, without payment, he made them return me the money, and threatened to impound the team if they did not do so; he would not even allow me to give them a small gratuity.

We had now to prepare for the greater trek. For this purpose we had a large fourgon, a covered roomy coach, drawn by three horses. My wife and our German colonist housekeeper slept inside, and myself and our driver (also a German colonist) under the vehicle. Taking as we did a circuitous route, as long as we were in the German colonies we had a roof over our heads every night, and we stayed a week with Mr. Cornies, the Government inspector of the Mennonite community. Contrary to the Mennonite tenets he had married a wife from Germany; he was also a man of great intellectual powers, and possessed a large estate, on a portion of which he had planted an extensive forest, thereby proving that the climate and soil of the Steppe were amply suitable for the vigorous growth of trees. Following his example, the Russian Government planted large tracts of Steppe land with forest trees, and it is in institutions connected with the development of these that the youth of the Mennonites receive instruction in forestry and first aid to the wounded instead of undergoing military service.

In this house one of the dishes provided for dinner was peacock, and a water melon of their own growing that weighed forty-five pounds. This was about our half-way house, from which we now entered on our Steppe journey, reinvigorated and refreshed. For many a long mile the driver and myself walked on foot; we started early in the morning, taking three hours' rest in the middle of the day, after which we proceeded until sunset.

The next stage of our journey was Einlager, where we stayed two days with our friends the Ungers, for whom I had erected the first mill, which I was pleased to find was making large profits. At that time it was the custom to work on the principle of barter, the owners of all windmills receiving one-tenth of the corn delivered instead of money, and this same principle was being carried out at this time with the steam mills.

The trade had so increased that those bringing corn, no matter what quality, could immediately receive in return barley, wheat, or rye already ground, without having to wait.

We then proceeded on our further journey to Ekaterinoslav, a city that had been founded within a few weeks by Potemkin to prove to Catherine the Great the prosperity of her newly-conquered Tartar territories. In this city we stayed with Mr. Tiesen, for whom I had erected my second mill, after which we took our last stage to Poltava and stayed with Mr. Schiller until we could establish ourselves in our new home. He was a colonist with some means, having a large carriage-building establishment and a farm in the neighbourhood. In this city I established a foundry, but owing to inability to obtain skilled workmen I was forced to return to Kharkov in the year 1867.

Journey from Keitchkass to Novo-Moskovsk

It was in the middle of winter, and urgent business forced me to take the journey of 128 miles between these two places. We had had a very severe frost of over 40 degrees Réaumur which had prevented my starting before, but this having given way considerably, I commenced the journey under a brilliant sunshine, in a large roomy sledge with a pair of horses, hoping to arrive at my destination at the end of two days.

The first fifty miles was over the Steppe, which being covered with snow obliged me to judge the direction by compass till my arrival at Ekaterinoslav, from which town I could get post-horses. Within about twenty miles of this town we struck the line marked out every winter by the Tchumaks (Steppe Riders), consisting of poles or withies, on the top of which are placed wisps of straw. These, however, in my experience are of very little use, owing to their being carried away by the wind. On this occasion, after wandering a considerable distance out of the direct line, the horses became so tired out that, coming accidentally upon a

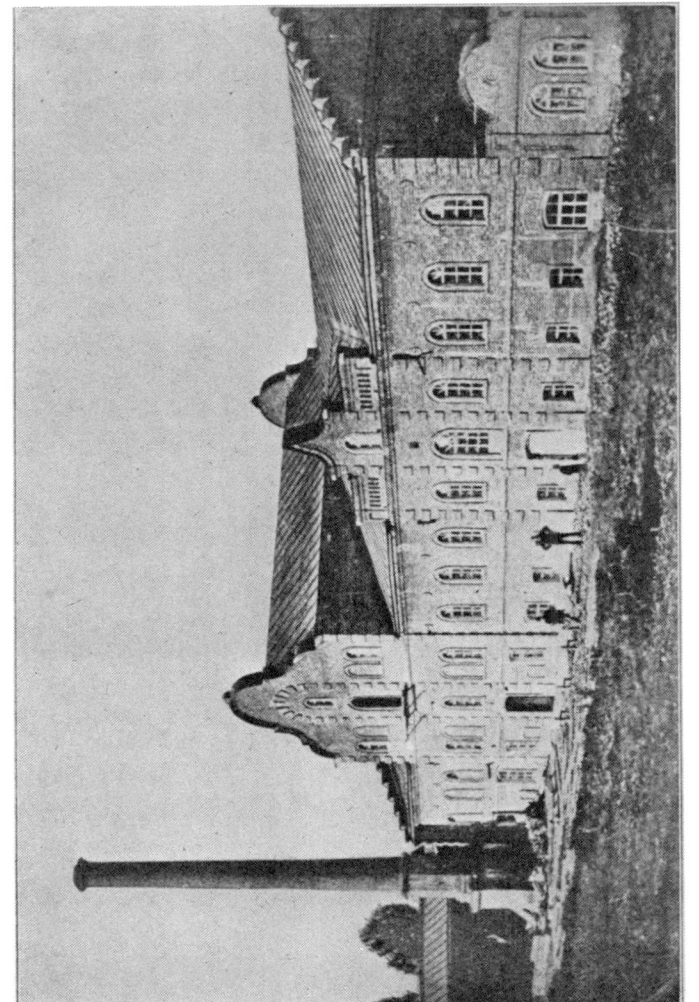

KHARKOV. MESSRS. HUME AND LISTER'S MILL.

small hamlet, we stayed for the night until early morning, when we proceeded and arrived at Ekaterinoslav between seven and eight in the morning.

The procedure at that time for all travellers by post was to obtain a travelling permit on presentation of their passports, which had been duly viséd by the police; when these have been registered at the post station, horses, if available, are provided. On this occasion, going to the postmaster immediately on arrival, I was told that he was asleep, and that I was to come again in two hours. At this I demurred, pleading urgency, but the caretaker of the place declared that he could not disturb the official's angel and would not wake him, so having been informed where he was sleeping I went and roused him. After some demur I obtained his signature, but it was only after middle day that I was able to obtain horses.

At the post station I found two Jews very thinly clad and looking very poor and haggard, who besought me in the most imploring terms to take them with me as they were going to the same town, and to this I acceded.

The post stations are generally ten to twelve miles distant one from the other, and the so-called post roads are mere unmetalled tracks marked out by ploughshares on either side, giving a width of about 120 feet. Each verst has a post marked diagonally with black and white stripes, and in addition on certain main tracks telegraph poles are erected, which was the case on this road.

After we had proceeded some little distance the wind began to blow, and the driver turning to me said, "We shall have a storm soon." The clouds began to gather, and before we got half-way between the stations we were in the midst of the driving drift, night was coming on, and the horses were worn out by the wind and weather. With the blinding sheets driven by a furious wind, and no shelter near, the position on these open roads becomes exceedingly dangerous, and it was so in this case. All horses when left to themselves wander in a circular direction, and in addition turn their backs to the blinding sleet and snow.

We discovered that we were out of the track; no marks were visible, and the driver wanted to leave the sledge and search for the telegraph poles, which I refused to allow. The Jews that were with me, not having suitable fur clothing, were in a parlous condition and in great danger of being frozen. They continually wanted to go to sleep, to prevent which I had to use physical force, as this meant death. Personally I had on a large wolf-skin coat (schuba), with a very large cape, so that I was warmly clad, and as far as I could was able to give them a certain amount of protection. We had proceeded for some distance at foot pace, with the wind, but whither we did not know, when all of a sudden, horses, driver, sledge, and passengers were hurled over a steep bank of over twenty feet in depth, fortunately falling into a great snowdrift which had accumulated at the bottom. The horses, half buried in the snow and struggling to find foothold, kicked and plunged, the driver was thrown over their heads, and I was shot two feet into the drift, while the two Jews were almost covered by the sledge, but happily uninjured.

We extricated ourselves at last, not much the worse physically for the accident, and found that we were on a tributary of the Dnieper, the river upon which Ekaterinoslav stands. Passing along the frozen stream under the protection of the bank, we ultimately heard the barking of dogs, a sure sign that a village was near. Here we arrived at about three o'clock in the morning, when I ordered the driver to wake up the owner of the first house we came to, so that we might obtain shelter. The man, so awakened, informed us that there was a caravanserai (kabak in Russian) in the village, where on arrival we were able to obtain a samovar, food, and shelter. We also found that we were within three-quarters of a mile of the place we had started from the day before.

We then proceeded to the original post station

whence we had started, and where we found great anxiety existed as to our fate, seeing that the horses ought to have returned the evening before. They feared that the great storm that had arisen had overwhelmed us, as so often happens to travellers in the winter-time. On proceeding again, nothing further happened, and we arrived safe and sound at our destination two days later than we had expected.

Kharkov and Poltava

Kharkov, the capital of the province of that name, is a city of the greatest strategical and commercial importance. It had, when I first entered it, a population of 75,000, which during the last fifty years has increased to over 250,000. Next to Nijni-Novgorod, it is the largest centre of commerce in Russia, having four fairs during the year, each lasting about a month. To them is brought all the merchandise and produce from the northern and central parts of the Empire. The most important of these is the great Wool Fair, held in the month of June, which attracts purchasers from all parts of Europe. On the plain in front of our house were stacked thousands of bales, like streets, consisting of all classes of wool of the merino, the long-woolled Russian sheep, the Angora goat, etc. Each of these classes, separately stacked, consisted of the washed, the half-washed, the swum, and those in grease.

In addition to its being the principal mercantile, it is, together with Kiev, a leading intellectual centre, having a University, Technical Institute, Veterinary College, large Secondary Schools, Libraries, Clinics, Clubs, etc. It was to this city that I migrated in 1867, owing to my failure to obtain workmen for the factory that I had founded in Poltava. Circumstances demanded that I should take an immediate resolution owing to my having entered into a contract of very considerable importance for the machinery of a large new distillery. The owner of the Karlovka estate was the Grand Duchess Helena Pavlovna, the aunt of the Emperor, and the distillery had to be completed and ready for work on October 1st of that year. In addition to much that had to be done in the foundry I covenanted to supply twelve large iron reservoirs, some 20 feet long by 4 feet in diameter, for holding the spirit. These I had to order from England, and I pressed upon the agent in London the necessity for their prompt delivery, there being more than ample time for their completion. Although the order had been confirmed and I had forwarded money for the purpose, the weeks came and went, the date for fulfilling the contract drew near, and in spite of my letters and telegrams I could get no news from London. At last they were sent off, but on their arrival in Odessa it was late autumn and the rains had already commenced. There being no railway at that time, nor roads, their transport through the mud became perfectly impracticable, no contractor being found who would undertake the work. The steward of the estate was furious; all the other machinery that I had contracted for had been completed, and had given satisfaction, but the result was that I had to make wooden vats at my own expense to contain the spirit.

This, however, was not the end. The mud was succeeded by frost and the transport of the reservoirs for 400 miles over the frozen ground had so shaken them through the constant jolting, that on their arrival, when tested, the water poured through the rivet holes as through a sieve, thus necessitating an almost complete reconstruction.

No one in England can have the slightest idea what the country tracks in Russia are like during the spring and winter. When once the spring and autumn rains commence, the surface of the Steppe is churned up into a thick, bad-smelling morass in which vehicles become embedded up to their very axles. It was during one of such autumn journeys that my coach, to which were harnessed eight horses and two pairs of bullocks, was engulfed, and it took me sixteen days

IN RUSSIA

to traverse the eighty miles that separated me from my destination.

On completion of the whole work it proved very satisfactory, so much so that, on the advice of the steward, the Grand Duchess authorized him to pay me in full for the wooden vats and half the price of the loss incurred on the contract. This was, however, considering my limited means, very appreciable, all the more so, that I was a great loser in the construction of a flour mill for Prince Dolgorouki. On establishing my foundry in Poltava, the first contract that I undertook was the above-named mill, consisting of a large water wheel, with all the internal machinery, and including the reconstruction of the dam, which involved the temporary deflection of the River Psiol. Unfortunately, I could not obtain skilled labour for the factory. All my patterns were completed, but mechanics and moulders would not leave Kharkov to work in Poltava, and after exhausting every means to secure workers, I was compelled to take the patterns to Kharkov, and pay an exorbitant price to have them cast. I thereupon came to a prompt decision to leave Poltava, and remove to Kharkov, thus abandoning all the outlay that I had made, and the whole of my savings up to date; and had I been compelled to liquidate my affairs, I should have been penniless.

I was, however, greatly helped in re-establishing my position through the steward of the Grand Duchess Helena, who, in addition to assisting me in the loss sustained, rendered me signal service by recommending me to paying work in the sugar factories which were at that time being introduced. This paved the way for my subsequent success. Although my stay in Poltava was adverse in a pecuniary sense, yet during this period I established friendships amongst Russian families which have been of lifelong duration. Among these I count the late Governor, M. Martinoff, the Karaishes of Sukarabovka (the lineal descendants of the great General Kutusoff, who withstood Napoleon), Count Kapnist of Dolgolovki, the Jukovskis, and many others, in whose society I and my family spent many happy hours. I would specially mention Madame Traskin and her husband, for many years Marshal of Nobility at Suma and Gentleman of the Chamber to the present Emperor. These I have known from their earliest childhood. The very considerable affinity existing between certain aspects of British and Russian characters, which renders social intercourse between the two races easy and agreeable, is not generally realized. It must not be forgotten that Russia is a nation in the making ; it has no middle class (which is the backbone of our own people), this being represented by the mercantile community, the majority of whom were either serfs themselves or of serf origin. Here also we met a dear friend who became the lifelong companion of my wife, and throughout all the years spent in Russia shared our experiences through good and evil.

In 1868, when the New Russia Company was founded, I had been invited to accompany the engineers from England to the rich coal-bearing estates in the Government of Ekaterinoslav. These gentlemen were proceeding there to construct the railway between the works and the main Kharkov-Azov line at Konstantinovka. Among them was a young man, Mr. William Gooch, nephew of Sir Daniel Gooch, the manager of the Great Western Railway, who on the completion of that work was very desirous of trying his fortune in some industry in Russia. His father, who was a promoter of the New Russia Company, and rich, had consented to give him substantial help, provided I was prepared to join him in the undertaking. On being consulted, we went thoroughly into the various possibilities, with the result that a steam flour mill seemed to offer the best prospects, but would involve a capital expenditure of £21,000. The business was eventually started, and from the outset everything looked favourable for a great success. Sales were effected in advance with promise of very satisfactory results. This being outside my own profession, it was arranged that Mr. Gooch should take the management under my supervision, and that he should live on the spot.

Two years elapsed, the mill was working, the business growing with every prospect of continued success. My partner thereupon went to England, married, brought out his wife and settled in a house adjoining the mill. Another year passed by, when early one morning a man came to my house in the town and told my housekeeper that Mr. Gooch required my presence immediately at the mill, adding that it had been burnt to the ground in the night. Of course, the shock of the announcement was severe, but really I had become so inured to misfortune that it did not seem to affect me so greatly as it otherwise might have done. It was found, on examination of the loss with the insurance company, that my partner, who had insured it, had consented to a valuation by the company, which, after excluding foundations and standing walls, had left a very small margin for the machinery, fittings, and all the woodwork of the interior. We had also, unfortunately, at the time a large supply of flour ready to be delivered in the morning, which, together with thousands of sacks, was burnt. This flour, having been insured, not in the mill, but in the stores, was a total loss. At this juncture Mr. Gooch's father declined to give any assistance in the reinstatement of the mill, and subsequently my new firm of Hume & Lister bought the place, and we established in it a factory for making pearl barley and cleaning rice.

About this time the news of the introduction of the steam thrasher had spread among the manufacturers of agricultural machinery in England. In consequence, Messrs. Marshall, Sons & Co., of Gainsborough, sent out a representative, Mr. Lister, with a view to establishing an agency for the introduction of their well-known steam engines and thrashers. Having been invited, I joined with Mr. Lister in partnership, he being quite unacquainted with the language and customs of the country, and we worked amicably and prosperously together for a term of over twenty years. Eulogy of the firm we represented would be misplaced, the reputation of Messrs. Marshall, Sons & Co. standing very high in the agricultural world.

With the first steam thrashing machines, however, there was trouble, owing to the fact that they were built on English models for an English climate and soil. In England, it being a damp climate, the haulm of the wheat leaves the machine almost unbroken, and gives very few " cavings." Owing to the climate of Russia, however, being hot in summer, the straw is easily broken up into cavings, and on that account a large quantity of grain passes over the shakers with the straw. This being the case, we suggested to the manufacturers the alterations necessary for their rectification. Thereupon they sent us out their foreman with men at their own expense, three years running, and on their report a machine was turned out that established their reputation as second to none.

On three separate occasions Mr. Henry Marshall came out himself, and I would emphasize my opinion that if all English firms were to act on the same principle and closely study the requirements of the importing countries, they need not fear competition in any market. In this case the main improvements consisted of: firstly, the equal distribution of the corn by self-feeders; secondly, the attachment of separate straw shakers; and thirdly, the delivery of the straw at long distances by means of elevators. I am fully aware that these improvements were almost immediately introduced and claimed by other manufacturers, but they were originally, as herein stated, introduced by this firm at our instigation.

On this ensued a long series of years of great prosperity. We erected large offices in the city, and established a good reputation throughout the district. The following incidents are connected with this period, and illustrate many aspects of Russian life at that time: Bankruptcy, the Baron incident, the carriage incident (chap ix); notes on first trial by jury, etc., the Nihilist movements (chap. x); the Russo-Turkish War, etc. (chap. xi).

A Case of Bankruptcy

To establish a business in Russia, either native or foreign, it is necessary to join a guild. There is no such name as shopkeeper, but all traders have to belong to one of three classes as merchants. A First-Guild merchant possesses the right of export and import. A Second-Guild firm is permitted to carry on internal trade in all its branches, but has to pay the guild subscription for each town at which it establishes an agency. The Third Guild are retail local traders; and the Tsek comprises all the small master hand-workers, such as smiths, carpenters, workers in tinplate, and all other forms of handicraft. Our firm, of course, belonged to the First Guild, being among the leading importers and exporters, and as we were the only British firm in the city we were constantly being requested to clear goods from the Custom House on the account of British merchants.

Among these was a large tea company, and often many hundreds of cases of their tea were held in bond in the Custom House under our name. On one occasion we received a letter from them, requesting our advice and assistance in connection with a business carried on in the town of Krementchug. They had been trading with a Russian firm in that locality with satisfactory relations. Unfortunately, however, the head partner of the Krementchug house had died two years previously. With his death the chief assistant, of the name of Alexeieff, took over the management of the business and was granted an interest in it. After some time he married the widow of the senior partner, who was very much older than himself, and the whole establishment was transferred to him. No notice of this change was sent out to the London house, although many transactions had been carried on subsequently in the name of the widow, who had also accepted the bills for the goods. Certain of these, however, on maturity had not been met, and the letters from London remained unanswered. In accordance with their request, we sent our book-keeper to Krementchug, who found on arrival that the transfer had been legally carried out and that the signboard over the shop exhibited the name of Alexeieff instead of that of the widow. On his return we consulted our solicitor, who advised that we had the right to call for an examination of the books, or declare a case of bankruptcy. This inspection was, however, refused, but almost immediately after we were invited to a cup of tea!

In explanation of this I may mention that when firms of the lower mercantile class decide to liquidate their debts, the practice is to invite all their creditors to meet them over a cup of tea, when matters are discussed, the books examined superficially, and a proposal made by the debtor of a certain percentage in the rouble as settlement, usually 20 per cent. At the meeting, which our clerk attended, there were assembled a large number of real and fictitious creditors, the voting being in favour of accepting the composition. We therefore advised the London firm, following the opinion of our solicitor, to accept the 20 per cent. offered. The solicitor wrote that he was fully aware that, as in all these cases, the books had been faked by many false creditors being added, but that a lawsuit would involve much expenditure and last a considerable time, with ultimately very little probable result.

In talking over this affair with a Russian merchant of high standing in our town, he said: "What is to be done? With us it is not considered at all a moral detriment to become bankrupt, and, as an insurance against all such cases, Russian wholesale houses provide for it in their books, as they consider that after five to eight years' trading they will be asked to drink a cup of tea. Not only so," he added, "but it is the general custom, under such circumstances, to make an arrangement with the defaulting firm that they should still continue purchasing from their former creditors." Should any of our English merchants having large dealings with Russian houses of second-rate standing read this, I should strongly advise them to take every precaution against such an eventuality. It is noteworthy that after trial and conviction for non-payment of a debt, the debtor can be imprisoned, but with the remarkable proviso that his upkeep during the period must be provided by the creditor. Should the latter fail in this respect for over a week, the debtor is at once released.

THE WITTE INCIDENT

Under the Russian form of government, personal responsibility finds no place. A spirit of distrust permeates every stratum of the executive, leading to a system of control over control, which prevails not only in affairs of State, but also in all commercial and banking institutions. For instance, in presenting a cheque for payment at a bank, the process followed is to hand it to a clerk, who on examining the client's account, initials the cheque, thus notifying that the drawer has sufficient credit to meet it. Thence it is taken to a second clerk, who enters it against the name of the drawer, and thirdly it has to be presented to the manager to be initialled, and then finally to the cashier. To the British mind such a complicated process seems a waste of time, and this I have often explained to the merchants and managers of banking establishments. On recounting the simple way that we had at home, they felt that it was quite impossible to introduce such a system into Russia, as they were under State control. On catechizing them, however, they usually admitted my contention that the control must end somewhere, so that some one at all events will remain uncontrolled.

On one occasion, when attending a meeting of

our Chamber of Commerce, to welcome M. Witte (who at that time was a rising young statesman), I had a most interesting conversation with him. I had made his acquaintance some years before, when he was the superintendent of the Odessa-Kiev railway line and resided at Kiev. He was a man of more than ordinary ability, having risen from the position of a clerk in the office of the railway. His great financial gifts brought him into communication with the Professor of Economics at the University, who took great notice of him, and ultimately became his attached friend. When the professor became Minister of Finance, he had him transferred with himself to his own department in St. Petersburg, and on his retiring after some years, M. Witte received the ministerial appointment.

In the speech which M. Witte made at our Chamber of Commerce, he referred in very severe terms to a petition that had been sent him from our Chamber calling his attention to the urgent need of an alteration in the commercial law. I well recollect that in it he made special reference to the lack of initiative in the Russian business world. The speech was listened to in dead silence; afterwards, however, in talking it over with the President of the Chamber (who was also the mayor of the city), the latter said to me, "You know as well as I do, Mr. Hume, that if we had carried out the suggestion made to M. Witte in our petition, without his consent, we should without doubt have received back an intimation that we were to mind our own business, and that most probably signed by M. Witte himself."

In one respect the Russians strongly resemble the Orientals. As long as a man occupies ministerial position, so long is he surrounded with an army of sycophants, who crowd the stations to see him off, or give him fêtes when he visits the provinces. But once superseded and gone into retirement, his devotees immediately turn with avidity to greet his successor.

The Cholera in Kharkov

In 1874 a virulent attack of cholera seized the city, and fearing that my wife and family might be endangered by it, I sent them to Berdiansk on the Sea of Azov, that part of the country having been exempt from its ravages. The only other British family in the city were a Mr. and Mrs. Cameron, her mother (Mrs. Innis), and their four children. One evening I received an urgent message to call upon them, Mrs. Cameron having been taken ill. On going to their house I found her almost in collapse. The doctor was called, hot bricks were placed to her feet and every means employed for her restoration, but before the morning she was dead. Deaths were so frequent that the ringing of the church bells was stopped and the burials carried out at night. It was indeed a stricken town, hundreds of deaths taking place every day, and deep gloom fell upon the city.

We had brought with us from England a servant named Martha to look after the children, who remained to look after my wants in town. When the cholera was subsiding I was called away to superintend some work on the estate of Prince Galitzin, which detained me over a week. On my return I found Martha ill in bed, and the daughter of a friend of ours looking after her. On inquiry I learned that the stupid girl had spent the money I had left with her, for her board, on fruit (plums, etc.), and she had been taken ill with acute spasms. Fortunately they had called in a doctor, who diagnosed it to be diarrhœa, and in a few days she had recovered.

Public Insecurity in the Towns

During the Nihilistic scare and as a consequence of the socialistic propaganda, life in the suburbs of the cities became very insecure; and owing to our residence being outside the town, special means of protection had to be employed. We had had for some years as night watchman a man of the class of nobles, who, according to his passport, must have been the descendant of a Circassian prince. The watchmen in Russia go round the houses with a clapper, which they beat at various times during the night, presumably to let the owners know that they are on duty; but I never thought the method a practical one, as it gave due notice to the evil-intentioned of the whereabouts of the guardian.

We had at the time as neighbours a French family, with whom we were on intimate terms. On one occasion I had been paying them a visit in the evening, and remained rather late. My intention had been to return without a light, but, acting on the urgent advice of my friends, I took the lantern which they offered me. The road lay between a high foundry wall on the one side and the boundary of my property (a high wooden fence), on the other, and was at that time of night absolutely lonely. Within a short distance from my friend's house, I noticed two men walking under the shadow of the wall, both having sticks in their hands. Suddenly their footfall died away, and flashing the light I saw that they were pursuing me. Fortunately only a few hundred yards separated me from my gate, and being unarmed I thought discretion the better part of valour, and sprinted for home, with the enemy close on my heels. I just got in in time to slam the door in their faces, leaving them shaking the gate with rage, and pouring out a volume of oaths. As I was, however, promptly reinforced by the night watchman and our dog Pompey, they beat a rapid retreat.

The prince in question had all the characteristics of being of gentle birth, and was treated with great respect by the general body of workers; but like the generality of the scions of the noble class, he would not put his hand to anything of a menial character. For instance, he would harness the horse to the wagon, but would not put in any goods that were handled by the general workmen, such as sacks of flour, etc. He stayed with us over a considerable period, and I left him still in the same position when I sold the property. The members of the nobility, however poor they may be, always act in the same manner; and as there are not sufficient positions in the professional, military, and civil services for all of them, and many of them have become impoverished through the freedom of the serfs or their improvident habits, there has grown up a half-educated proletariat highly prejudicial and dangerous to the State.

In Russia there are fourteen degrees of official rank (Tchin), many of which confer privileges of nobility, ranging from Collegiate Assessor through various gradations to the head of all, the Emperor. It is, however, possible for the same person to advance from the lower to one of the highest grades, even as Minister under the Crown. The form of address, however, varies with the step attained; in the lowest it is " Your Honourable," followed by " Your Well-born," " Your High Well-born," " Your Councillor," " Your Privy Councillor," etc. The only title indigenous to Russia is that of Prince; all others, such as Barons, Counts, etc., are of exotic origin, though all are addressed as " Your Brilliancy." These form a class much more numerous than we have in England, owing to each child taking the title of the father. It is interesting to note that in the elected chamber, the Duma, all parties are represented, from the peasant to the Prince. I am quite of opinion that this institution may in time grow to full fruition and become the real representative of the enfranchised people of this mighty empire.

Sidelights of Russian Life

Many of the Russian estates lie at a considerable distance from the main towns, so that the life of the country families is often very isolated, and their visits to the large cities few and far between. Under these circumstances, they every year receive into their houses milliners, shoemakers, etc., who travel from property to property, to carry out all the renovations of the family wardrobe, and incidentally, as in mediæval times, distribute local news from house to house throughout the country-side.

Again, among the frequent callers are the pedlars, mostly Hungarians, by which name they are called in Russia, who bring goods of all kinds, from the glaring prints of saints and heroes to the finest fabrics then in fashion—in fact, all goods suitable from kitchen to drawing-room.

Lastly, at stated intervals appears the professional beggar in his horse and cart, for whom are gathered the crusts of bread used by the poorest classes in their soups, all the débris of the kitchen and the "rummage" of the house. In addition food is supplied for his horse, and he generally leaves with a few kopecks in his pocket for the journey.

The Baron Episode

One day a gentleman came to our office with a letter from the leading banker of the city, introducing a Baron G. v. H. to our good attention, as he required two portable engines and a steam thrashing machine for his estate, which was situated some two hundred miles from Kharkov. The Baron, who was a man of very aristocratic appearance, informed us that the corn harvest would be ready in about a month; and as he required a certain amount of credit, I informed him that the terms required in such a case were that the machines remained our property, being on hire to the proposing purchaser until they were fully paid for. To these conditions, which were the usual ones in the trade, he was quite willing to accede, and said, as he was going to Moscow and not returning to the estate, that he should like to have the contract signed and closed before he left. The purchase was for a considerable sum, amounting to over £700, a third of which had to be paid down in cash; this was duly carried out on the signing of the contract.

All these details being arranged satisfactorily, I

KHARKOV. MESSRS. HUME AND LISTER'S OFFICES.

IN RUSSIA

drove with him to the bank, where I received confirmation of the letter; and the banker added that on the Baron consenting (as they had bought the whole of the harvest) he was willing to pay us the money due, proportionally to the quantity of corn delivered, and a letter to that effect was immediately drawn up and signed by both banker and baron. We then proceeded to the notary, who drew up and legalized the contract in accordance with the conditions explained to him—namely, one-third cash had been paid, one-third was to be paid on August 1st, and the balance at the close of the harvest, but in no case to be later than November 1st. The machines were to remain our property until these conditions had been fully completed.

These formalities having been arranged, the machines were sent off in charge of the engine-driver, who was to work them, and who, though in our employ, was to be paid by the Baron until the completion of the contract. After some time we received news from the Baron, that he was perfectly satisfied with the machines, and our driver also wrote that they were working admirably and giving every satisfaction.

Some weeks passed and we heard nothing further; when we suddenly received a telegram that the machines had been placed under arrest, and that it was necessary to take immediate legal steps or they would be sold by auction within a month. On this we at once sent off our chief clerk to the estate with strict orders to remove the machines forthwith, which he duly carried out in spite of the remonstrances of the Jewish creditor, and placed them in the yard of the priest's house. We then took legal advice how best to have the arrest annulled; but the Jew, having been informed of the contract by our clerk, took the arrest off and put it upon another machine that the Baron had obtained from one of our competitors on the same conditions. This was eventually sold, the owners taking no steps in spite of a warning which I had given them.

The bankers who had recommended him to us had

also sent representatives to act under their contract immediately after I had informed them of the telegrams I had received, and it was agreed to work together in unison. During the whole time we could obtain no information of the whereabouts of the Baron ; no one knew where he was to be found, no information being obtainable, either at the estate from the steward in charge, or from the place that he had given us as a reference. He belonged to a very high family, his mother having been lady-in-waiting to the late Empress, and it seemed scarcely possible to believe that a man with his bearing and his aristocratic connection could be associated with an absolute swindle.

November 1st, which was the last day of the contract, came and went, and we removed our machines ; but the corn which the bankers should have received was not forthcoming, so that we had no claim upon them. The various proceedings that we had been forced to take had caused us a very great expense ; in addition, the machines could never be sold at their original price again, but only as second hand, and therefore at a considerable loss.

The news of the Baron's action had got noised about in the city. Dining at the Grand Hôtel one day, the owner, who was a Frenchman, mentioned the matter to me, and whilst we were talking, by a strange coincidence, a telegram was brought to him which on his opening it was found to be from the Baron, stating that he expected to be there on a certain date and engaging a room. Hereupon I saw the hall porter and told him that he would receive twenty-five roubles if he or the night porter would let me know the moment of his arrival, day or night.

On the date specified in the telegram I was awakened by gravel thrown at the window of my bedroom by my watchman, who told me that the man had come from the hotel to tell me that the Baron had arrived, but was renewing his journey next day.

Early in the morning I drove to the hotel, and I do not think that I ever saw a man so surprised as when we stood face to face. I had the contract in my pocket, preparatory to such a meeting, and explained to him the great danger that we had passed through with regard to losing our machines, and that he must go at once with me to the notary, undersign a paper confirming their return, and pay me the amount I claimed for the loss incurred. This he at once agreed to do without demur, took out of his pocket a large bundle of hundred-rouble notes (ten pounds each) and paid me in full. We then proceeded to the notary, where the return was duly undersigned, so that we came out of the episode without loss except for the anxiety and trouble.

The sequel of the affair was of an extraordinary character. It appeared that the estate which the Baron had represented as his own in reality belonged to a young widow lady, to whom he had been making court. He had persuaded her to give him over the whole estate by legal contract for a term of fifteen years, with its inventory of crops, cattle, sheep, etc., on condition that at the end of the term the land should be returned together with the inventory; but the contract having been made through an astute Moscow solicitor, the land could not be recovered before the end of the term, and the rent only be sued for as a debt. Immediately after the contract was signed the Baron sold off all the movable property on the estate, cattle, sheep, etc., and had it not been for the arrest it was very evident the whole of the corn crop would have been realized. As it was, when I met him at the hotel, the Baron was on his way to Paris, where he remained until such time as his lawyer had arranged matters with the widow, she being obliged to forgo all indemnities for the wrong done her, and in addition pay a large sum to recover the estate.

The Carriage Incident

On one occasion during the absence of my wife in England, I decided to give her a surprise on her return, by presenting her with a new carriage, harness, etc., on her birthday. The one that we had had for some years was beginning to look very shabby and had been used latterly by our housekeeper when driving to the bazaar of a morning for the purchase of provisions. In the purchase of a new one I spared no expense in its decoration or stability ; it could be used for one or two horses—that is to say, with either pole or shafts— and being built on the droshky plan, could carry four, the whole with the new harness and coachman in his uniform having a very smart appearance.

My wife, on her return, was extremely gratified with the gift, but unfortunately our coachman Mattvae, who had been with us many years, had become so addicted to drink that no reliance whatever could be placed upon him. After repeated warnings, I fully made up my mind to give him notice ; the man, I believe, was sincerely attached to us, and my children were fond of him, or I should have long before got rid of him.

The Patriarchal system was at that time in full vogue. Although Mattvae was a man of about fifty years of age, he received no wages except gratuities that I gave him, but on the first of every month his old father made his appearance to draw his son's money. He was a fine old fellow with a long, white beard, and a long staff in his hand, and bowing low he would ask, " Barin [Master], how has the boy been behaving during the month ? " Had he been very bad, I would shake my head and say I had no good report to make, upon which he would turn to his son and say, " Down on your knees and ask pardon," and then while he was prostrate would give him several strokes with his staff until I stopped him. This comedy had been enacted many times, but the poor fellow was incorrigible. We have known him come in with the carriage and after removing the horses go out of the yard, after a quarter of an hour returning so drunk that he could scarcely stand, then he would lie down in the stable beside the horses until he recovered. But at last it became impossible to retain him, and the groom took up his duties for a time.

Living on the estate contiguous to our own was General Rashkine, the Cavalry Commander over the general Government stud, who was very neighbourly with us. So I went to him and asked him if he could recommend me a satisfactory coachman, more especially as he must have been brought into connection with so many of that class. Mrs. Rashkine, who was present, said to him, "What do you think of Ivan, who has been here asking a recommendation to the stud from you?" She explained to me that he had been acting as her coachman for some time when the General was in the regiment, and only a fortnight since had called to see if he could get him a situation. He had left his address, and the General thinking he might probably suit, I finally engaged him.

The man who thus entered into my service was a tall, lithe, reddish-haired, military-looking individual, and certainly he fulfilled his duties to our horses (of which we had four at the time), but my wife never liked him. One morning, after he had been with us about three months, he came to me and said he had an offer to take charge of a stud of forty horses and he would have to leave at once or lose the place. He therefore asked me if I could release him, saying that our groom, Peter, was quite able to look after the horses till we got another coachman. I told him I would think over it and give him an answer next morning, and took the opportunity in the meantime of consulting my wife, who was quite agreeable. So I told him to come to the office next morning, when I would pay him off and return him his passport, only that he was to instruct Peter in everything that he required to know about the stables, feed, etc.

On the next day, before leaving for the office, I told our housekeeper that he was going and I had instructed him to give her the keys before he left, as he was coming to the office to be paid off. A short time after I reached the office Ivan appeared, was paid and received his passport, but within an hour our gardener arrived on horseback to know if it were true that I required the carriage forthwith. Ivan had come home and told the housekeeper that I wanted the carriage in town immediately, and she had foolishly given him the keys, whereupon, he had put our very best horses in the shafts, with the new harness, coachman's attire, etc., and driven away. On the housekeeper telling my wife that I had asked for the carriage, she said, "I do not believe it for one moment, and he must not go without the children." But I have often thought afterwards that it was very providential that he had gone without them, for we have never heard of him or the carriage again, and who knows what might have become of the children had they been with him, as a man of that character would probably have taken them out on to the Steppes and in some way or other have got rid of them.

I immediately went to the Governor, and related to him the whole circumstance, upon which he telephoned to the police-master of the city. On his arrival, the inspectors of the Police District were instructed by telephone to place a watch on all outgoing roads, and a special messenger was sent with me to the head inspector of my own district, who without delay sent mounted men to scour the neighbourhood. In addition official telegrams were sent in to the neighbouring surrounding towns, but all in vain.

The police were of opinion that the man had not left the city, and for a long time afterwards called upon me to go with them to see if I could recognize my property. I have been taken to places where nobody could possibly have thought that any animal could be found, a long, descending pathway leading to an underground stable which contained, perhaps, from fifteen to twenty horses, probably every one stolen and faked. If our horses were there, owing to this cause it was impossible to recognize them, and the inspections consequently proved useless. I was told that there were several of these underground stables in the city belonging to

Gipsies, all of which the police informed me they had inspected.

My neighbour, General Rashkine, was very much concerned, as he had seen the carriage and much admired it. Mrs. Rashkine also expressed her deep sympathy, and told us that she was perfectly sure that they had been fellow-sufferers through the same man. It appears that when Ivan had been in their employ for some time, one day he asked permission to take a holiday for three weeks, in order to go to his native village. This the General allowed, and he left. Two nights after, their stable was broken open, and the best horse in it, a black stallion, was stolen. It was an animal that had cost them a large sum of money, and like our own, it was never afterwards heard of. She said that they had always considered it a remarkable fact that not a sound had been heard that night from the two rather savage dogs that were kept in the stable yard, and she was now fully assured that it was this man that had stolen the horse.

The inhabitants of the village where we lived, and with whom we stood on the very best relations, expressed to us their deep condolences through the mayor on the loss we had sustained, and showed their sympathy in practical form by sending out men in all directions to scour the country.

CHAPTER X

LAW COURTS AND NIHILIST CONSPIRACIES IN KHARKOV

Introduction of trial by jury—First case—Basis of Russian laws—Amusing case in the Courts—Origin of Nihilism—The *Kolokol* or *Bell* newspaper—Results, incendiarism and assassination—The Emperor's speech—Establishment of martial law—Appointment of German Governor—Riots at Kharkov—Wholesale deportations of peasants—Imposition of fines on us by Governor—Incident of English governess—M. Jukovsky—Petition of Zemstvos for national education—Attitude of Tchinovniks—Petition refused—Causes of student discontent—Zemstvos' action paralysed—Triumph of arbitrary government—Contrast in political status of Bulgaria and Russia—Ferment among students in Kiev—Building of sugar factory—Yard man, or Dvornik, in Russia—Dvornik shows unexpected abilities—Visit of police inspector—Arrest of Dvornik—Police placed at gates—Discovery of dynamite—Method adopted to dispose of same without discovery—Artel system at Kiev and Kharkov—Accuracy of Russian carpentry.

NOTES ON THE FIRST TRIAL BY JURY IN THE CITY OF KHARKOV—FEBRUARY 1868

NOTICE having been given by the Government that the new system of trial by jury would be introduced into the courts at Kharkov, I received from the Governor a ticket of admission. The crowd was so great because (although the courts would in future be free and open to the public) the *élite* of the town desired to be present on this the first occasion, and it was therefore necessary to limit admission by the issue of tickets.

The prisoner to be tried was a young man who had been a clerk in a Government office, but on account of his sympathy with revolutionary ideas, he had one evening in the theatre called out an offensive remark, which led the Governor of the town to deprive him of his situation without inquiry or trial. He had been in receipt of a yearly salary of £100, and having no other resource and no money to fall back upon, he had tried every means to get a living. He had applied for a situation as coachman or yardman, but no one would engage him, and in his extremity he had stolen clothes from his landlord to the value of 300 roubles (or £30). The advocate for the prisoner being a very young man, and feeling doubtless the presence of so many notabilities (it was his first appearance in the courts), became frightened, and spoke very tamely, passing off the arbitrary conduct of the Governor without remark.

In all criminal cases, the law requires three judges to be present on the bench, and also a Public Prosecutor, called a Procuror, who, as a representative of the Government, sums up the prosecution. In addition, there are the two barristers for the prosecution and defence respectively. In the present case, the pleadings having been completed and the Procuror having given his opinion, the senior judge summed up to the jury, placing before them five counts upon which they were to return their verdict. He explained to them clearly the law on the subject, telling them it was not sufficient to bring in a verdict of guilty for the theft, which would make it only an ordinary case. They must also answer the fourth count, as to whether he had broken into the room in which the clothes were lying, as if so it would be house-breaking or robbery with forcible entry, and in that case the punishment under the code was far more severe. The jury retired, and were absent for some time. On returning, in answer to the question by the judge they stated that their decision was unanimous, bringing in a verdict of guilty.

The various counts were recapitulated one by one. When it came to the fourth, with or without forcible entry, they gave no answer, and a second retirement was ordered. Returning after a shorter time, the same question on the fourth count was asked, and the answer given was, amidst the laughter of the assembly, " God only knows—we don't." Upon this the judge ordered them to be seated, giving them a good lecture, and telling them that speaking in that way under the new law was equivalent to contempt of court, which might incur a year's imprisonment. On this they were sent back again, duly humbled, and brought in a verdict of " Not guilty." The judge, rather indignant, was forced to accept the verdict on that count, but on the four other counts the prisoner was sentenced to lose his civil rights and nobility, and his name was ordered to be removed from all Government employment lists.

Nihilists' Conspiracies—Kharkov

It was from the year 1864 that the so-called Nihilist movement dates its origin, and it may be said that it represents an advanced stage of socialism. It began with the wild theories of Bakounin which received a definite Nihilistic sanction in a Congress held at Basle in 1869. The culmination of the movement in murderous terrorism followed the depression resulting from the Russo-Turkish War of 1877-8. The object that Nihilism had in view was the overthrow of all existing systems of Government and substituting in their stead one of pure communism, and was accompanied by the negation of all religion.

Nihilism, fostered by the organs of the revolutionary paper the *Kolokol* (*Bell*) published in London by a Mr. Herzen, spread with remarkable rapidity to the Universities and higher-grade schools, and among the so-called *intelligencia* of the country. This paper, although proscribed by the Russian Government, found its way by thousands into Russia, and scarcely any family of standing was to be found, in whose possession there were no copies.

At the commencement of the propaganda, committees were formed in each Province, and every effort was made to incite the peasantry against the proprietary class. The plea advanced was, that at the time of the emancipation the Emperor's Ukase had been falsified by the landowners, who had robbed the peasants of their land. As in all similar cases these committees gave rise to men of advanced opinions, followed in due course by the militant system. Under it incendiarism, bomb throwing, and the murder of highly-placed officials were perpetrated, and considered venial and doing efficient service; thus in our city of Kharkov, Prince Krapotkin, the Governor of the Province, much beloved, a very near relative of one of that name living in England as an exile, fell a victim to the conspiracy, he being shot in his carriage on leaving the Institute for the Girls of the Nobility, where he had been distributing the prizes. This was all the more regrettable, owing to the fact that only a few days before he had presented to the city a Maternity Institute.

At this juncture incendiary fires were nightly being reflected on the clouds, and, as the Russians express it, " the Red Cock flew." Thereupon a reign of terror ensued, and the proprietors left their domains in the country and transported themselves and their families into the towns. It is interesting to note the action of the Government in their dealing with this campaign of crime. It had reached such a point that it might almost have been termed a state of civil war, the Nihilists being ranged on one side and the Civil Government on the other.

On November 20th, 1878, the Emperor Alexander II, before the representatives of all classes in Moscow, gave expression to the following celebrated and deep-meaning words: " I hope [said the Emperor] with your assistance to stop the erring youth from that ruinous road in which evil-disposed persons are trying to lead them. Yes, may God assist us and give to us calmness to direct our dear Fatherland gradually to develop in a peaceable and legal way. Only in that way can be secured the future peace of Russia as dear to yourselves as us."

At a meeting of one of the Provincial Zemstvos, the President spoke as follows: " The new crime committed in Kharkov [the murder of Prince Krapotkin] demands that the Zemstvos, agreeable to the above call of the monarch, should rise to fight to the death this ever-recurring evil. The wise word of our Emperor should direct us into that road for the protection of our social and political life, into which also the Government itself called us, in its communication printed in the Government Messenger No. 186 in the year 1878."

According to street law, every peasant residing out of his village had to send his passport yearly to his commune for renewal, together with the poll tax, 3 roubles (6s.). Many hundreds, however, after receiving their freedom, had taken up their permanent residence in the cities, and had lived there for years without having renewed their passports, under the mistaken idea that with their freedom they would be allowed to reside in places other than their own village without further payments.

The first step taken was to place the whole of the country under martial law, and the streets of the principal cities were patrolled by Cossacks, who with their heavy whips were empowered to disperse any assemblage of above fifty people. The Governor-General was invested with autocratic power, under which all prisoners became subject to court martial, and could receive administrative punishment, even to the extent of being transported to Siberia without trial.

In our city a German Governor was appointed, who, in a similar position in another province, had made himself so hated by the tyrannical manner in which he had carried out his duties, that he had been mobbed by the women. Immediately on his taking over his duties, he issued his proclamation that any householder harbouring tenants without a passport should be fined 500 roubles (£50). The result was that hundreds of families, together with their young children, were turned out of house and home during the inclement autumn nights. This gave rise to a serious disturbance in which not only the students, but the hooligans of the city took part.

Early one morning I, together with my youngest

son, had visited General Kartsoff, the Head General of the Province, who had taken a great liking to my boys, and had invited them to call upon him. On this particular occasion he had one of them on his knee, when an aide-de-camp arrived, and informed him that a great demonstration was taking place on the plain in front of the first gymnasium in the centre of the city. The whole of the people were at fever heat, and ready to take part in any revolt should the occasion present itself. Two policemen had overturned the basket of a poor woman, who was selling fruit on the plain at a spot where she usually stood. On her refusal to remove, they had brutally dragged her off to the police station. On this the mob assembled, the police office was sacked, and the effigy of a police constable hung by the neck from one of the so-called fire towers that are erected at every police station in each quarter of the town. Upon this a free fight took place, many of the police using their swords; but being severely handled, they had to be withdrawn and the military were summoned.

On quitting the General, after leaving my sons at home, I proceeded to the scene of action, arriving at the same time as the fire engines. On the plain there must have been several thousands assembled, and no sooner had the engines drawn up, than they were immediately broken up by the mob, and the spokes of the wheels, the poles, and the other débris were used as weapons against the force. The General came galloping up on horseback, and riding into the midst of the people, kindly advised them to disperse, in his fatherly manner calling them his children. His advice, however, was not followed, the passions of the mob being too greatly excited. Thereupon he gave orders for the soldiers to fire high, and from some unexplained cause an officer standing on a balcony was shot dead. Further action followed against the mob before the riot was quelled, and a number of casualties occurred, not only amongst the rioters, but also among the officers and men.

In furtherance of the Ukase issued by the Governor, domiciliary visits were made by the police, and the passports examined so that the landlords, to escape fines, turned out any defaulting tenant into the streets. At the house we had erected in the main street, we had not only our own offices, but various tenement flats which we let out. Amongst our tenants was a General, and on one such visit by the police a servant girl in his employ was found to be without her passport, upon which the Governor fined us, the landlords, 300 roubles (£30). It appeared to us that the action was so grossly unjust that I at once drove to his office and represented to him that I considered it a gross injustice that I should be fined in the place of the General, seeing that I had not the slightest possibility of interfering with his domestic arrangements, and had no control over the people in his employ. On this he told me that he would cancel the fine, which was done.

In the meantime the streets were encumbered with those that had been turned out of their houses, and amongst them was a plasterer who had been employed in the erection of our offices, a highly-respectable and honest workman. He came to me in great distress and begged of me to take pity upon his wife and three children (the youngest only three weeks old), they having been turned out from their home. We felt great pity for them, so I went to the police inspector of our district and explained to him the circumstances, offering to stand bail for them if he would give me his word that no fine would be imposed upon me for giving them temporary shelter. We were on the very best terms with him and he readily agreed on his part to accept my verbal statement, but added, "You know I cannot take bail, owing to the order issued to the police, and these domiciliary visits take place without my being consulted, direct from the Governor's Chancellory, but on my part you have nothing to fear."

We on this gave them shelter, and, as fate would have it, on the very next day a visit was paid to us, and we were fined 500 roubles (£50), which we had to pay. The man and his family were taken off by the police to walk their weary way from 200 to 300 miles to their village, where they would arrive as perfectly unknown strangers.

A further episode of a Nihilistic character arose with an English governess, a lady named Mrs. Zerman, a widow, who had been engaged for some years in the family of a general. As before stated, there was scarcely any home without some evidence of the young people being more or less tainted with Nihilistic principles. In this case there were two sons, students of the University, who were no doubt members of the Secret Society and had a large number of the proscribed journals in their possession, and also portions of a machine which Mrs. Zerman was fully convinced formed part of a bomb. She informed us that on one occasion, in the absence of the General, there had been an explosion in the attic, but the fact had been promptly hushed up. The lady came to us very early one morning in great distress of mind, seeking advice under the following circumstances: She said that they were fearing a visit at their house from the police every day, as every student of the University was a suspect and watched, and already many had been arrested and taken away. That morning she had found that a big box had been placed under her bed unlocked, and on opening it, noted that it was filled with papers and Nihilistic publications of a compromising character, of which she brought us samples, and wanted advice as to what she should do. My counsel was, either to return them to the lads or to let the police know they were not hers. But this she would not hear of; so I said if she would bring them piecemeal as much as she could carry, we would burn them, and this was carried out. At the same time it showed the spirit of chivalry that animated these young conspirators in placing the box of incriminating documents under her bed!

After the declaration of the various reforms that

had followed on the freedom of the serfs, the nation, being in the first flush of the new enthusiasm, was much influenced. There also existed a great desire to carry out the wishes and edicts of the Emperor, and there were many broad-minded Russians, members of the Zemstvos, who had become inspired by the monarch's words. These considered that up to the present time the punishment of the criminals had failed in its purpose, and that the stern repression by the authorities, through the police and military, was causing a revulsion of feeling in their favour. The method provided no curative remedies, but was driving the evil from outside inwards, until it had become a deep-seated disease. Thereupon they presented petitions to His Majesty praying that there should be established a national system of education.

Amongst many friends that I had gathered, and with whom I could converse freely on the real needs of the country, was one of Russia's truest patriots—the late M. Jukovsky—the proprietor of a large estate, who, when in town, would call upon me to chat over the education problem I had deeply at heart as well as himself. On his estate and in his district he had founded schools out of his own resources, and had influenced the Zemstvo to memorialize the Government for the establishment of a national system.

On this several other Zemstvos took up the question with avidity, and sent in petitions representing that, in their opinion, only in education could be found a remedy for many of the social evils that afflicted the country. They added that they as a body were ready and willing to co-operate with the Government in bringing into operation a national system for each class of the community. It was hoped that on this being established it would draw to them all the best strength of society, and they might rightly have considered themselves entitled to expect from the Government the fullest possible consideration and assistance in response to their petitions. To their great sorrow, however, the petitions met on the road from the

KHARKOV. MR. HUME'S GARDEN.

Tchinovniks and the intermediate authorities, through whose hands they passed, every possible hindrance instead of the assistance that the Zemstvos had a right to expect. When, however, they reached the Minister of Public Instruction, the Zemstvos were prohibited from taking any part in the undertaking, on the plea that the lower and middle-class schools would not be strong enough to prevent the introduction of dangerous ideas.

It was with deeply depressed feeling that my friend called upon me and told me of the result, and that he was quite unable to go farther into the matter than to support his own private establishment.

In Russia, in the middle-class schools, the eighth part of all pupils failed to pass their final examination. These, without finishing their course, formed a clique amongst themselves, their youthful faculties being in a condition favourable for the reception of false ideas.

With regard to those who have finished their educational course, and have passed into the higher institutions, these are immediately brought into situations of a most unpropitious character for their future development. They meet with suspicion and vexation from the authorities under whom they are placed, and there are very few of them that have sufficient time for the quiet pursuit of their studies. These methods, which are of a provocative character, give rise at first to dissatisfaction and passionate anger, and ofttimes, if persisted in, lead to student riots, which at that time had become chronic in all the Universities and colleges. It was not by such means, in my opinion, that sentiments of law and order could be developed amongst the youth, whose generous and social instincts naturally caused them to cohere for good or evil.

The want of a good sound education in Russia is felt, not only in the institutions of learning, but in all social positions and professions, among which may be mentioned Justice and Medicine. The Emperor gave the Zemstvos to Russia as a pledge for the peaceful and lawful development of his people, but unfortunately, through the criminal actions of the youth amongst the advanced class of the Nihilists, the independence of these institutions was taken away from them. Requests of the most ordinary character remained unnoticed, not even being considered worthy of an answer.

An independent, truthful, quick, and honourable justice is an absolute necessity for a civilized people, and it must be accompanied by the preservation of respect and obedience to the law. Such a court of justice was supposed to have been presented by His Majesty on November 20th, 1864, and was established in Kharkov in 1868. Owing to the various administrative dispositions under martial law, the worst possible features of autocratic government had been introduced, governors, police masters, and subordinates having the liberty of the subject in their own power at their own will.

Under these conditions the influence of the new courts was being drawn out by the roots, and the power of the law as a protection was nullified, so that it refrained from protecting the subject, who came entirely under the despotic rule of the administration. In this manner the very best possible ground was being prepared for the growth and spread of anarchical ideas. These would have met with a dangerous enemy in the printing press, but this, as is well known, was deprived of all possible independence and subjected to the most stringent censorship, so that at the very time when the number of secret organs was increasing and permeating the country, those of the legal press were obliged one after another to close their publications. All these unfortunate conditions at that period of Russian life will doubtless in time and under the progress of civilization be remedied, but this cannot be done unless there should be a great national spread of education.

It is an anomaly that after the Turkish War the Emperor of Russia, in granting freedom from the Turkish yoke, gave to the Bulgarian nation privileges far exceeding those enjoyed by his own people. Thus they have their own parliament, independence in debate and meeting, freedom of person, free press, and free justice; and I venture to hope that the Russian people may, in their ever readiness to serve, and their deep-seated reverence to, their Czar Liberator, soon be in a position to profit by those same gifts, and in the words of the Czar " enter on the path of a gradual, peaceful, and legal development."

NIHILISTS' CONSPIRACIES

At the time of which I am writing, there was great ferment amongst the students of every university town in the country, and in Kiev they were constantly passing down the Kreschatek three deep, singing patriotic songs and shouting themselves hoarse against the Government. The most stringent measures under martial law were unavailing, although the leaders were being deported, and I have seen gangs of them, manacled, standing at the station ready to be sent away. Yet, hydra-headed, fresh ones started in their place, and still the conspiracy went on. It is strange that I, a law-abiding British citizen, should become dangerously involved, and in such a manner that diplomatic interference might have ensued. The facts are as follows:

We had at our office a big work in hand, connected with the building of a new sugar factory. For much of the machinery we had already contracted and had partially prepared the plans. One day my Polish engineer brought me a certain number of sheets to look through and confirm, at the same time mentioning that we had no one in the office to make the tracings, which had to be done as soon as possible so as to be sent off. At the time, unobserved by me, cleaning out the office was our yard man (in Russia called the Dvornik), who has to be employed in every business house, and is more or less under the supervision of the police, who at that time used them as spies upon the occupants.

The next day this man came to me in the office and addressing me, said, "Excuse me, Barin, but I heard the engineer say yesterday that you required some tracings made of certain plans. I think, sir, that if you entrust them to me I should be able to do them to your satisfaction." I stared at him, and said: "You would be the last man in the world that I should have thought would have proposed such a thing. Wherever did you learn it?" I called my draughtsman, and asked him to bring Number One sheet, and giving it to the yard man, told him to take it home and bring it to me in the morning finished. If carried out to my satisfaction he could have the others, and I would pay him the usual price charged, only the work must be done thoroughly. The next morning he brought it, perfectly accurate in every respect, so much so that I cross-questioned him as to whether he himself had traced it. To this he almost indignantly replied, "By God I did it, sir!" I then gave him the others, which were completed satisfactorily.

A short time after, the Assistant Master of the Police came to the office, and on settling himself down, and as usual accepting a cigarette, he began confidentially to tell me that he had become aware that I had Nihilists in my employ, and that he would like to inspect the clerks that were engaged in my office. He said that he did not wish to cause a scare by going into the general offices; perhaps I would send for my head clerk, and request him to call the clerks into a room apart for inspection. Having no other room vacant beside my own office, I left him there, and he catechized each one to his satisfaction, afterwards informing me that his suspicions had not been confirmed. Of course our people had become very much alarmed, more especially as immediately afterwards police officers were placed at our entries, both of offices and yard. These were separate, the big gates opening on the main street, while those of the office were at the other side.

A few days later he again called, and said that I must have others on the premises, his information being explicit. He then asked, "Have you a Dvornik?" at the same time showing me a portrait, which was that of our yard man. I sent for him, and on his appearance the police officer called in two of his men, who were waiting outside, at the same time ordering him to be handcuffed and taken away.

At this period, men of high education were hiring themselves out disguised as yard men or persons occupying menial positions, and it was difficult for the police to recognize them owing to the perfection of their disguise. In this case the man must have so altered his appearance that, though in constant touch with the police, he had remained unrecognized. We had then to engage another yard man; and on making a personal visit to the yard building, which consisted of stable, coachhouse, a workshop and three storehouses, I found them in disorder. One of them was especially so, with empty boxes carelessly thrown in, which I told the new man to put in order. After doing this, he brought me a list of things he had found in the store-room. Amongst them were six cases of black turf, and he asked me what he should do with them. I instructed him to bring me in a piece, and immediately on seeing it knew it to be dynamite. On examining the cases privately, I saw that there was enough in them to have carried destruction over a very large area.

The position was an extremely serious one, and if the police had had cognizance of it I should without doubt have been put under arrest as having this explosive in my possession. Seeing that the town was under martial law, I might have been deported without trial, and ended my days riveted to a barrow in the mines.

The problem that I had before me now was how to dispose of the boxes without any one having any inkling that they contained an explosive. The plan I carried out was the following: As I was continually dispatching goods to my other yard near the river, I sent one or two cases at a time, so concealed that they could pass the police officer at the gate, and in this way I got them delivered at my other yard. Here I disposed of their contents by throwing them piece by piece into the river. Nine years after, on visiting my old offices, I saw, to my astonishment, that although no police officer was at the office entry, yet my successor had the privilege of being constantly supervised by the policeman at the side gate. Thus ended my first adventure as a Nihilist.

In the city of Kharkov a similar ferment existed, and it is a curious fact in all these agitations there was a solidarity throughout the country between the students attending not only the Universities, but also all the colleges, such as the Veterinary, Agricultural, and Polytechnic Institutes. This was astonishing, for they seemed to act in unison as if controlled by some central authority.

In the city of Kharkov we had erected a large building in the main street, which contained not only our offices, but fourteen separate suites of rooms, in one of which my partner resided, and the others were let out in flats. When we erected the building, the work was given out to Artels—that is, bodies of workmen who undertake at a certain price to carry out the work under the supervision of an architect or surveyor. In this case we ourselves were the supervisors. The Artel system is one that I have often thought might be well studied by our own labour leaders.

In the interior of Russia there are whole villages in which the male inhabitants all follow the same trade, such as carpenters, plasterers, bricklayers, etc., who elect from themselves their own leader. We had for several years as the Artel leader over the carpenters a man of the name of Ivanoff, who came regularly at Eastertime to visit his old customers, and to ascertain how many men we might require in his special branch during the coming season—which ends on October 5th, Old Russian style. He then went back to spend Easter and take on his men, in due time appearing with them. His duty was to find them in food, lodging, and all necessaries; and at the end of the season, when we made up our account with Ivanoff, he would divide it into equal shares, reserving to himself a double one, and to the boys a half.

Beginning at an early age (about eight years), these latter became exceedingly expert with the axe, which is the common implement of the country. So much so, that on one occasion I set a task to a young lad of twelve years of age, by drawing a line along the edges of two floor-boards with pencil, instructing him to cut the pencil mark in halves so that on holding up the two boards to the light I should be able to see how far he had succeeded in levelling the two edges. On holding them up, I could only discover five or six gleams of light, and this was confirmed on ruddling one edge of a board and rubbing it against the other, thus showing the mark of attrition, which proved undoubtedly the success achieved.

CHAPTER XI

RUSSO-TURKISH WAR AND PENJDEH INCIDENT
(1877-8-85)

Origin of Russo-Turkish War—Effects on money exchange—Negotiations with English firm—Final decision—Purchase of wheat and storage—Failure of transport—Severity of winter of 1877-8—Osman Pasha and Turkish prisoners—Precautions taken to preserve wheat at stations—Incident of purchase from Prince L.—Final settlement—Penjdeh incident—Anxious moments—Volunteer fleet—Incident with Chief of Custom House—Reasons of unpopularity of police—Introduction of universal military service—The old system—Length of service based on education—Terms of service—Cossacks—Comic incident connected with Cossack's purchase of machine—Co-operative purchases of machines by Cossack—The Zaporozhski—Russian Army as fighting force—Importance of religious or racial motive.

THOUGH mainly with the view to asserting a predominant or equal position with the Roman Catholics in the Holy Land, on April 24th, 1877, the Czar proclaimed war with Turkey, avowedly for the purpose of avenging the wrongs of the Christians in Bulgaria. The Turks, having cruelly quelled the insurrection of the Christians in that land, had incited their army in occupation to commit atrocities which horrified Europe to so great a degree, that it left the Turk without any ally against the mighty power of the Czar.

The task seemed an easy one to the Russians. The peasantry took up the cry, " They are murdering our brethren," and from the farthest confines of the Empire hastened on the war. The Russian Army under General Gurko crossed the Danube into the Dobrudja at Galatz in June, and pushed forward into the enemy's country, when after various successes and defeats, advances and retreats, the actual fighting of the war ended in favour of the Russians on November 13th by the fall of Plevna. There Osman Pasha surrendered with 40,000 troops, and at the same time Kars was stormed and taken by Louis Melikoff.

During these two years, the question arose, " How has the war influenced the material interests of the country and to what extent has it affected trade and commerce ? So far as our own firm was concerned, all import and export business came to an abrupt stagnation. Immediately on the declaration of war, all private transport by rail was prohibited, the Government having attached every railway van or wagon in the south, for the transport of the army and stores, to the seat of war. Kharkov, being a great strategic point for both Europe and Asia, could not give the private merchant any transport facilities whatever, for over two years. The position of our firm became exceedingly critical, and from the very first we communicated our fears to our principal creditor, regarding the steps to be taken should war eventuate. It came with startling suddenness, and we found ourselves totally unprepared.

At the date on which I write, I can recall the circumstances of these times, almost day by day as they happened. We had only one creditor to whom we owed any large sum, but this amounted to £20,500. Our business was a credit one, dependent on the harvests, and therefore it followed as a corollary that if the purchasers could not realize on their crops, they could not pay their debts. It was a species of barter that we instituted, under which we lent the steam machines on hire to the proprietor, on condition that he paid a third with the order and the balance with 6 per cent. interest equally divided at the end of the harvests of the next two years. We were generally by this means well covered, and during the best years of our trading it worked well. On the increased duty being imposed, the buyers were unable to pay the extra price, and we on our part were unable to give an adequately longer credit.

At this particular juncture, a very large amount was outstanding, and although the crop was a good, medium one, there was no demand for the produce, and to exact payment of arrears was impossible. An additional cause for anxiety arose from the fact that the sales had been completed when the rate of exchange was eight roubles to the pound sterling, and instead of that it had fallen to thirteen roubles, which meant on the large sums outstanding a loss of several thousands of pounds.

I therefore went to England to consult our friends, and proposed that (owing to the complete stagnation in the corn trade, the Sea of Azov and the Black Sea being practically closed) advantage might be taken of the very low price of produce to accept corn at the current rate from our customers instead of money. This would be stored at the ports of Sebastopol and Taganrog, until such time as the war should end and rolling stock be available. We on our part agreed to renew our bills at intervals with interest until sales could be effected. This being accepted, we received from our customers large consignments of wheat, which we stocked at many stations on the railway lines, awaiting transport. To our dismay, however, most stringent orders were received to close every station against the reception of merchandise of all descriptions. We were thus landed with thousands of bushels of wheat, spread over a large area, on uncovered wayside railway stations, open to the air, and thus subject to the inclemency of the weather during the fast-approaching winter season.

The winter of 1877 proved a very severe one, and, in spite of a large number of tarpaulins that we had in stock, the railway transport difficulty made it quite impossible to get them delivered at the various stations where the corn was deposited, and they had to be brought thither by carts. In many cases the sodden grain had split the sacks, from which large quantities of the contents escaped, and were being used as food for poultry by the station master and neighbouring villagers.

We had at that time two clerks continually on the road, stitching sacks, replacing coverings displaced by the wind, and generally watching and reporting upon prospects of removal. Unfortunately, there seemed little hope of a speedy relief. Day and night the trains rushed on bearing relays of men and stores. These, on their return journey, brought the thousands of sick and wounded from the battle-fields of Bulgaria, and later the thousands of the gallant defenders of Plevna, who had proved themselves the real heroes of the war. Of these Turkish prisoners there were interned in Kharkov about ten thousand men, the pick of the Ottoman Army, together with Osman Pasha, the indomitable defender of the place. Had he been adequately supported by his own people, his heroic defence might have turned the tide of war. I had many interviews with him in the hotel where he was living and receiving every possible honour from his captors, who for hospitality and generosity under such circumstances are unrivalled.

I received from Osman just before his release his signed portrait, which I still possess. I should add, that he kept himself strictly private, otherwise, so generous is the Russian character, he would have been lionized in the city circles. He also made himself very popular amongst the general public by his urbane and modest bearing, and especially with the droshky drivers, as he invariably gave gold on his short drives. He spoke French a little, but most of his conversation was carried on through his doctor, or one of his aides-de-camp.

I have never forgotten the impression left on me at seeing day after day the rank and file of the prisoners marching from the train to their bivouacs, past our offices, their fine physique being in sharp contrast to that of their Russian escort. I had many opportunities of making closer acquaintance with their good qualities, as they were allowed out in gangs (accompanied by a Russian soldier as guard) to work at private jobs in the city, and I constantly availed myself of their services in my garden, and other work connected with the house and grounds.

The siege of Plevna, which taught all armies the value of spade work, cost the Russians dear; and at one most critical period of the war, had the Turks taken the initiative and received the necessary aid, a different and an extremely difficult task would have faced the invaders.

In the meantime with us month followed month in unvarying, ever-increasing anxiety, sacks were rotting, poultry were feeding, and when I went in the spring to examine our various deposits, I found in many places, where the tarpaulins had become displaced, corn was growing out of the uppermost sacks to a respectable height. The general aspect of all the stations was that of green fields, for all of them were encumbered with produce to their fullest capacity, and no more could be received. We were infinitely better off than the great majority of the depositors, owing to the precautions taken, and in the summer when we had sun-dried and resacked all that could even be suspected of deterioration, the sequel proved the value of our precautions.

In addition to the corn at the stations, we had contracts with proprietors for delivery on call—that is to say, they let us a barn or other suitable building, where the goods could be stored. For the corn we settled with them in full, and also agreed to pay a small rental for the store, securing the place with our own locks and insuring it fully. Under these conditions, of course, such goods required little supervision, the storage places being in our possession.

One of these proprietors was a certain Prince L., who had agreed to pay his debt to us of about £700 in corn; in his case every possible precaution was taken, seeing that not only he himself, but also his Polish steward, did not enjoy the best of reputations. The corn we had thus bought and stored in a separate barn had been taken over in liquidation of his debt, and the keys being in our possession we had perfect confidence that the goods were intact. Judge, therefore, our surprise when sending our representative on inspection service, we received a telegram stating that the barn was empty and asking for instructions. Following on the telegram came a letter explaining that the steward had been instructed by his employer to open the door at the back of the store which had been overlooked, sell the contents and remit the money, he laughingly saying, " The estate does not belong to the Prince at all, but to the Princess." He added, " Your people have no claim against either, as the contract with the Prince was void in law."

On this barefaced robbery, I consulted the best-known advocate in our city, who advised my going to St. Petersburg, ask audience of the Princess, and if possible obtain from her confirmation of the contract. He advised that, seeing this year there was no more corn on the estate, we should agree for the next year's harvest, on condition that all interest due should be at once paid, and both be made parties to the new contract. Having obtained the address of one of the best commercial lawyers, I proceeded to St. Petersburg. He, on consultation, thought the advice good. I then called upon the Princess, but was received into the Cabinet by the Prince, who at once said : " Oh, I was just writing to tell you I had been forced to sell the corn, owing to having to meet a very pressing debt. I also felt certain that if I paid the interest you would prolong the payment over another year."

I thought the man was off his head to talk to me like that, seeing that, if matters were not settled, I should take criminal proceedings forthwith. He had sold me corn under seal that was not his property, and further stolen the goods that were not his, but mine. The Princess must have been listening, for she burst into the room and fell in a faint upon the sofa.

I thereupon went to the lawyer and, relating to him the result, instructed him to interview the Princess, and if possible come to a definite arrangement. The episode so far ended in a notarial contract with the

Princess for the harvest of the next year, and all arrears of interest were paid together with the lawyer's fees, the Prince being in addition made a party to the contract.

The next year duly arrived, when we sent our clerk a fortnight in advance with the sacks. On arrival the steward took him round an estate not belonging to the Princess, but to that of a neighbouring owner, in order to assure him that at least four weeks would be necessary before thrashing could commence. Thereupon our clerk returned, and on sending a fortnight later, he met convoys of carts carrying the corn from the estate, which proved to be our corn that had been sold by the steward to a Jew.

Again the same comedy was played, the lawyer advising that we were practically in the Prince's hands. The latter was an influential man in the Foreign Office, and if we decided on a lawsuit it would probably last for years, so we again prolonged the settlement for another year on the same terms. Then having been apprised by telegram that the corn was again sold, and the Princess was passing through Kharkov by a specified train (our local solicitor having taken preliminary action for detaining her), he met her at the station, and at last obtained the return of our money from her.

The war at length came to an end, but after the conclusion of the Treaty of Berlin the cars were for a long time occupied in the repatriation of the troops, the stores, the sick and wounded. Kharkov again became the centre for the return of the army that had been engaging the Turks at Kars and Erivan. The troops were billeted on the inhabitants both coming and going, and in my own case I had to supply board and lodging for several of these poor fellows, who had been torn from their wives and families to fight their country's battles at the bidding of the Czar. Needless to say, they were generously treated, and each man had received (on leaving for the war) a copy of the New Testament to be a consoling element in his hard life. It was very gratifying to us that several on their return journey called to thank us once again and to bear testimony to the consolation the Word of God had brought to them amidst the dangers through which they had had to pass.

Two years passed away before the transport could be obtained for our corn, but at last an end came to our waiting, and the remnant was stored in the ports of Sebastopol, Theodosia, and Taganrog. Upon making up the final accounts, which had taken our head clerk and myself a considerable time, and the last quarter of corn had been disposed of, I said to my partner at his desk opposite me, "I want you to look over this balance sheet to see if it is quite correct"; to which he replied, "I don't want to look at it, or hear about it, as I am quite prepared for the worst, so tell me a month hence." "Well," I said, "it is as much your duty as mine to know how the business stands, so here goes. Of all the corn we purchased, by weather, pigs, poultry, thieves, etc., we have lost in bulk a little over one-third; but having bought at between seven and eight roubles per quarter and sold at thirteen, we have covered every expense, all interest and incidentals, and have cleared out of the transaction nearly £700—not much, I admit, but still far better in its results than we had ever expected."

Penjdeh Incident

Another war scare that caused us the gravest anxiety was the incident of Penjdeh, when the Russians were threatening Herat with intent of invading India, and, we were expecting hourly a diplomatic rupture between Russia and our Government, which must have proved disastrous to our interests.

At the very height of the dispute, when war seemed inevitable, subscriptions were invited for the formation of a Volunteer Fleet, which was to serve for the destruction of vessels in the British Mercantile Marine. Nearly every philanthropic effort at that time had to have Imperial sanction, and from the course of origin and the high positions of those forming the Committee, there is no doubt that in this case also the initiative was Imperial.

One day an officer from the Customs House called upon me and said the Director of Customs wished to see me. On my arrival I was ushered into his office, and on taking my seat he informed me with much detail of the proposal to start the fleet forthwith. Turning to a long list of names of the local merchants, he said, " We are getting on very well, you see ; these have all subscribed, and your name is entered for a thousand roubles."

I looked at him, and told him politely that there must surely be a mistake, as I had not consented or even been asked for any such subscription. " Doubtless," I added, " being a British subject and a guest of your Empire, it is a mistake, for I should hardly have expected so insulting a demand." I therefore refused to subscribe a single kopeck to be used in warfare against my own countrymen. Thereupon, starting up from his chair, he shrieked, " Then I will get you expelled the country ! "

I then left, and on arriving at my office I informed my partner of the interview, a German commercial traveller being present. Some time after, I received a newspaper from Germany containing an account of the incident ; and, to do them full honour, we received from many quarters expressions of regrets from our fellow-townspeople, and I am convinced that had we brought the matter prominently before the superior authorities, the action of the official would have been repudiated.

The great unpopularity of the executive, and more especially of the police in Russia, arises from the fact that the whole system of government is based on the assumption that autocracy is not the attribute of the Emperor only, but pervades and governs the actions of every subordinate official in their respective spheres. Thus the aphorism so often quoted by them, " God is

KHARKOV. MAIN ALLEY IN MR. HUME'S GARDEN.

high, and the Czar is far," is carried out in every gradation of the hierarchy, which means that every one in authority makes his own laws and carries out his own will. Thus the Governor of a Province, often as large as the whole of England, would interpret his authority not as a servant of the State and the public, but as having an autocratic authority equal to that of the head of the State. The police master, tearing through the streets with his attendant Cossacks, is far too often a man who carries his autocracy to the extreme, and woe betide the burgher who falls under his displeasure; and thus it is throughout all the grades of the executive.

In our own case, we were so pestered by the police and sub-inspectors, through some trifling mistake in the book that every householder had to keep of his tenants, their lodgers, servants and visitors, that much against the grain we were forced to fall into line and pay a monthly subsidy to the police officer to keep the books himself. The whole system of Urban Government at that time was usurpation of authority by officialdom, and redress of grievances was rendered thereby abortive. Like the strain of the refrain that runs in music through the most intricate of variations, so is the characteristic Eastern strain ever present in the Russian official world, which summarized means, subservient to those above, imperious to those below them.

I must add, however, that I have known examples, and many of them, of true Russian gentlemen belonging to the ruling class that have deeply deplored the evils that arise from autocracy, and, themselves being men of the highest honour, benevolence, and integrity in their various spheres, have set an example by the strictly honourable performance of their duty.

Universal Military Service

Under the former military system, the army was recruited by a yearly levy of the serfs, the percentage varying according to the nature of the demand. When once a soldier was incorporated in the army, it became his life's profession, and his service under the colours continued for twenty-five years. After this term was finished, he received a passport of release, enabling him to live in any part of Russia, quite independent of his Commune.

A large number of these veterans, who on retiring had received a certificate of good character, were drafted into the employ of the railway companies, where they formed a very efficient guard or police at the stations. As this has become an institution under the present military system (there being no pensions), the means of living for old soldiers is assured, and the men (in general of fine physique) are very noticeable on the platforms in their handsome uniforms. In addition to their acting as guardians or police of the stations, the many thousands now employed, not having reached veteran age, are liable for military service, and can be recalled to the colours for duty at home.

Under the old system, recruits were largely enrolled from the scum of the population, not only the proprietors from amongst their serfs, but also the Communes giving up their worst and least desirable members to the service. This had a very bad effect upon the villages where the regiments were quartered, owing to their immorality and misbehaviour, and most of all they were largely responsible for the syphilitic diseases which infest many of the provinces of South Russia. The pay of the Russian soldier at that time was three roubles a year (six shillings), the smallness of the pittance being a strong incentive to all kinds of peculation and theft.

The new military system became universal, and was put into full force in November 1874. Service was compulsory, beginning at the age of twenty and extending to the completion of the forty-third year of age, but under it, the number of years to be served in the ranks was dependent in some extent upon the educational status of the recruit.

Under this fundamental law the term for actual service to-day in the field is :

(1) The infantry and field artillery : three years followed by fifteen years in the reserve.
(2) The cavalry, horse artillery, sappers, etc. : four years followed by fourteen years in the reserve.

After completion of service in the reserve, the soldier passes into the Opolchénié (or Territorial Army) for a further five years' service.

The Opolchénié is divided into two distinct parts. The first part consists of not only all trained men who have passed through the reserve, but also all the young men who have not been drawn in the yearly contingent for service, but are nevertheless liable for service in time of war.

The second part is a general levy *en masse* for home defence only, and includes all those previously exempt from service, whether as students or only sons, etc., and also those not conforming to the physical standards of the regular army, and the older classes of surplus men already partly trained.

But under this system of universal service the priests and all Church servants, who had finished a course of study not lower than a clergy school, are exempt, and terms of service are abridged in varying scale to the following :

(1) University and higher-school students who have, on completion of their courses, been able to pass an examination for Ensign of Reserves.
(2) Teachers in higher schools and all who have been occupied as teachers previous to reaching age of service.
(3) Those of the Academy of Arts who have been sent abroad at the expense of the Crown.
(4) Those from various corporations who have been sent abroad for the completion of their scientific studies.

The exemptions for family causes come under five categories as follows:

(*a*) The only son of the family.
(*b*) One son in the family only capable of work, the father being incapable.
(*c*) A son capable of work, but whose mother is a widow, unless he has a brother older than sixteen, or one already in actual service becoming free the next year.
(*d*) One capable of work, but having unmarried sisters, and brothers under age who are incapable.
(*e*) A grandson capable of work having to support a grandfather or grandmother.

In the third category are included:

(1) An only son capable of working for a father who may not yet have attained the age of fifty years.
(2) A person following in age immediately after a brother who has been lost in military service.
(3) One following in age next after a brother in actual service, who will not be released in the next following year.
(4) Persons not having received exemption under the previous category because of the existence of a brother about to attain the age of sixteen years, or within a year of finishing his service; such persons are allowed one year's exemption.

THE COSSACKS

The Cossacks are the direct descendants of the wild tribes who for many generations have inhabited the Steppe lands of the Don. They are grouped in colonies (so-called Stanitzas) scattered throughout various parts of the Empire, and are subject to military laws from their birth. In return for a portion of land and certain privileges, which each male receives from the Government, they must always be prepared to obey their call of service. This, until the introduction of universal service, consisted of three years under arms absent from their homes, and three years in their villages. In former times these military communities rendered very valuable aid to Russia Proper, by preserving the borderland from incursions of the marauders. One of the methods adopted was by pushing forward successive lines of their Stanitzas. This eventually brought about as a result the domination and incorporation of the Steppe country.

All these semi-barbarous tribes, under the special privileges, nominally enjoyed the right of electing their own officers as also that of their chiefs, from among whom the Ataman or General-in-Chief is eventually chosen. Amongst my many friends I think I may count the late Prince Swiatopolski-Mirski, who for some years occupied this high position among the Cossacks.

This privilege of election, however, only continued until the year 1874, when, as before stated, universal service was introduced and their old organizations, with their rights and privileges, were modified. In return for land allotted to them, they have to equip themselves at their own expense with horses, saddles, etc., and all necessaries except arms. Instead of the three-years' rotation formerly existing, they have under the new rules to serve twenty years, three of which are in training, twelve in active service, and five in the reserve.

These Cossack contingents now number 330,000 men with 236 guns. In active service they are for the most part massed along the whole of the western frontiers—that is to say, on those bordering Germany and Austria. Their duty in warfare consists in acting as light cavalry scouts. The Cossacks of the Empire which are best known in Europe are those of the Don and Ural, though there are many others on the Volga and in the Caucasus. The latter are men of good physique and martial demeanour, who serve as escort to their Majesties the Emperor and

Empress on all gala occasions in the metropolis and elsewhere.

Those so selected are the *élite* of the Circassian manhood, and present a striking appearance clad in their handsome Caucasian uniform. The Cossack cavalry, being especially trained for scouting, are very effective against small bodies of the enemy, though less valuable in frontal fighting. The Cossack mode of attack is one peculiar to themselves, and is known under the name of "Lava." They advance in a crescent form—that is to say, with a centre and two wings, the object being to encircle the enemy; and their onslaught being fierce, they are much dreaded when this formation is adopted under favourable circumstances.

In the immediate neighbourhood of our city along the Ukraine were a number of Cossack villages; the inhabitants of these formerly knew no law, and occupied themselves with raiding and pillaging the Tartar tribes. They have long since settled down, and are now engaged in agriculture and cattle breeding.

In connection with this people, it may interest my readers if I relate a rather comical occurrence in the practice of our firm. On one occasion entering my office after lunch, I met a man in Cossack clothing coming out of the door. As it was lunch time, when most of the clerks were absent, I asked him what he wanted, to which he replied, " I am come to purchase a set of steam thrashing machinery."

Sets of these machines cost, according to power required, between £500 and £600 sterling; had I not known that many of these Cossacks are rich with the money hoarded by their forefathers, I should have felt surprised that a man of his appearance should be able to lay out so large a sum of money. He was dressed in the ordinary Cossack peasant uniform, in large full blouse embroidered in front in red, wide blue trousers, very full, and of home-made linen, a high fur cap, and jackboots. I accompanied him myself to the stores, where he examined very closely the various engines without speaking a single word; at last he came to one over which he lingered long, then producing a piece of chalk he marked it with a large cross, saying, "That is mine." He then proceeded to the thrashing machines, which he likewise minutely scrutinized, and it became evident to me that he very well understood the machinery he was choosing. After marking one with a cross, as he had done with the engine, we proceeded to the office. On entering, my partner looked up, evidently surprised. It was a very curious thing that although he had lived many years in the country, with the exception of a few conversational phrases, he had never learned the language, but it was often extraordinary to me how he could make himself understood by the commonalty of the people.

The Cossack, after I had taken my seat, put his hands into the very capacious pockets of his trousers and drew out a large towel; then he began to count out £10 notes (100 roubles each) to the full amount of the cost. Our head book-keeper having by that time arrived, I instructed him to complete the formalities and give the necessary receipts. While waiting for these documents, he went again into the yard to inspect his machines, and saw there a heavy plough that had been sent us by some one on approval. This, being far too heavy for the Russian oxen, had remained for several months unsold, and we had repeatedly requested the sender to remove it, as we had never dealt in these implements and had no intention to do so. On the Cossack returning to the office, he asked my clerk the price, when I told the latter to sell it for half price to get it out of the yard, and this our client also took and paid for.

On his leaving, my partner (Mr. Lister) said to me, "I confess to having put my foot into it that time, for when he first came in and walked up to my desk, I took him for a beggar, and waving my hand at him said, 'Go with God,' and he was going, but you fortunately met him." The Cossack proved to be a very valuable acquisition, as he subsequently introduced several adjacent villages for the purchase of sets.

It had already become the custom for a whole village or Stanitza to unite its financial resources in the purchase of these machines. In this way the harvest is thrashed, and the grain cleaned, sorted, and sacked all in one operation. The routine for the use of the thrasher is fixed by lot, and many of the villages make a good profit out of the machines by hiring them out after the completion of their own harvest.

Perhaps the most important of the military communities that inhabited the southern part of the Ukraine were the Zaporozhski, who were not of the real Cossack order, but, as belonging to the Orthodox Church, enjoyed special privileges along the district of the Dnieper. Their history is one of special interest, seeing that they formed a separate tribe, ever willing and ready to take service with either side of the border for a subsidy. They were on that account very dangerous and unreliable, even when apparently friends, a higher scale of payment taking them promptly to the enemy's side. Their final act, leading to their dispersion, was taking part with Charles XII of Sweden against Peter the Great; eventually they were disbanded by Catherine II.

One of these tribes is still in existence, and has a special history. Its name means "Beyond the Rapids," and its tribal rights are still in force over the forty-six miles of rapids which extend between Ekaterinoslav and Alexandrovsk on the Dnieper. At the time when the tribes were expelled, those that remained retained certain exclusive privileges in connection with the navigation of the river. On the breaking up of the ice, enormous volumes of water cover the exposed rocks of the cataracts, when opportunity is taken to bring down the stream the immense rafts of timber which have been prepared during the winter in the northern forests. The members of this tribe have the sole privilege of piloting either vessels or rafts through the rapids. They have an extremely manly appearance, and in their bearing their long independence and self-consciousness are reflected. Their martial qualities render them very valuable as scouts, and during the Russo-Turkish War they displayed their military qualities to the fullest extent in that capacity.

I have often been asked to give my opinion of the Russian Army as a fighting force. This is a difficult question for me to answer, not being a military critic, so that I can only give an approximate opinion, which must be based on an estimate of the moral qualities of the peasants, who form the fighting line of their military organization. The principle features of the Russian peasant are stubbornness of character and fearlessness of death, causing them under discipline to undergo the most adverse circumstances, and to remain firm and unwavering at the command of their superior officers. A fair judgment of them cannot be formed from the result of the late Russo-Japanese War. For an inert machine of this kind it is an absolute necessity that they should have good leaders, there being no initiative in the great ignorant mass of the rank and file. Such efficient leadership was absent in the above-mentioned war, and the Russian Army laboured under great disadvantage, owing to the enormous distance that separated it from the base of operations.

Under these circumstances the energies of the great bulk of the executive were exhausted in overcoming the difficulties of transport, which could only be carried over a single line of rails. But it is quite possible to conceive that a very different result might accrue if they were called upon to fight with a neighbouring European enemy.

The Empire of Russia, although composed of so many different nationalities, as a fighting unit is homogeneous, and is able to place in the fighting line from four to six millions of men, in many respects more inured to fatigue than those of any other country. It is noticeable that in most of the wars that have been waged by Russia, the essential motives have either been religious or racial—that is to say, the peasantry have had their enthusiasm excited by appeals in the name of the Slav Brotherhood or by statements that the Holy Places were in danger. The Russian Army is therefore, in my opinion, a unit that has to be reckoned with by any European country with which it may be brought into collision. The men as a whole belong to a hardy and enduring race, for whom the most ordinary food of other nations would be a luxury, and extremes of temperature have to them no significance.

CHAPTER XII

JOURNEY FROM LONDON TO KIEV

Incidents of stormy passage—Cologne incidents—Sociability of Continental traveller—Arrival in Berlin—Methodical arrangement for vehicles—Hotel Kaiserhof, Berlin—Methods of Berlin advertisement—Beaconsfield's room at Kaiserhof—Ambassador's ball—Predominance of military element—A feature of militarism—Impressions of Berlin—Method of visiting new places—What a German working-man found interesting—The opera—Emperor William I—Tipping in Germany—The start for Breslau—The forgetful clerk and the obsequious conductor—My travelling companions—Breslau—Cracow—Wieliczka salt mines—Conversation on Cologne—Plague and quarantine—Method of isolating epidemics—Apathy of officials in Russia.

Incidents of Travel

Letter home from Berlin dated Feb. 11th, 1879

"I ARRIVED here safe and sound last night at seven o'clock, and, being thoroughly tired out, after a bath and meat tea turned in, and feel quite fresh this morning with only a slight train rumble in my head. I started, as you know, from Charing Cross at 7.40 on Sunday morning, and arriving at Dover found a very strong south wind blowing; looking seaward the white-topped, frothy, heavy-rolling waves betokened a bad passage, and so in very truth it proved.

"In the harbour itself, close by the jetty, the steamer was rising and falling with the heavy swell, so that, to be prepared for all eventualities before starting, I fortified myself for a rough journey with a good breakfast of ham and chicken. We had on board a good many passengers, amongst them being several ladies, who, I observed, were preparing themselves for the inevitable before the boat had even cast itself off from its moorings. Already the sailors were busy placing those ghastly white basins, many of which were already in request, and wherever you happened to glance they peeped out from under the seats and coamings.

"I took my seat on deck under the bridge on the lee side of the boilers, wrapped myself well around with my fur coat (Schuba), put on my fur cap, and, well warmed and ballasted, settled down for the journey. Exactly opposite me was the door of a private cabin in the paddle box, occupied by two ladies, and it was a sight not very exhilarating for squeamish outsiders to see the poor creatures buried in wraps, with their faces anxious and blanched, showing how deeply they felt their critical situation. The sight of the preparations made by the attending sailors turned one's reflection homewards on probable eventualities. I was glad, therefore, when the swinging of the door caused the sailor to put it on the hook, thus hiding the picture from my sight.

"Next to me sat a young man who informed me that although he had very often crossed the Channel, he had never yet once been sick. This delusion in his case is for the future dispersed, as I can yet see him sitting in despair with a white basin on his knee; and although I turned my back to him and resolutely steeled myself with stern resolve, the sound of upheaval worked havoc upon my nerves. Time went on, and with it the rolling became more intense and the misery the greater, as the ship made its way through the cross-cutting waves and the wind swept the crest, driving it in blinding spray across the deck, drenching my coat and cap. The sailors, looking like ants bearing eggs, were making desperate rushes from stanchion to stanchion, bearing the basins to the vessel's side.

"Ever and anon the steward would come up to ask after my health and to dose my neighbour with brandy. Oh! the smell of that brandy is still in my nostrils, and I do not think that I shall ever hear of that spirit without bringing to my mind very forcibly my present Channel passage. In my own case the movements of the boat, the sight of my fellow-passengers, the howling wind, and the drenching spray had an effect, and I felt within a kind of flutter that told me that my chicken was far from being at ease, and although I tried to deaden its sensibilities by doses from my brandy flask I felt that its successive plunges were gradually weakening the barriers of its cage. And finally came the dénouement. Although it had cost me so much, it seemed to me that the old sea god was not yet satisfied and would fain have my stomach too, and the frantic attempts to frustrate his purpose has made it so sore that I can feel it still.

"Do you remember a picture in *The Illustrated London News* of the arrival of Channel passengers at Dover after a rough passage? If so, you may faintly picture our arrival after a delay of one hour and twenty minutes beyond scheduled time, and the pale, woebegone, washed-out people that crossed the plank from ship to shore.

"The kind-hearted Custom House official was exceedingly gracious in looking over the luggage, and for myself, when he asked me my name, I could only mutter ' Nameless,' and when asked if there was anything I had to declare, I added, ' No, I lost all *en route.*' Yes, my back was bowed, but not with age; 'tis true my limbs trembled, but not with pains—for sea-sickness, at its worst, takes only the starch out of you and leaves you crumpled and flabby, but not broken. Once again on *terra firma* your pluck returns, and I feel perfectly sure that before arriving at the station my neighbour had already returned to his delusion.

"It was very evident that my fellow-passengers had fully realized, like myself, that a Thames Tunnel would have been to us a blessing under the circumstances, and the food that the meat-eating Briton demanded was strictly confined to soup, which I also ordered, and when the waiter demanded ' What to follow, sir?' I answered again ' Soup,' and if he had reiterated the question I should have been inclined to say 'Toothpicks.'

"On starting by train I ensconced myself in a first-class carriage and tried to sleep. I wooed her, but she would not come; that boat haunted me, the rolling and the plunging were still there, agitating my brain, and sleep I could not. The French carriages were an abomination, and the continuous rattle of the windows made me feel quite nervous after the sea experiences. It seemed like a continuous shiver accompanied with teeth rattling, and the carriages swayed backwards and forwards in a continuous movement.

"France at last is left behind and we have reached the frontier of Belgium; again that ordeal has to be passed of scrutiny by the Custom House, after which we rattle on our way to Brussels. Ever since we left the frontier my appetite has been returning, and by the time I had reached Brussels I felt ready to eat a bullock. Having only twenty minutes allowed me for the experiment, I ordered a portion of one to begin with, which greatly fortified me and gave me sufficient stamina to reach Cologne, where we arrived at eight o'clock.

"Here we were informed that owing to the delay in our boat we should have to wait all night, as no train would be in connection to Berlin till seven o'clock next morning, so being recommended by the station official to a so-called first-class hotel near, I went there, got a room, ordered my supper and a glass of lager beer. The very obsequious waiter informed me that in that hotel they never kept anything but Bass's Ale and London Stout. 'Oh,' I said, 'is that the case? What is the price?' 'Well, sir, 2s. per bottle.' I hesitated; but drink I must—the sea-salt is in my mouth and stomach. 'Bring a bottle of Bass,' and it is brought. Oh, ye shades! Is Bass guilty of so great an abomination? Perish the thought! Burton-on-Trent will repudiate him! There it stands, a long-necked bottle, evidently in the past service of a Bordeaux wine merchant, and it looks ashamed of the deception it is practising. The waiter uncorks it by holding it between his knees, and with a peculiar flourish, as if he had performed a tremendous feat, holds up to you a scraggy, lean, consumptive article that had evidently done duty in many a former campaign. No 'pop' accompanies its extraction, but it is drawn as if already accustomed to the trick and would fain by silence give its protest to the sham. The liquor that is then poured into the glass is a dead, watery, sour-looking fluid, with nothing of Bass in it. I sent for the landlord and asked him what he thought of it. He shrugs his shoulders and says he buys it for Bass. I ask him if he does a good trade in it. He says, 'Oh yes, I keep nothing else.' I again ask if he sees his customers a second time. 'Oh yes, very often,' he replied. 'English?' 'Well, yes, sir.' 'More German than English?' 'Yes, certainly.' 'In that case, then, I advise you to keep a separate bin of the real stuff for the English, and sell it for 1s., and give this only to the Germans, if they like it.' As for myself I tried half a glass and was more than satisfied, so I left the rest in the bottle to be filled again with water for the next guest, suggesting to the waiter that it must be an income of itself.

"Now to bed, and they certainly have given me a very nice room and clean mattress and linen with, what is in general use in Germany, an enormous feather bed, which is generally used as a counterpane, but which in my own experience I have generally found on the floor in the morning. I laid me down and could not help laughing to myself to think what a sight I should appear to a second person entering the room, to see so small a head peeping out from so colossal a body. The window was in front of me, but looking in a direct line all that I could see was about six yards of white ceiling, just above the bed, and it seemed to me in thought most ridiculous.

"I tried hard to sleep, but for a long time it was in vain, a mixture of seaway and train rumble are bad soporifics. At last I dozed, but not for long. I woke to find myself suffering torments of heartburn, doubtless arising from that half glass of Bass. Blessed be the man who discovered bicarbonate of potash, and thrice blessed I felt myself in having put a bottle of it in my bag. I took a dose of it, and its gushing effects of a most generous character repaid me and proved the efficacy of the alkali. A happy thought strikes me to tell German landlords always when they manufacture their Bass's Ale to do so with potash, when they may be assured the effect would be instantaneous and refreshing.

"Following on this I slept a dreamless sleep, but to awake at half-past five as if a hundred sledge-hammers were banging at my door. Mentally I ejaculate, 'Drat that fellow! I have only just come to bed and have scarcely been to sleep, surely I can have another quarter of an hour,' when the thought comes rushing over me that the train starts at seven o'clock, that there is the packing, breakfast, and the station intervening, so stern resolution forces me, and out of bed I jump; and a good wash, refreshing me, makes me feel a greater love for humanity, in general, and thankfulness to that waiter who had roused me, in particular. All the preparations being now completed, I descend, breakfast, and pay my bill, the dining-room waiter trying to do me in the change by giving me a Belgian franc instead of a German mark, which would have meant twopence to his benefit.

"Escaping this slight imposition, on going out to inspect the weather, instead of a brilliant sunrise, I find it a drizzling, Scotch-misty, damp, foggy morning, with the views circumscribed, and the cathedral only a few yards distant, rising out of a thousand mixed impurities for which Cologne is celebrated. Still worse was the wet fog, that impresses you with a fear of bronchial troubles, so, holding my breath, I passed through it, arriving at the station twenty minutes before time. In order to pass the interval I order a coffee as the Germans call it, which, in addition to the lager beer, is the best possible beverage obtainable

TARTAR CART, CAUCASUS

in the Fatherland, and this supplemented by two small Cologne breads with a neat pat of good butter is, next to Maria Farina's Eau de Cologne, the best product of that city.

"The train arrives, and after the interval we depart. So thick is the fog that we appear to be cutting our way through it, and the smoke from the engine blowing past the carriage windows, being luminous with flame, seems to my imagination a spectral train rushing through a phantom world. Onward we move, daylight grows stronger and so does the rain, now mingled with sleet; outside, the snow has turned to water, the rivers have overflowed their banks and stretch out their many arms like an octopus across the plains. The passengers at the stations are standing in their damp clothes and dripping hats; from these the water is forming courses down their faces, and finding no other outlet is dripping in spasmodic drops from off their noses. Rain-soaked and half frozen, these form very undesirable companions in the carriage, for their umbrellas make small rivulets on the floor, and when placed on the netting overhead, drip in uncomfortable drops down your neck.

"I certainly find the general Continental traveller far more sociable than with us, and more polite one with another than the sullen Briton. The German on entering the carriage greets you with a hearty 'Good morning,' and on leaving with 'Adieu,' or a "Grüss Gott," and in the interval helps to beguile the time with pleasant chat. I find Beaconsfield's policy with regard to the Peace Conference to be universally approved, and Russia, from all I gather, receives no sympathy from the mass of the German people.

"As usual we lunch at Hanover, and the guard comes round to each carriage to take orders, which he telegraphs to the station before our arrival, when we find a *table d'hôte* prepared, and sit down to a good luncheon of four courses and cheese for the price of half a crown.

"The Hanoverians do not forget that they were once British subjects, and most assuredly, had their preference been gratified, they would have wished to remain so. It is a curious fact that every German who can talk English pretty well likes to be taken for an Englishman by his countrymen, and this peculiarity I have also noticed in nearly all Continental travellers, except the French, who, like the English, glory in the title of their own nationality. It is evident to me that the general body of the people are not in favour of Bismarck's protectionist policy and would decidedly remain as at present, being at heart staunch free traders.

"We are now nearing the last station, Berlin, and I am forcibly reminded on our arrival that there are many things which we could copy with advantage. An official in uniform asks you politely if you wish a cab, and on your assenting you receive a metal plate with the number of the cab on it. There is no noise, no bargaining; the price is one shilling with extra for luggage to any part of the town, and the cabman receives back his badge only then, when all is in order. I drove direct to the hotel, the Kaiserhof, the largest in Berlin, and was allotted Room No. 169. This hotel is a most comfortable and well-arranged place and of a very high class. I have still remaining a tremulousness in my hands and the noise of the train in my head, but the good night's rest and the sleep that I have enjoyed has greatly refreshed me. To-morrow I propose calling on my agent and friend, Mr. S., whom I have to see on business, and shall not resume my journey to Breslau for probably three days. I see from the papers that the plague that had invaded Russia in the Volga district has been nearly stamped out, and that vigorous energetic measures have been taken to circumscribe the malady; and I pray that He who has brought us unscathed through so many dangers will still protect and keep us as He has done hitherto."

*Letter from Kharkov. Continuation of letter of
February 11th, 1879.*

"MY DEAREST WIFE,

"Your father asked me to give a full detail of my journey, stating that my narratives give much amusement. I will try therefore to continue the letter that I left off on my arrival at the Kaiserhof.

"This hotel to the German mind is the very acme of perfection, and its guests have for the time being all the prestige that a high title can procure. To lodge at the Kaiserhof you cannot pass unnoticed, for the very next day in the *Berlin Post* I found amongst the list of fashionable arrivals the name of George Hume, Esq., engineer, from London. It will interest you to know that this information is conveyed to the Berlin public not in the smallest of type, and occupying an obscure corner on the fourth page, but in bold characters on the front page of same. This distinction bears fruit, for cards of invitation issued by tradesmen pour in thick and fast, and in glancing through them clothiers take up a most prominent position, evidently being of opinion that the Briton newly arrived from London could not possibly do without being clothed in the latest German fashions; beyond this, the shoemakers are advertising their goods of the latest and best Paris fashion, and these again are followed by hosiery, millinery, opticians, and I even find malt extract figuring in the list.

"It seemed to me, on looking at this mass of material, that the waiters of the hotel must get a fixed income by presenting the same set to each arriving guest, and that these same had already done duty for perhaps a month, being taken from room to room as the guest departs. I may say that I left mine as a legacy, and doubtless they are still being imposed on new arrivals.

"In addition to the cards the Kaiserhof has its own newspaper, which informs the travelling public that it is the property of the hotel. It is brought up to your room with the coffee in the morning and consists entirely of advertisements, principally of houses recommended to the visitor where he could obtain anything that he might require, from a pin upwards, at specially cheap prices. The list, however, to my mind casts reflection upon all the other houses in Berlin that are not included in its columns.

"The Berlinese in general when I mentioned that I was lodging at the Kaiserhof became immediately most reverential—that is to say, a very much higher degree than respectful. They cast down their eyes as if dazzled by your brilliancy, and speak to you with bated breath, but doubtless on anything you may purchase full charge is made for it in their bills.

"This hotel has also its reminiscences, and if you happen to be an Englishman, you will be sure to be invited to look at the door of the room which Disraeli occupied during his recent visit for the Conference on the treaty between Russia and Turkey, after the late war. You are also told that he was here visited by the Crown Prince and Bismarck, and, duly impressed, you gaze upon the door of that henceforth historical apartment, putting the sixpence into the ready hand of your guide, and go thence a happier and an ennobled man. Should you, however, be a hero worshipper, and only an ordinary shopkeeper, leave out any mention of the latter from the book they bring for you to inscribe your name and titles, but put in instead, knight, lord, or marquis, for the Kaiserhof cannot harbour a Jones or Smith unless he happens to be a professional or titled.

"The hotel is certainly a very superior one; and its dining-hall, similar to the Slavonic Bazaar, Moscow, has the quadrangular inside court, covered over with a glass roof, whilst the dwelling-rooms occupy its four sides. It is therefore as lofty as the house, and the guests can look down upon it from all the corridors of the building. Around its second story inside the court are placed the statues of the principal German Generals, the Emperor, of course, who gives his name to the hotel, occupying the place of honour. On the evening of the day of my arrival, a brilliant Ambassadors' Ball was being given, and at it I should think was congregated all that is fashionable in Berlin society, including the Chinese Ambassador and his secretary, who sat at a table apart, dressed in all their gorgeous Chinese robes. These guests seemed to me to be quite ignored by the general company, and looked very uncomfortable amidst their barbarian friends. I noticed from my window that they ate nothing, but were engaged the whole time talking to one another, doubtless comparing the half-naked fashionables of our civilized lands with the well-robed beauties of their flowery and celestial country. The attending lady guests were very brilliant, many of them quite sparkled with diamonds on their heads, necks, and dresses, but did not give to me, a Briton, a very impressive idea of high society. The noise of the conversation rising from below was indescribable; it was as if an immense murmur ascending upwards had been met half-way by one descending from the roof, which had been unable to escape, and the two opposing phalanxes meeting just at the height where I was standing, seemed to me to be rising and falling in furious controversy.

"After writing my last letter from Berlin I sallied forth to Karlstrasse to look up my old friend, Mr. Selig, who, you will doubtless remember, was our guest in the early part of last year. He was delighted to see me, and wanted immediately to take me from the hotel to stop with him as his guest, but feeling, however, that I was far more independent in my movements by remaining where I was, I declined the invitation, but accepted one for the opera the next evening.

"You can scarcely move three steps in Berlin without being reminded of the predominance of the military element; the officers, looking as if they were wearing stays, parade the streets trailing their sabres along the pavement, looking to my mind very despotic and supercilious. On one occasion, being desirous of smoking I found I had left my matches in the hotel, but meeting with an officer with a cigarette, I politely saluted him, and, as is usual everywhere on the Continent, asked him for a light, to which I received the answer ' He who smokes should take his light with him,' and he walked on. I do not specify this as being the general German character, for I have always found amongst the civil population, in my many promenades and visits to dear friends in that country, the greatest hospitality and courtesy.

"What the Kaiserhof is to Berlin, so is the Unter den Linden the one street in the world to all true patriots of the Fatherland. In comparison with it the Champs Elysées of Paris, the Ring-strasse and Prater of Vienna, are scornfully rejected; and whilst the visitor is in Germany, when that street is mentioned he is expected to sink his own private judgment and lift up his eyes in ecstatic wonderment at its mention.

"Having got thus far on my road to Karlstrasse, I must say that, while not ignoring the fine surroundings in the metropolis of other countries, the view from the Thiergarten end towards the Schloss embraces undoubtedly a very fine avenue, which may give rise to a very legitimate pride in the heart of every dweller in the city. To my mind, however, it is a great pity that the houses on both sides are not built on a specified plan somewhat similar to those in our own Regent Street. The existing shops in my opinion are more appropriate to a third-class street than a first-class avenue.

"I visited Mr. Selig in business hours, and may mention here that it seems strange that I should come to Berlin to purchase British goods, but we required both for our sugar factory machinery and our steam engines various kinds of indiarubber goods, of a thoroughly reliable character. We had tried repeatedly those of German manufacture that gave us no satisfaction, so were obtaining them from Mr. S., who has an office in London. I would here remark upon the careless apathy which leads our manufacturers and merchants to ignore the vast field that exists in Russia for that class of English goods which is far superior to any others existing. The country is inundated with German travellers showing all classes of their wares, much of which come from England, but I cannot recall a single Englishman ever calling upon us at our offices with technical appliances.

" It may be interesting to the general reader to give them an idea on visiting new places of a plan which I have adopted, and found efficacious. It is to get on to the top of the first tramcar one meets, no matter whither it may be going, seat yourself near the most intelligent-looking passenger, and getting into conversation with him, ask him to point out to you the various buildings and localities of interest on the road. This I have done in most towns that I have visited for the first time, the idea having first struck me in Copenhagen. I, therefore, on this occasion, finding that the tram was bound for the Potsdamer Thur, sat down next to one whom I took to be an intelligent workingman. On commencing to talk I found he was a shop porter by trade, but he did not have a very exalted idea of what constituted places of interest. In his view they were the public-houses where you could get the best beer at the cheapest rate, and refreshment places which he pointed out he could highly recommend, because there you could get a good dinner of potato soup and roast pork, with sauerkraut, for fourpence. Of course, I took his word for it and expressed my great surprise. Another object of intense interest to him was a dingy, four-story building, with windows begrimed with at least a twelvemonths' dust, to which he suddenly called my attention after a long pause, with the exclamation, 'Look there, at that house.' Well, I looked. 'What about that house?' 'Oh. that is the wholesale house where my master buys his goods ; they are worth millions, but you would never think it, they are so simple.' Here apparently he had exhausted his whole knowledge of the city, of which he really knew nothing, although he had been born and bred in it, and had very rarely been outside its confines. To the many ʻquestions that I asked him, he could give no answer; he had never been in a museum, picture gallery, or any of the great historical buildings which teem in Berlin, his little world being circumscribed by his daily rounds, the places to purchase cheap beer and refreshment, and his simple family connections.

"The following day being my last in Berlin, I had accepted the invitation of Mr. S. to take tea and afterwards supper with them. I proceeded at half-past five to Karl Strasse, and, after a very cordial reception, we sat down to tea, which was not the vile German decoction usually presented, but quite of the English brew, and after this we proceeded to the opera.

"I had been previously informed that ladies in Germany always took their needlework with them, never dressed themselves up in evening costume on these occasions, and always worked during the intervals between the acts. I can vouch personally that this is a fallacy; there is no work, but, unlike us, there is no show. They appear to be good, plain housewives, without any pretension to dress or extraordinary ornaments. Mr. S. informs me that although knitting is not to be seen at the opera, the women do take it with them to the music halls, and that it is amusing to see the number of stockings in various stages of their construction.

"The opera was over at half-past nine, which I thought a most excellent idea, as it allowed every one to get home, have their suppers, and to bed, without interfering with their usual family arrangements. I may say in this connection that in Vienna similar times are in vogue, and it is very amusing to see the people rushing down the streets homewards, after the entertainments, the reason being that the houses there are in flats, built round a quadrangle court, with a doorkeeper who has the right of exacting a small payment for any desiring to enter after ten o'clock.

"After the opera we retired to supper at a restaurant which was patronized by the royal family. It was a very unpretentious-looking place, plain, but very comfortable, and Mr. S. informed me that it had acquired its good reputation by its good cookery and excellent wines and beer. My arrangements now being to leave Berlin the next day, I retired early to bed, giving orders to be awaked early to do my packing.

"Not having to start before the afternoon, I strolled down to the Schloss, where I had been informed the old Emperor William I. could almost daily be seen at the window of his working-room. This palace is of very modest dimensions, and the workroom has four windows looking out towards the University. It was a lovely morning, and one of the windows was wide open. Standing by the statue of Frederick the Great I noticed a great crowd of people looking towards the palace. These I joined and saw the fine old gentleman with his arm in a sling pass and repass the windows, and then he came, before retiring, and stood for a short time saluting the people. Adjoining the Schloss is the palace of the Crown Prince Frederick, which was made a present to him by the people.

"The time of my departure was approaching, of which I was fully aware by the attention paid me by the service. For instance, Boots came bustling into my room, very attentive and obsequious, waiting for my luggage, but very evidently expectant of baksheesh. 'Are you contented with me, sir? Have I well cleaned your boots? Have your clothes been well brushed? Could he help me to pack?' Such politeness was worth a price, and he got it. Next came the head waiter, with the bill. 'Had my noble born slept well? Should he send the porter?' I glanced at the bill. Oh yes, I see service is charged, but not politeness, so again a tip. The porter lounges at the cab, giving the last finishing stroke to the proper disposition of the luggage, pats up the cushions and adjusts the seats. This is extra, so again drink money; but I have forgotten to say, outside my bedroom door stands the chambermaid, who wishes me good morning and a good journey. This must also evidently be paid for, so again pin money, and last of all the grandly-uniformed hall porter asks after my health, whither he should send any letters or telegrams received; this has to be settled with a gratuity, and thus I depart.

"With what feelings I get into that cab I cannot describe. I feel debased within myself, and questions come over me, such as 'Are all these service-mongers talking about me, as a shabby, close-fisted, mean traveller, daring to come to the Kaiserhof and give his shilling or two?' and so on. Did I give in proportion to their merits, standing, or service? or how should I ever dare to face them again if I came to Berlin! Ah, well! all I know is that I have paid, in addition to the service already charged in the bill, seven and sixpence for the short time of my stay, and now I am off."

[In a subsequent visit to Berlin, during the Boer War, and having supper in the most-frequented restaurant of the city, boys came in and threw on the tables fly-sheets with telegrams just arrived, of which I obtained a copy. On perusal I found that they announced the British defeat at Colenso. One of the guests at a central table stood up, and read it out aloud to the three or four hundred people assembled, on which they rose and cheered the Boers to the echo, a practical evidence of the depth of their " affection " for the British nation.

During the same visit, journeying from Charlottenburg I entered an omnibus, and found myself seated next to an elderly gentleman, who, evidently recognizing me to be British, began declaring in a loud voice that the English would never conquer the Boers unless they engaged two or three German generals. Subsequent events in South-west Africa discounted this hypothesis, seeing that to overcome the resistance of Herreros they were obliged to seek the assistance of a British police officer.]

"I now enter the booking office, take ticket for Breslau, receive my change, find it fifty pfennige short, so remark, 'Beg your pardon, sir, but you have made a mistake. No matter—no excuses—mistakes of that kind may be rectified—hand over the cash—adieu.' On the platform the conductor asks, 'Where are you for, sir? Breslau—oh yes, sir. Would the Herr like to travel alone?' 'Oh, no, I prefer company, in reason, you know.' 'All right, sir, I understand,' and he busies himself in placing my luggage in the netting, calls for a fresh foot-warmer, asks if I am comfortable. 'Oh, perfectly,' but obdurate to his blandishments. 'Is your baggage booked?' 'Yes.' 'Will you dine at Sommerfeld?' 'Perhaps.' It's no go this time; I'm steel, acarius bronze, fourteen-inch armour plate, in fact invulnerable—no more tips; so in revenge there are ushered into my compartment two men, and presently two females, evidently mother and daughter, and the conductor looks around for any other passengers he could accommodate me with. I of course know and feel that this is aimed at me personally, so as he holds the door I say to him, 'There is still room,' and he slams it at me.

"Did you ever notice the composition of the German carriage, non-smoking compartment? These are an exception on the train, smoking ones being the rule; the non-smokers are used indiscriminately, either for the general non-smoking public or ladies' special compartment. How is it that this is always, or nearly so, empty, and the women will patronize the smoking-compartment with the gentlemen? It has always been a puzzle to me whether smoke has the drawing tendency or whether the men themselves are the attraction. Do they run away from the company of their own sex merely to avoid each other, or do mothers with daughters speculate upon chances? Personally I have not been able to solve the mystery, but it is a fact that the ladies' compartments are nearly always empty, and you will find their proper occupants ensconced amongst the men.

"I will now ask you to take a glance at my travelling companions. We are five passengers; opposite to me sits a spare pale figure, who informs me that he is an optician, having a shop in Unter den Linden. I should have taken him for a straw-hat cleaner, blanched from the sulphur fumes. He soon wants to know who I am, what part of Germany I came from, and these questions I evade. 'Are you from Westphalia?' he asks. 'Why?' I respond. 'Well, your accent is South German.' 'Oh, indeed! I come from a much more northerly government than that.' 'Ah, I see, you must be Dutch, or even perhaps a Dane.' 'Neither,' say I. Evidently the man is very puzzled, and as a last shot, 'You are a Russian, I am sure.' After a lengthened silence and great cogitation on the part of the little man, evidently at his wits' end, he says, 'I am quite sure you are a German,' but being forced to say 'No,' I avow my nationality, much to the amusement of the ladies, who had been quite agog listening to him.

"My companion next to me was a man of middle age, well developed in front, who had produced from his baggage a bag with fur inside, in which to insert his legs. It was extremely comical to see how the poor fellow puffed and blew in his frantic endeavour to get his legs inside it, which caused great merriment to myself, and the ladies giggled. This bag is a contrivance for keeping the legs warm, and when drawn up to its full height reaches to the hips. I should fancy it must be a piece of work for even a thin man to get into, but compressed into the narrow space of a train compartment, it seemed almost an impossibility.

"Just fancy him for a moment: he takes the bag with both hands, holds it open, stretches it out at arm's length and raises both his legs. As his legs rise, so do his arms, and the bag is drawn up above his knees, but his legs are outside; another frantic attempt and the same result. The poor fellow looks round and must notice that we are trying to repress our mirth. He then takes the bag in one hand, but raising his leg for insertion brings his body over on to me, and our mirth cannot be restrained. Following on this, all has to be recommenced with the same results; resting his body on his arm, he changes his tactics, but in vain, so coming to his aid I assist him to insert his legs in the bag up to his knees, which enables him at last with various wild convulsive twitches to get it into place. By the time he had succeeded, the perspiration was running down his face from the exertion, and I could not help picturing to myself that should any accident require his immediate descent, he would be obliged to hop like a kangaroo.

"The two ladies, who were evidently mother and daughter, had baggage sufficient to half fill a separate compartment, and I was much incommoded by a portmanteau placed by my knees. I should think that they belonged to the higher middle class, but the dress of the old lady reminded me forcibly of that of a Quakeress, her bonnet being a cross between that of the Quakeress and a coal-scuttle. The younger one was dressed in a more modern style, but not by any means of the most fashionable character.

"Before leaving the Fatherland and entering Austria, one of the most crying evils that the traveller meets with is the constant annoyance arising from tipping. This has grown into a system, and I feel very strongly that it should meet with strenuous opposition. It is not only in Germany, but also in Austria that it is growing, and in both countries it seems to me that it has already become endemic, and is now being calmly accepted by the traveller as a lawful claim. Thus the conductors on the trams and public vehicles expect to receive a tip with the ticket, and if not voluntarily given, will stand hesitatingly before you for a moment, apparently with the view of calling the attention of your fellow passengers to you; and should not this tax upon you be liquidated, you may expect petty annoyance being inflicted on alighting, either to yourself or any lady passenger you may have with you.

"It will be seen by the foregoing narrative that it works differently in different spheres—in the hotels by obsequiousness, accompanied by questions of health and perfectly unnecessary fussiness, in the trams and public vehicles as already stated, in the railways by crowding your compartment with passengers when there is plenty of room elsewhere, and in my case by the fraudulent withholding of the right change for the ticket.

"The optician attempted conversation, but, I not being in the humour, his effort failed. My other companion, in the sack, snored loudly, having evidently been prostrated by his over-exertion. At last, however, we are all aroused by the guard opening the door at the station before Sommerfeld, to ask if any of us would like to dine there, where on arrival we find we have to wait twenty minutes to enjoy the good *table d'hôte* provided by the company for two and sixpence; this is well worth the money and the inevitable tip that follows. This institution has, of course, died out with the arrival of the corridor trains, but before their advent it was excellent, as it avoided all delay, confusion, and loss of time on arrival.

"Here also we change guards, and the old one has the impudence to come to our department to wish us good-bye, with the question, ' Have you had a pleasant journey, ladies and gentlemen ? and have you dined well ?' when on this I take hold of the door and slam it in his face; after a few minutes we have been handed over and have been paid a visit by the new guard. The one that now appears is certainly one of the biggest men that I have ever seen, and in contemplating him I cannot help the thought of how many yards of cloth are used in his uniform, and also wondering how ever he gets into his clothes of a morning. Does he have to sleep in them ? or live in them till they wear out ? And does his tailor manufacture new ones on him like ships are armour plated ? And you are lost in wonder that the human skin can stretch so far without bursting. As he waddles up the platform he has to lean back as far as possible in order to counterbalance the protuberance of fat in front of him; and, unable to stand upon the step to examine our tickets, quite out of breath, he stands at the door, and his assistant hands to him the tickets from the passengers to be clipped, after which we see no more of him.

"I came to Breslau in order to pay a long-deferred visit to an old friend, the British Consul at that place. I telegraphed the time of my arrival to him from Berlin, and he met me on the platform, greeting me in the heartiest manner, and taking me and my belongings in his carriage to his house, where I met his wife and family, and enjoyed the greatest hospitality in their beautiful home.

"Breslau is situated on the River Oder, consisting of two towns joined by a bridge, and enjoys a series of very fine promenades, constructed from the old demolished ramparts; the streets in the centre of the old town are narrow, but the suburbs are beautifully situated and arranged. I was shown most of the public buildings, as I had not previously visited the city, and amongst them are noticeable the Cathedral of St. John's, with its high altar of beaten silver, the Town Hall, dating back from the fourteenth century, and the University (founded in 1702), which possesses a library of three hundred and ten thousand books and four thousand MSS. This city, which was formerly an appanage of Austria, reverted to Prussia in 1757. It is now a city of over five hundred thousand inhabitants, and a great commercial centre, being in close proximity to Russia, Austria, and the extensive coalfields of Upper Silesia. As I could not spare more time, after two days I had to say good-bye to my kind host and take the train for Cracow.

"The real aim of my journey to this part of Europe was to visit the great salt-mines of Wieliczka, Cracow itself being known to me through my having been there many times. Cracow was formerly the ancient capital of Poland, and is situated on the left bank of the

Vistula, which here becomes navigable. The fortifications, as in Breslau, have been turned into promenades, the only relic of them being St. Florian's Gate and a round tower, Orandel, which was built in 1498; the Stanislaus Cathedral, so named after the patron saint of the Poles, was consecrated in 1539, and the whole history of Poland is indissolubly connected with the Cathedral. At the Congress of Vienna in 1815, the town became a free state, and was neutralized under the protection of Russia, Prussia, and Austria, but reverted to Austria in 1846, with the consent of the same Powers.

"The Cathedral, built on an eminence called the Wawel, dominates the town, and is sacred and revered by the whole Polish nation; within it the kings were crowned, and it serves as a Pantheon for many of them and for the great patriots of their race. Here lie the remains of John Sobieski, Kosciusko, Poniatowski, and Mickiewicz, and also a part of the old Polish Regalia; the paintings and sculpture are specially notable, being works by Veit Stoss, Guido Remi, Peter Vischer, Thorvaldsen, etc.

"On entering Cracow the Koscuisko Hill is most prominent, surmounted by a monument to the memory of that Polish hero, and in the suburban district of Podgoritsa stands the monument to Krakau, the founder of the city and from whom it takes its name.

"I now proceeded to the main object of my visit, the before-mentioned Wieliczka, a small town in Galicia, nine miles from Cracow, noted as being on the summit of the most celebrated rock salt mines in the world. These are on several different levels, connected with the surface by eleven shafts, and have over sixty-five miles of chambers and passages. The length at present worked is $2\frac{1}{2}$ miles, and has a breadth of 1,050 yards, with a depth from the surface of 1,880 feet. The mines have been worked since the eleventh century, and since the year 1814 have been the property of the Austrian Government. They are remarkable for the many chambers which have been cut, some of them with statues and candelabra, including two large chapels and high altars with all their appurtenances complete, a large dancing saloon, the Kronsleuchter saloon, and the Michatosits room, all of the greatest interest to the visitor, each of them having been cut out of the rock salt. Within them is also the Lake Prysikos, 195 feet long, 120 broad, and varying in depth from 10 to 26 feet.

"Cracow, as a city, seems to my mind sunk in the lowest depths of Judaism, having a very large Jewish population; in consequence the old town seemed fragrant of damp schubas and garlic. Having carried out the object of my visit, I took train for Russia.

"At first we pass through forest land, and coming out on to the open plain I notice the long ropes passing over pulleys which were being worked from waterfalls, and by this means the various mining and mechanical operations are being carried out economically.

"In my compartment, one of my fellow-travellers was a German from Cologne, who seemed lost in wonder at my having left it only a few days before. Mentioning that I was glad to have left so malodorous a place, he felt almost to take it as a personal offence: for instance, 'What,' he says, 'Cologne smells? Cologne is dirty? Why, sir, this is quite impossible! The Rhine, the cleanest river in the world, runs by it.' To which I reply, 'Oh yes, it is quite true, but that is the worst of it.' 'How, what do you mean?' 'Well, the fact is that having so fine a river flowing by it, the municipality are too lazy to use the water at hand to wash their city with, and consequently it remains noticeable as the dirtiest city of the Rhine.' He then told me that he was born and lived there, but had not been in the town for twelve years, so I told him I was glad to hear that, or I might have asked him to sit at the other end of the carriage if it had been under ten years, but, I added, 'We will not discuss that, as I think you are purified.' He then began to abuse London, and to this I agreed partially—that it might be nearly as bad, but the difference between London and Cologne was that of new-mown hay in the one case to assafœtida in the other.

"Thus discussing, we reached the frontier, and found that the passengers on the train coming from Russia had had to undergo disinfection owing to plague that had entered Russia in a village near Tsaritzin on the Volga. I fully sympathized with these passengers, as they came out from the quarantine perspiring and rubbing their eyes after their three-hours treatment under carbolic acid. My sympathy was so much the greater that I had to undergo the same treatment on my leaving Russia for home two months since.

"The question of the plague and the possible introduction of it into Europe gave rise to all kinds of rumours both in Austria and Germany, and the very strictest of preventive measures were being employed against its introduction; in Russia itself every carriage of the trains smelt strongly of disinfectants. Under certain circumstances, autocratic government is certainly beneficial, and it was so in the case of the plague, which, originating in China, forced its way through Turkestan on to the Caspian, and was on its way to devastate the western countries of Europe, when the prompt measures employed stamped it out at the village near Tsaritzin.

"I was informed by an eye witness, whose credibility I could not doubt, of the measures that had been taken, which were very similar to those usual in Russia when the cattle plague is prevalent in a district. The village was surrounded with black flags, and a neutral zone having been marked out, sentinels were posted to prevent exit or ingress on the part of the villagers. Within the neutral zone food and the necessary medical comforts were placed, and in this manner the village was entirely isolated. In the meantime, tents were erected some few versts away, to which the inhabitants of the village were moved with all their belongings. When the plague had been stamped out, the village was burnt to the ground;

thus the black death was stayed, and Europe saved infection, the quarantine regulations being ultimately relaxed. A new village was subsequently built for the dispossessed inhabitants of the stricken locality.

"I have often made the remark on my arrival in England from Russia how deeply my mind had been impressed with the sight of our beautiful country, in contrast with the barren, bare, extended views of Russia. I have seemed to enter a miniature world in which everything is so small and so neat; the roads winding in and out seem scarcely wide enough for two vehicles to pass, and the beautiful green hedges make the fields that are bordered by them look smaller than the reality. On crossing the frontier of Russia, however, I have always been struck by the vastness of the view, the distance of the horizon, and the state of sleepy apathy that seems to pervade everything.

"The contrast is not only in the agricultural districts, but also in the cities; for instance, in London, you find the feverish rushing of its teeming population and with it the movement of trains and trams, the quick, impetuous slamming of the doors, sharp, shrill whistle sounding its commanding tone, and the starting to the moment. This impresses the mind with the strange emotion of a people borne along on an impetuous current, upon a stream carrying everything and every one helplessly before it, without any possibility whatever of staying its headlong course. Here, however, in Russia, everything and every one seem asleep or apathetic. In the Custom House, the officials, unlike their German colleagues just over the frontier, talk and smoke lazily, looking through the luggage, and with the most nonchalant indolence shrug their shoulders at any remark you may make. The train also sleeps as it starts off on its express speed of twenty-five miles an hour! The three rings of the station bells sounding at several minutes' interval seem a sleepy effort to awaken the officials and driver of the train to overcome the inertia of its languid organism. The conductors who come round to clip your tickets have evidently just emerged from somnolence, and will again (their painful duty finished) relapse into that state of oblivion.

"The oxen on the road moving at their solemn steady foot pace, and the post-horses returning from their relays, hang down their heads asleep, dragging along the sleeping post-boy in his telega. The stations are full of sleeping peasantry stretched out on the floors or platforms, with pillows of enormous size, upon which they rest their heads. These are awaiting patiently and somnolently the arrival of their third-class train the next day, and so it is throughout all the degrees of Russian society. Industry, progress, education, all sleep; and looking out of the carriage windows at the vast expanse of snow, the mind naturally receives the idea that it is the counterpane of a sleeping nation. 'Tis true that occasionally she wakes and stretches out her giant limbs, heavy and overgrown, into some neighbour's domain, placing her feet into some province such as Turkestan, or some Asiatic Khanate, after which she once again falls into a state of sleep and for a time the nations are at rest.

"Our next important stopping-place was Elizabethgrad, but on the way we had to change trains owing to the line being held up from an accident that had taken place three or four days previously to a military train, owing to which close on a hundred soldiers were killed and wounded. The wreckage was on both sides of the line, and a large breakdown gang was engaged in its removal and restoration.

"On arrival at the station, I found that the very usual practice on Russian lines prevailed here, and that the train for Kharkov had left punctually two and a half hours before the frontier express had arrived, so that I had to stay there from two o'clock in the afternoon until two-thirty a.m. before the next train started. It was extremely fortunate, however, that I had a very old friend in the town, who founded and was carrying on a large engineering establishment. Of course I called upon him, and was most hospitably received, staying with him till midnight, when he accompanied me to the station, where I remained till the arrival of the train.

"Having telegraphed the time of my arrival, I was met at Kharkov by my partner and the heads of our several departments, receiving the heartiest of receptions. I found that during my absence, owing to the Nihilist agitation, the city and province had been placed under martial law, and the town was being patrolled all night by Cossacks on horseback."

CHAPTER XIII

THE TRAGEDY OF KIEV

Failure of important firm—Meeting of creditors—Our firm and Mr. Leiste appointed liquidators—Meeting at Dessau—Return to Kiev—Suicide of Mr. Leiste.

ONE day in the early part of the month we received a letter from our Kiev agents, intimating that they were not in a position to meet their bills as they became due, and that therefore it was absolutely necessary for them to stop payment, at the same time asking me to go over at once to advise them. This intimation was of very serious import to us, as not only were they owing us on bills the sum of £5,500, but had also in their possession, on sale or return, goods to the value of £2,200. The firm in question was the most prominent one in the machine trade throughout the district in South Russia, and had a reputation second to none for honesty and enterprise. The news was so startling in its suddenness, that within an hour of its reception I had packed, and was at the station just in time to catch the early train.

On arriving at the town and proceeding to the offices, I found that the principal of the firm was absent in Saratov, where he was in negotiation with the town for a tramway concession, and that the notice in question had been sent by his partner. Going with him to the bank, I found that the cause of the notice was the withdrawal of credit, and as a matter of fact they had over a long period been trading on borrowed capital. I immediately advised that his partner should be telegraphed to return, and that a circular letter should be drawn up apprising each creditor of the position, and requesting their immediate presence. To this we soon had answers, followed by a meeting held on a specified day, which was largely attended.

Being the principal creditor, I was called upon to preside, and as a matter of course I suggested that the first thing to be done was to call in an expert and reliable accountant, place the books in his hands, take stock, and draw up a balance sheet, which, when done, would give us a basis upon which to act. This seemed to the creditors the right course of procedure, and I being on the spot, they pressed me unanimously to accept the position of chairman and supervisor. Our solicitor strongly advised them a friendly liquidation, being fully aware that any estate going into bankruptcy in Russia, once in the hands of the court officials, would, in so far as the creditors were concerned, remain there until the whole of the assets were exhausted. Having laid these arguments (which were fully endorsed by our solicitor) before the meeting, I accepted the position, on condition that the remaining creditors on their part would elect some independent person as their representative to be my coadjutor to act on their behalf and to be paid out of the common fund. Subsequently they appointed a gentleman named Leiste, who took charge of the office under my supervision and controlled the accountants who were drawing up the balance sheet.

Owing to the very large stores of spare parts of various machines, many of which were quite obsolete, but still remained on the books at current value, stock-taking occupied a considerable time, all the more so that no order had been observed in their storage, and the goods had become mixed.

In the meantime the season came into full swing. Orders were coming in ; specifications connected with sugar factories and distilleries had to be drawn up, if the business were to remain a going concern. All this caused double work, as the accounts between the old and new stocks had to be kept separately, and it took the accountants, with a large staff, fully six weeks to finish the balance sheet. This, when completed, showed the assets of the business to be worth, errors and omissions excepted, 27 per cent. net. Thereupon copies were sent out to each creditor, and I suggested in my covering letter that a further meeting should be held; and seeing that the larger number of the creditors were manufacturers in Germany, I offered to meet them at any central place they might find suitable.

Ultimately, the town of Dessau, midway between Russia and Germany, was selected. During the whole of this time I had been oscillating between the two offices, Kharkov and Kiev, because Mr. Leiste, having had no experience whatever in the machine trade, was in constant need of supervision, and my presence was equally required in the city of Kharkov. We had in our office a young Polish engineer, who had studied in Germany and had proved very competent in the higher branches of the business, so that I could trust him to draw up the details of all such work.

Also at this time Mr. Leiste had been living in my hotel, the Belle-Vue, and it was my custom every morning to invite him to breakfast with me in my room, and we would afterwards walk together to the office. I noticed, and frequently remarked to him, the small amount of solid food that he took, for his principal diet consisted of milk; and seeing that he was a man 6 feet 3 inches in height and proportionately broad, I thought that he required a more substantial dietary.

As the time for the meeting approached, he seemed to become exceedingly anxious that I should not attend it, but remain with him in Kiev. Even on the very day when I was leaving in the evening, he put his hand upon my shoulder, begging me to remain, stating that the Germans were only making a tool of me for their own purpose. "I am certain," he said, "knowing them as I do, that nothing will come of it, and I am sure that the work you are engaged upon will have no corresponding benefit. You have done all the work and prepared the balance sheet, and they will take the assets and steal the business out of your hands." I remarked to him that I was not a child, and that he was as much concerned in the matter as myself, seeing that he had undersigned the balance sheet and agreement, which latter had been notarially confirmed; also that so far as my experience went in Russian law, there was not the slightest chance that they should act in the manner he surmised. I told him we had also acted in conformity with the advice of the first legal authority in the city, Mr. Kupernik, and that in any case, now that the meeting had been arranged, I must and should go.

On receipt of the balance sheet, the principal creditors had written their approval of my work, so I left the city in the fullest assurance that I was doing the correct thing. In the events that followed, I proved to be right, whilst his objections, I am confident, arose from a diseased imagination. On arriving at Dessau, I took up my abode in the hotel which had been previously arranged for the meeting, and on the day appointed we met together to a man, when I was again asked to preside. I felt at once that I was amongst friends, and that it was not at all likely any opposition would arise. Addressing them in German, I presented the balance sheet, which was accepted as read, and point by point explained the whole circumstances of the case—that is to say, of the reckless speculation arising from forfeited contracts, and the defalcations of their head clerk.

On the accounts being agreed to, I told them that I had come from my firm with an offer; if they would accept a certain percentage of their claims as shown by the results, I had the authority of my partner to pay them cash down the agreed proportion before I left. I then proposed that the meeting be adjourned until the next day to give them time for the consideration of this offer. Before the meeting closed, I explained to them if they thought it right in their own interest to refuse my offer, I should expect a fair remuneration, together with all out-of-pocket expenses, such as hotel bills, both for myself and Mr. Leiste, which otherwise were included in the offer. The upshot of it was that it was accepted, and much to my surprise the very first to give adhesion to the proposal was the man who had up to that time done his best to oppose the agreement, and had advised letting the law take its course.

Although, as afterwards proved, I had done good business in the transaction, which enabled us in course of time to recoup ourselves the total cost that had been incurred, I had also made a good bargain for the creditors, and we feeling in honour bound to continue them our patronage, the transaction eventually proved satisfactory to all parties concerned.

After having settled with the creditors, I telegraphed Leiste that I was returning on a certain day, as I was obliged to go to Königsberg to inspect work which some manufacturers were carrying out for our firm, and which it would take me two days longer to complete. I was, however, very anxious to get back as soon as possible, as it was the very heart of the season, and August 12th again found me in the city, having arrived by the night train.

The host, having been apprised that I should return at midnight, had prepared for me a substantial supper, after which, thoroughly tired out with constant travelling for two days and a night, I retired to a well-earned rest—all the more restful that the worry and anxiety of the business were at an end. The following morning, when the waiter came in to take my clothes away to be brushed and receive orders for breakfast, I asked him to go to Mr. Leiste's room, acquainting him of my arrival and inviting him to join me at breakfast. He told me, on returning with my things, that he had knocked at the door, but had received no response, so, thinking that business had called him away earlier than usual, I ordered my breakfast and had it.

After the meal it occurred to me that the night porter, who had not left, might be able to tell me whether Mr. Leiste had gone out that morning; but the waiter brought me back word that no one had passed out of the hotel, and that Mr. Leiste must be in his room.

Accompanied by the waiter, I myself went to Mr. Leiste's door, tried it and knocked, but without result. I sent at once for the proprietor, who, when he came, ordered a step-ladder to be brought, Ascending this and looking through the fanlight over the door, he exclaimed, "The room is in complete disorder, and what look like pools of blood are on the floor." I then went up myself, and from what I saw immediately sent for the police, when having forced an entry, we found ourselves in the presence of a never-to-be-forgotten scene.

The room had pools of blood in places, and lying across the bed was the poor man's body with the dagger from a sword-stick still piercing his heart, and on examination it was found that five wounds had been inflicted. Of course the usual protocols and formalities connected with such scenes in Russia had to be performed, the rule of the country demanding that the nearest person to a murder should prove his innocence; under the present circumstances it was the police officer who had been first in the room, so the general course was abandoned, and the body was removed to the hospital, where the inquest was to be held. This took place in the dissecting-room, all the witnesses being present, and on opening the head the operating surgeon called me to him, and showed me the diseased portion of his brain. The whole affair still remains a mystery.

At this time the Nihilist agitation was more or less prevalent throughout the whole country, and found its greatest centres in the Universities, which were seething with disaffection. The police had a suspicion that he was the victim of a Nihilist plot, arising from some connection that he probably had with the anarchist conspiracy. My suspicion that it resulted from hereditary taint may, however, have been the correct one; both his father and his elder brother having committed suicide, the latter by throwing himself from the fourth-story window of an hotel.

My theory seemed to have some further foundation on recollecting that once when going into his room unannounced, I saw him standing before his window, which was open to its full extent. He was looking down into the street, and I should not wonder if my entry had not then stayed his purpose of following his brother's example. But it has always puzzled me why he should have so persisted in his endeavours to prevent my going to Dessau, and whether, if the truth were known, his homicidal mania might not have endangered my own life had I remained during that time in the city. To me it is still all mysterious. I had a very sorrowful duty to perform, to break the news to his wife. She was living at the town of Graievo, where their two sons were receiving their education, and it came upon her of course with unexpected suddenness, as a bolt from the blue. I met her at the station, having previously taken for her a comfortable lodging, and the next day accompanied her to the funeral, which was followed by all the people connected with our firm. I was very glad, however, to receive from her the information that she would be comfortably well off, as he was a man of some substance and fortune.

CHAPTER XIV

AN ADVENTUROUS JOURNEY HOME IN 1881

Family temporarily removed to England—Settled in Cheltenham—Education of my two sons—Business delays at Kiev—Intention to reach home at Easter—General inquisitiveness of Russian travellers—My fellow-passengers—Sluggishness of Russian railways—" Dead-heads "—Rise of blizzard—Train stopped by snow in middle of forest—Yelping of wolves at midnight—Difficulty of obtaining provisions—Sixty hours' stoppage—Train service dislocated—Starving third-class passengers—Arrival at Warsaw in early morning—Food obtained under difficulties—Arrival in England by night boat—Failure of connections—Stay night in Gloucester.

In order that our sons might receive a thorough English education—though hitherto this had not been neglected, they having been well grounded in French, German, Russian, and English, by governesses and a tutor—we felt that home influence was of such importance that we decided to make the sacrifice, and give them a home for a time in England. I therefore bought a house in Cheltenham and arranged to spend a portion of each winter with them, returning to Russia for the spring and summer, and our two sons were placed as weekly boarders in a private school at Stroud.

My journey home this year had been delayed, owing to very unexpected work having come in, requiring my personal attention at Kiev. Instead, therefore, of my reaching England for Christmas, owing to the postponement I was only able to make a start hoping to reach home by Easter.

The train was the ordinary one, running in connection with the Warsaw-Berlin express, and the weather being bright and crisp on starting, with a steady barometer, there seemed little prospect of a change; but owing to the immense distances to be traversed, little faith could be put on local indications. On arrival at the station I found a large number of passengers, mostly of the second and third classes; but having taken the precaution to book my seat in advance, I found myself in a good *coupé* of a first-class compartment, with the bottom sleeping-berth that I had engaged.

On sitting down I found that we were four all told, two occupying the upper, the third passenger and myself the lower berths. These the guard prepared beds for at night time by lifting and suspending to the roof the back part of the seats used during the day. It does not take long in Russia for fellow-travellers to grow communicative, and we soon grew unreserved. One was a professor of the Odessa University who was going to Lodz and Berlin. He was intimate with an old friend of my own, Professor Sherzl, who spoke sixteen languages and was Professor of Philology in Odessa. The second was a very near relative of the Scottish General Virchaw, and the third was one of the old Russian nobility, and owned large estates in the district of Kursk.

The inquisitiveness of the Russian travelling public, more especially amongst the women, is very annoying, and I have had on occasion to appeal to them to desist from troubling my wife, as I could see she was irritated almost to tears. They would take hold of her dress, examine the material, criticize the make, and ask details of her family rank, etc.

We started from Kiev between seven and eight o'clock in the morning, and the time passed pleasurably chatting and smoking, until we arrived at the station Kazatin, where there was a full hour's stay for lunch. There is one remark about the Russians that cannot be gainsaid, that they are undoubtedly, next to the Spaniards, the greatest spendthrifts of time. "Why do you hurry?" says one, "there will be a to-morrow,"—a remark one constantly hears.

Lunch time being completed, the first bell is rung by the porter, who has been holding the clapper of the bell by a string during the whole of our stay, doubtless with a view to preventing it awaking the engine driver too soon. However, the porter is now alert, the station master makes a sign—ting, ting, ting speaks the bell, and thus ends the first signal. On this there is dead silence, the porter boy stiffens to his heavy task of holding on to the clapper, but not a single passenger has moved to the train. After a lengthened pause, ting, ting, again is sounded, the second time of asking, and on this a few of the first- and second-class passengers walk to the platform leisurely smoking, whilst the third-class and "dead-heads" take their places. At last that long-suffering bell and patient porter give the third and last signal to the remaining passengers, who then take their places. First a single, then a double whistle by the station master is answered by the driver, and the train moves out slowly, groaning violently.

The English reader of this chronicle will naturally ask what is meant by the word "dead-head." It simply means that a very large number of the poorer class of passengers pay the guard a small sum to allow them to travel without a ticket, but as at any station an inspector might join the train, on a given signal they crawl under the seats. It is more than a surmise that the inspectors are in the game, and it is reported that on one occasion an inspector, seeing a man's leg protruding, kicked it with the remark "Keep your luggage out of sight." Once in Warsaw I was about to take a ticket for the south, when a young Jew sidled up to me, and in a low voice said, "I can get Barin a ticket, a real one, for half price." I asked him what he meant by making me such an offer, when he slunk away, doubtless to find some one more amenable to his offer. I have not the slightest doubt that the booking clerk must have been a partner in the swindle, as the offer made me was for any station on the line. The "dead-head" rascality is affecting very materially the revenues of the lines, so much so that the Government is adopting severe measures for its repression.

Once on the road the train moved on at its slow pace, stopping at every station with the same formalities as previously described; as evening drew on, the guard, entering the compartment to examine the tickets, told us that a bura (storm) was upon us, but they hoped to reach the forest, where they could find shelter before the full blast fell.

The traveller always notes with amusement the various titles by which those of a lower station in life address him, notably in Russia, and in a lesser degree in Germany, and especially by those who are in full expectation of tips. These service-mongers instinctively graduate the titular prefix according to your appearance, age, etc., and in the case of railway servants by the class you travel and the tip expected. These titles, I must admit, are graded and applied with great discretion. They commence with Sir, and proceed in extended scale to Hon. Sir, Gentleman (Barin), Your Well Born, Your Very High Born, Your Excellency, Your High Excellency, Your Privy Councillor, and to crown all, Your Brilliancy (Siatelstvo), and it must be a keen disappointment to a poor fellow, after having exhausted his vocabulary of the highest grade, if at last he should only receive sixpences or even less.

Yes, the dreaded bura was upon us. Driven furiously by the cruel north-east wind, the frozen snow was swept before it in horizontal swathes that, looked at from our carriage, appeared like winding-sheets, and it is no uncommon thing for whole parties of workmen and even wedding groups to become engulfed in these sweeping storms (the metels). On several occasions I have been caught in them, and though clad in wolf-skin travelling-coat with a large collar, I have felt the wind blow through, when there was not more than 10° F. frost, as if my clothes were made of canvas. The thought came to each one of us, accompanied by no formal prayer, that God might grant relief to both men and beasts in this hour of peril.

Our own position was growing more grave with every minute. We had left the plain behind and had entered the great forest of Minsk. A pine forest at its best offers little of beauty to the eye, but with each snow-laden branch bent almost to breaking-point, it looks lugubrious in the extreme, and has always given me a feeling of deep depression. The train, which had been thudding along for some hours, at last came to a standstill at the entry of a deep cutting, and the forepart of the engine was embedded in a thick snowdrift, the driver not being able to move the train either backwards or forwards. He had, however, before leaving the foot-plate of the engine, taken the precaution to transfer a fair supply of coal from the tender to the luggage-van, which being in a corridor train had communication with the compartments. We had, therefore, sufficient fuel for our carriage heating and snow melting.

We were quite isolated; in front the engine was half buried in the cutting, and behind the accumulation of snow was so great that nothing but a snow-plough could clear the rails. Night was now upon us, and nothing could be done until the morning. Only a short time before the stoppage we had entered the Minsk Province, so that we were about 120 miles from our starting-point, and 10 miles from the nearest station. Shortly after midnight we were awakened by the violent barking of the little dog which the landed proprietor had brought with him, and this was followed by the long-drawn yelp of the wolf, terminating in a yap. Looking through the windows, we could discern the silhouette of their forms and the bright glint of their eyeballs. It was very evident also that the pack was a large one and very ravenous.

It behoved us, now that we knew the full extent of the disaster that had overtaken us, to discuss the best means for meeting it, so we summoned the guard, who informed us that he had already communicated with Kiev about our position, and asked them to send provisions by sledge, as the passengers in the third class were already famishing, and under the very best conditions we were imprisoned for at least three days. On the Russian railways the conductor has in his possession means of communication by an attachment to the ordinary telegraph wires, which is a great safeguard under perilous conditions. It is always the custom in this country, at all events amongst the first- and second-class passengers, to take with them a supply of provisions for the journey, and we had among us in our compartment a sufficiency to hold out, with care, three days.

Two days and nights had already passed before we heard the whistle of the distant engine on the Kiev side; and hour after hour dragged slowly awaiting the longed-for food supply. We could now hear the workmen, and by midnight of the second day we were harnessed to the locomotive ready to drag us back to the station we had quitted sixty hours before. The foreman of the relief gang reported that the snow was bunched for quite ten versts along the line, in many places to a height of twenty feet, and they had had to work under the very worst conditions, the snow having been frozen into blocks which had to be cut out in pieces. He brought with him a plentiful supply of black bread, and on arrival at the station the excellent hot Russian soup (borsch), and the hot tea with lemon, refreshed and reinvigorated us.

Towards the end of our imprisonment a collection had been made from the first and second classes of provisions for distribution amongst the eighty people in the third class, and the remaining tea having been reserved, and given to the women and children, we had exhausted the resources of our commissariat.

Our difficulties were, however, not over, for the railway cutting had yet to be cleared; but owing to our train being out of the way, a more rapid advance was possible, as the work could go on from both ends. The number of wolves in packs prevented night work,

IN RUSSIA

so that we were detained at least another thirty hours before we could start. The great blizzard had dislocated the whole of the train service to the south, and as there were only single lines of rails, we were continually being shunted, and arriving at stations unexpectedly, or closed for the night, with no possibility of getting anything to eat. In this way we arrived at Warsaw at three o'clock in the morning, not a soul on the platform, and as hungry as hunters. The professor was the only one of the quartette alighting beside myself, the other two having changed at Brest for various destinations.

Standing on the platform, it was interesting to notice how the various nationalities disposed themselves for the night. The Poles kept their distance from the Russian, and also from the Jew. As for ourselves, we tipped the conductor to take charge of and deposit our luggage at the Railway Luggage Office in the morning, and we started to walk to the town in search of food and shelter from the cruel winter wind.

Like most Russian railway stations, the Warsaw one is about three-quarters of a mile from the town. I have often visited the city, which, in spite of its many attractions, seems to me always in a state of chronic depression and gloom, added to by the black costume, bordered at the bottom by a white band, worn by the ladies, when out walking, as a sign of mourning for their lost freedom. The city is endowed with many public and private buildings devoted to art and science, and a library with a collection of 500,000 volumes is attached to the University. Its public gardens are very noticeable; the Saxon Garden, situated in the centre of the city, is 11 acres in extent, and is of rare value both as a lung resort and during the heat of summer, affording a resting-place under the shade of its old trees. The great out-door attraction is the Lazienski Gardens, laid out by the Polish King Poniatowski. They have in them an elegant palace on a small scale, beautiful alleys, fish-ponds, a theatre, and a monument to Sobieski, once King of Poland. The population of Warsaw is 757,000, of whom a third are Jews.

But to return to our journey. Accompanied by the professor, I walked through the Praga quarter and over the Vistula bridge into the city, to find every hotel and restaurant closed. Meeting with a policeman, we inquired if he knew of any place that would be open at that time of the night, when he said that he could take us to a place (a traktir) open all night, suitable for the droshky drivers, but not for gentlemen. However, the necessity was on us, so we bade him lead on, and we found the place he mentioned to be in a narrow side street down some steps into a cellar. On opening the door we were received with a spray of snow caused by the hot air from the room becoming condensed by the frost outside, and the smell that accompanied it was most malodorous. We did not stay longer than sufficed to obtain a loaf of black bread and some dried fish, when the policeman took us to his comrades' shelter, where we were able to enjoy our meal with the tea they generously contributed. Having, in the morning, secured our baggage, I parted from my excellent companion, who was bound for Lodz (the Polish Manchester), and I took tickets by night express for Berlin, sending first a telegram home of my movements.

I have on several occasions spent some days in Warsaw in connection with my business, and, to tell the truth, have always left it without regret. Will Russia never learn that "force is no remedy," and that some day her necessity may be Poland's opportunity?[1] There is no love lost between the Teuton and the Slav, and should the heart not replace the heel, Russia may one day find herself with a stern enemy within her gates. To my mind it seems indisputable that no proud, self-respecting community, such as

---

[1] This was written before the promise of Czar Nicholas II, in 1914, to reconstitute the kingdom of Poland, at the conclusion of the European War.

the Poles, can submit with equanimity to the coercive measures of the Russians, who are striving by brute force to denationalize them, destroying their individuality by the abolition of their national and religious rights.

Arriving in London by the night boat, I just caught the last night train to Gloucester, when on arrival I found the last train for Cheltenham had left some time, and, not being able to hire a cab at that time of night, I was perforce obliged to spend it at an hotel and proceed home the next morning.

CHAPTER XV

EVENTS LEADING TO THE DEATH OF ALEXANDER II

Autocratic character of Nicholas I—Military insurrection, December 1825—Effects of Crimean War—Alexander II ascends throne—Transformation of principles of government—Emancipation of serfs—Difficulties with peasants and land distribution—Opposition of proprietors—Appointment of committee by Emperor—Methods adopted—Village communes and their powers—The Zemstvos—Usual limitations of autocracy—Emancipation of serfs directly due to Emperor—Start of Nihilism in 1877—Reign of terror—Attempt on General Trepoff—Acquittal of Vera Zasulitch—Prince Krapotkin's murder—Attempts on life of Emperor—His assassination, March 13th, 1881—His character—No advantage accruing from his death.

BEFORE Alexander II ascended the throne, the political life of Russia had been of so autocratic a character, that the whole country felt widespread dissatisfaction, and was fully prepared to adopt more liberal ideas. The system favoured by Nicholas I was one of extreme autocracy. He was a man of iron will, a stern, despotic ruler, who carried to an extreme the aphorism, "L'empire c'est moi," and brooking no adviser, declared that his will was to be law. At the time of his accession to the throne, in December 1825, there had been an attempt at a military insurrection in St. Petersburg, which had its origin amongst the young men of the nobility. This he vigorously repressed, all the leaders being executed or exiled.

Nicholas had very little sympathy with any liberal sentiments; he repressed as far as he could all intellectual and scientific activities. Many authors of high professional standing were exiled to Siberia, where they died, and their works with them. He himself was a soldier with the mailed fist, and demanded of every one who was in his service immediate and unquestioning obedience. He ruled as a tyrant, and the whole administration was bound to bow to his iron will, being practically deposed to the condition of State serfdom. In his actions, being guided entirely by this spirit of militarism, he had not the slightest strain of sentiment, and looked at everything not from an intellectual point of view (which found in him a most uncompromising opponent), but from that of administrative officialdom. He was, in fact, the very embodiment of autocracy.

Immediately on his death, it became evident that, with the accession of Alexander II, a new era would be inaugurated, and that a monarch had ascended the throne who had no sympathy whatever with the repressive system of his predecessor. It was at once obvious to the public, that under Alexander II a complete transformation would be effected in the principles by which the country would be ruled, and in his first proclamation that he issued he appealed for support to all classes of his people.

The Crimean War, although the Russians were defeated, proved the commencement of a progressive era of a very far-reaching character. It was the death-blow of Imperialism, and led to the inauguration, under the auspices of the new monarch, of that long series of reforms that made his reign memorable. Of these reforms, which followed each other in rapid succession, the first and greatest was the emancipation of the serfs. The idea of such emancipation was no novel one, for from the time of Catherine II successive monarchs had entertained it, but the difficulties had been considered of so far-reaching a character that every plan projected had to be abandoned.

The main point upon which differences had arisen had always been in connection with the distribution of land to the peasantry, the question being whether, on the abolition of serfdom, the liberated serfs should receive land or not. It will be readily understood that the issue was thus of great economic importance. The proprietors had hitherto depended on the work of the peasants for the tillage of their fields. If freed without land, the peasantry would be forced to migrate from their villages; on the other hand, should they have to receive land, the proprietors would of necessity have a considerable part of their estates appropriated to satisfy the requirements, and this could only be carried out by the indemnification of the landowner.

Alexander II, in this respect quite opposite to the character of his father, was of a most kind and beneficent disposition. Wishing to obtain the opinion of the proprietary class of his kingdom upon the emancipation question, he placed the whole matter for ultimate decision before a committee that he had formed to examine the question. After long consultation, it advised that each male peasant should receive a certain amount of land from his former proprietor, to be paid for by him over a term of forty-two and a half years. This was ultimately authorized (in spite of the opposition of a large number of the proprietary class) under the sign manual of the Emperor himself. The resulting settlement that was agreed to was as follows:

The Government arranged to issue bonds bearing interest, which became a medium of ready exchange.

We in our firm took these bonds in payment for our machinery, and they passed readily from hand to hand as interest-bearing ready money, they having coupons attached. It is interesting to note that on May 1st, 1881, the payment by the peasants for the land was remitted by the Government.

The amount of land that each male peasant received in the southern agricultural districts was three dessiatines (8 acres), so that if a peasant had a large male family the quantity received would be considerable. In other districts the area ceded was variable, differing according to its value. Every three years, redistribution took place, according to the number of males forming the commune at that date. It should be noted that half the area allotted to a village always remains communal, and serves as pasture land for the whole community; the arable and the pastoral portions are interchangeable, at every triennial distribution that which was arable becoming communal and the communal arable.

It is but little understood in England that the village communes are essentially self-governing institutions in which every male adult has voting power. By them the mayor of the village is elected, and the incident of the taxation determined by Government is distributed and collected. They have legal powers so wide that any member who is a disgrace or a danger to the community can be judged by it and sent to Siberia. Formerly these sentences were without appeal, but owing to many abuses having crept in, the Government appointed land assessors who constituted a Court of Appeal.

The meetings of the Mir[1] are quite informal, presided over by the mayor, every adult having the right of speech and freely giving his opinion. It will thus be seen that the constitution of the village Mir is representative of real democratic ideals, and to such an extent, that, if it were supplemented by a wise system of national education, it would in my opinion represent the most perfect form of democratic self-government obtainable. As it is, owing to the ignorance of the peasantry (a very small percentage of whom are able to read or write, more especially of the veterans from whom the mayors are chosen), they are entirely under the domination of the clerk to the commune. These are men of a certain education who can read and write, but are, however, unfortunately too often inebriates. Frequently very grave circumstances have arisen, involving loss of money belonging to the commune, owing to these men placing a document of a compromising character before the mayor for his signature without his being aware of its contents. The manner of legalizing the document con-

[1] The Russian word Mir in English signifies " the world."

sists of the seal being blackened and pressed to the paper submitted.

The Communal Assemblies date from long before emancipation time. On freedom being granted, a certain number of communes (seven of them in our district) were grouped into a larger unit (the Volost). A given number of these, in their turn, formed the district council, or local Zemstvo, each of these again sending their representatives to the chief Zemstvo of the Province. These various institutions serve as the medium between the Government and the peasantry for dealing with such questions as the levying of taxes, conscription for military service, maintenance of roads and bridges, education, and many other minor duties, thus serving as a relief to the central Government.

As each male adult has a vote, the Zemstvos at first were extremely popular; but like all other institutions in which different classes of society are brought together, the one representing the intelligence and the other limitation of outlook, considerable divergence of opinion has developed. It followed, as in all similar cases, that the best qualified by education and position became despondent, and, finding more profitable fields for their activities, did not offer themselves for re-election. In consequence, confidence in these councils rapidly diminished. Although in this manner certain defects have developed, I am strongly of opinion that when placed on an intelligent and solid foundation, based on a system of universal education, the Zemstvo undoubtedly will form a sound basis for representative local government. These institutions, which were founded long before our County Councils, were considered by Lord Randolph Churchill to be of great importance, a view that led him to visit Russia in order to study their constitution.

It is quite a misconception to suppose that the Emperor in issuing his Ukase (which in our Constitution is equivalent to a Proclamation by the King) does so without the proposed edict having been exhaustively considered by his Council of Ministers. It is quite true that he is the supreme power in a very much higher degree than is the case with any other European monarch, one of the attributes of his authority being that he can theoretically take the initiative in any reform he may consider imperative, even contrary to the expressed opinion of his councillors. This is, however, so rare an occurrence, that during the reign of Alexander II, I can only recall the case of the law for the freedom of the serfs, which was commonly considered (and I believe rightly so) to have been drafted in the Chancellery of His Majesty, and passed under the power of his autocracy, in spite of opposition from the proprietors and interested parties.

Immediately after the emancipation a great popular movement took place, incited by foreign agitators, resulting in the formation of a social democratic party amongst the peasantry, who felt that they had been wrongly dealt with by the proprietors in the distribution of the land. In course of time the social democracy gave place to a still more extreme party, the Anarchists, who are well known under the term Nihilist. Between these groups and the so-called Liberals a great gulf existed. The latter were desirous of having reforms carried out in a pacific manner, these including the peaceful elimination of the hitherto-existing autocratic system, whereas the Nihilists (as their name implies) were prepared to use any violence in order to overthrow established government.

At this time a reign of terror was inaugurated, leading up to the assassination of high-placed persons, the burning of buildings, and many other extreme forms of intimidation. The movement was also accompanied by labour troubles, such as strikes, forcing the Government, by their frequency and severity, to adopt strong means of repression by the military. The great body of terrorists were recruited from the students of the Universities, technical colleges, and high-grade schools, a circumstance which caused these establishments to be closed.

Being intimately acquainted with professors of the

University, I had every opportunity of learning the effect of the subversive teaching of the Socialistic Committees. The agitation grew to so great an extent, that inflammatory speeches were made by the ringleaders to their fellow-students, in assemblies held in the Hall of the University itself. This resulted in a complete revulsion of public opinion, bringing with it the introduction into the Universities of a deeply-regrettable coercive system.

It was in 1877, during the time of the Russo-Turkish war, that Nihilism had its inception at Lipetsk in the Government of Tambov, and an ever-increasing reign of terror was inaugurated, culminating in assassinations on the one part and cruel repressions and executions on the other. Owing to the state of war thus created, conspirators became increasingly bold, so that in February 1875 the Prefect of St. Petersburg, General Trepoff, was fired at and wounded. His assailant, a woman of the name of Vera Zasulitch, was arrested, and having been brought to trial, was acquitted by the jury. This verdict had a widespread effect, increasing the momentum of the movement, so that the so-called Executive Committee gave its orders for the execution of some of the highest and most respected of the public functionaries, which orders were carried out.

The long series of these actual or attempted murders increased with alarming rapidity. The Police Master of Kiev, the Rector of the University of that town, Prince Krapotkin of Kharkov, and many others, fell victims to the conspiracy.

This culminated in several attempts on the life and finally the assassination of the Czar Liberator. The first of these was made on April 14th, 1879, near the Winter Palace, where a schoolmaster named Soloviev fired at him several shots from a revolver. On December 1st, 1879, the imperial train, bringing the royal family from Livadia in the Crimea, was wrecked by a mine hidden under the rails near Moscow, the imperial family having owed their escape to travelling by the pilot train which preceded their own. On February 17th, 1880, a third attempt was made to blow up the imperial family, when at dinner in the Winter Palace, by dynamite. This attempt failed through their having been delayed, but the explosion, which took place in the guard-room beneath the dining-hall, made a large number of victims, killed and wounded.

On March 3rd, 1880, an attempt was made on the Emperor's life by a Jew, said to be converted, an act which was repudiated by the whole of the Jewish community. On March 13th, 1881, a bomb was thrown at the Emperor's carriage, when he was returning from a drive, by a man named Risakov. This bomb, however, miscarried, killing several of the guard. The Emperor himself descended from the carriage, and hastened to assist those who were fallen or wounded, when his death was caused by the launching of a second bomb by a man named Griniavitski, a crime which horrified the conscience of all civilized humanity.

Alexander II was a man who during his beneficent reign had acted throughout the whole period of his great reforms from purely conscientious motives. These reforms he had planned and introduced for the benefit of his country, and it seems an irony of fate that he who had granted the peasants their freedom, should have received his death-blow from a bomb thrown by the hands of a peasant. The question arises forcibly before us, what advantage accrued to the conspirators by so cruel a murder? They had surmised that by his death the cause of socialistic democracy would receive a strong impetus. Instead, the only result was to bring Alexander III to the throne—a man of strong will and reactionary tendencies, who, influenced by these cruel acts, through drastic measures brought this Nihilistic movement to a collapse. Many of the leaders were executed, and all members of the revolutionary committees were sent into exile. With their departure, the agitation which had so long terrorized the nation came temporarily to an end.

At the moment the terrorist agitation has transformed itself into one of social-democratic character, marked by trade strikes and a more peaceful agitation for political liberty in the higher centres of education. It is to be hoped that the Duma, representing Parliamentary institutions, may lead the way to the inception of a dominating healthy public opinion in the country.

CHAPTER XVI

RUSSIAN POLITICAL PROBLEMS
PART I. THE JEWISH QUESTION

Jewish question perplexity for Russian Government—Relations between Jews and dominant power—Characteristics of Jews—Extent of Jewish pale—Sections of Jewish race—The Sephardim—The Karaim—The Ashkenazim—Congestion not the cause of problem—Basis of antagonism between Jew and peasant—Non-intolerance of peasantry—Economic causes—"The cry of Christendom"—Origin of special laws—Smuggling—Universal military service—Remedial laws by Alexander II—Their effect—Evasions of law—Oppression of peasantry by the Jew—Jewish colonies—Their failure—Jewish jargon—Jews in London—East End Ghetto—Summary—Kotlinski incident—Conversion for purposes of gain.

I HAVE been frequently requested, since taking up my permanent residence in England, to give my opinion on the Jewish question in Russia—a question that has perplexed and worried the rulers of the nation for generations, and still remains a problem unsolved and unsolvable. Like all questions of policy connected with this class of subjects, there are two sides when dealing with a nation of over five millions of people, living, moving, and having their being amongst a dominant power, differing from them in religion, language, race and tradition. Firstly, there is the Power, infinitely superior in numbers, which makes the laws, imposes the taxation, and generally watches over the interests and internal organization of all classes of the people. Secondly, there is the Jew, between whom and the Russian there exists a marked line as regards thought, feeling, and aspiration. The Jew is so elusive in his character and so keen in his conceptions, that he defies and circumvents, with the utmost facility, every law made for his repression. He has talents and attributes vastly superior to those of the general population of the peasant Empire, and were these attributes properly applied, they would have a most civilizing influence and cause him to become a sustaining element of the community.

I am forced to admit, in spite of all preconceived British traditions, that, as the Gulf Stream flowing through the ocean never mingles with it, and bears a separate fauna, so the Jew remains, in his characteristics, a separate people, as a class apart, not always zealous of good works. During my prolonged stay in the country, I lived just without the confines of the Jewish pale, which embraces the whole of Poland, the west province of Lithuania, White and Little Russia, Mohilev, Grodno, Volhynia, Podolia, Minsk, Vitebsk, Kiev, Kherson, and Bessarabia. I had every opportunity of becoming thoroughly acquainted with them, and had, amongst the superior class, many intimate friends, and many also in my employment, as messengers, correspondents, and clerks, and found them, for the most part, reliable.

There are existing at the present time three distinct sections of the Jewish race—the Sephardim, Karaim and Ashkenazim. The first may be termed the aristocracy of the race, and has become more or less incorporated with the land in which it resides, not being distinguishable from the general population either in language, dress, or manners. The Karaite sect of Jews is evidently a very much higher class than the Ashkenazim and enjoys equal privileges with all its fellow-citizens. It is distinct in race and religious observances, and looks with contempt upon the common but more numerous race. Its members are good, settled agriculturists, employing themselves principally in the culture of tobacco and the breeding of horses, often having studs numbering many hundreds. They are supposed to be descendants of the Samaritans. The ordinary Jew first entered Poland after the Crusades, from Germany, but these emigrants came direct from Palestine.

BLIND BEGGAR, TIFLIS.

The Ashkenazim, on the other hand, have differences strongly marked. Their long, lank forms and lean faces are to be seen within their Pale in ever-increasing numbers, and from below their fur caps two obnoxious ringlets fall down the sides of their faces. Dressed in their long kaftans, they present a picture arousing natural repugnance. The new Ghetto already formed in the East End of London furnishes many similar characters. It is to this latter race that the Jews of South Russia belong, and the German-Jewish jargon spoken by them is corrupting our language, as it is fast becoming the common language of the East End. Therefore to this class I refer when speaking of the Jews, numbering as they do between five and six millions of the population of the south-western provinces of Russia. Writers have affirmed that the dominant evil feature of the commonalty of the Jewish race arises from their congestion, and that, owing to this cause, expansion in civilization is impossible, and the means of living have been circumscribed. I think that this argument must be considered baseless, seeing that the Pale given to the race embraces a district comprising fifteen Russian Governments, which in themselves cover a space many times greater than the whole of Great Britain, sustaining a population of over forty millions.

In my opinion, one great cause of their demoralization lies in the fact that they produce nothing that adds materially to the real welfare of the nation, or enriches it with the economical employment of their wealth, but, on the other hand, that they have by usury, extortion, and corruption, more especially among the rural population, brought upon themselves the repressive measures of the Government, and still worse the pogroms of the peasantry. Personally, I cannot conceive of any Government imposing repressive measures on any portion of its population out of mere caprice, but it may take such a form that the innocent may be made to suffer with the guilty and the penalty inflicted exceed the bounds of moderation.

The first thing in considering this question, I think, should be to discern the basis of the antagonism which undoubtedly exists between the Jew and the peasant—that is, to diagnose the disease and then, if possible, discover and suggest the remedy. I find that, as a rule, most people with whom I have spoken on the subject consider that it arises from fanaticism or an outburst on the part of an ignorant proletariat against the religious services of a meek and inoffensive people; on this point I take issue.

From my long residence among all classes of the population, I have not found that the moujik [1] is actuated by intolerance against any other form whatever of religious worship that may differ from his own, or by any motive for the propagation of his own ritual. He has a strong religious instinct, but, unlike the Mohammedan, is tolerant to all others. He uncovers his head and crosses himself before the funeral procession of a Jew or Christian with the same devout reverence as it passes before him, and not even when incited by the Holy Synod in authorized sermons has he risen against the ever-recurring dissenting forms of worship. In his case, fanaticism is not the incentive to violence, unless his conscience be outraged by some real or carefully-planned false reports of the persecution of his Christian brethren in home or other lands.

I am convinced that all other incentives to rioting and bloodshed have been economic in their character. Socialism, which of late years has made such gigantic strides among the artisan and labouring class; Nihilism, which is the negation of all law amongst the students and half-educated; political unrest amongst the well-to-do and proprietary class; the ever-recurring strikes among the mechanic class; the great land hunger amongst the peasantry which rages throughout the country, together with the Jewish question, have each and all a common origin, and that of an economic character.

[1] The Russian peasant.

Each of these separate causes is a formidable danger to the State, and a combination would be fatal. In opposition to these various elements, which are essentially of a dangerous and explosive character, though they be at the present moment disorganized, we find a weak Government making an abortive attempt to organize itself into some semblance of an autocratic Parliament (a contradiction in terms), writhing in the pangs of its new birth, and subject at any moment to have its very existence terminated at the uncontrolled will of the Emperor. Putting aside, however, these questions of a purely domestic character, which only concern the internal policy of any Government, and returning to the question of the Jew, it may be asked what steps have been taken to meet " the cry of Christendom," to stay the hand of persecution, and give full protection to life and property to so large a portion of Russia's subjects. These justly claim, and should have that claim allowed, to exercise full rights of citizenship in the State. On the contrary, up to the present time the sole answer that has been given has been the repression of the Jew and the accumulation of his disabilities.

I am no special pleader for the Jew, who, I admit, is a difficult problem for any nation, and increasingly so even for ourselves, as evinced by the experience of every magistrate in the East End of London. It is becoming a question how best to deal with the 385,000 at present in the British Isles, and whose numbers are constantly increasing. If it be admitted as an axiom that all subjects of a nation are equal before the law, then I take it as a corollary that all subjects are subservient to the laws and the general restrictions governing the economical administration of their country. The question then arises, for whatever reasons have specially oppressive laws been enacted against one section of the people, thus imposing upon the Jew the status of an alien in the land of his birth, as also that of his forefathers, for many generations? The reason for this, to my mind, is obvious, and arises from the fact that the actual position at present between the Jew and the Gentile Government is that they are standing in direct opposition to each other, with evasion on the one part and repression on the other.

Under such circumstances, the commonalty of the Jew in Russia has become the parasite of civilization, preying upon the vitals of the country, and, following on this, the laws of repression have become increasingly severe. Thus, only 10 per cent. of the Jewish population are permitted to enter as students in the Universities, to the great detriment of the country, which forces the most intelligent and astute portion of the community to use its unrivalled talents in fomenting conspiracies and plotting against the State. Again, they are forbidden to purchase land in Poland, and are not allowed to dwell within fifteen versts of the frontier. Their answer to this has been that, while deprived of the ownership of the land, they purchase its produce over a series of years, thus holding the proprietor in perpetual thraldom, and to such an extent that one cannot purchase a chicken from any of the estates without the intervention of the Jew. On the frontier question much can be written. They are the most consummate smugglers, and have brought their actions in this respect to such perfection, that they will undertake to deliver all kinds of goods, without duty paid, to any part of South Russia. As an instance, a merchant in a large way of business received, over a long period, big consignments of contraband goods, particularly tea. He was thus enabled to undersell his competitors, whose jealousy and suspicion being aroused, led to the source of his supply being discovered.

Thus the Jew, compelled to live by his wits, and debarred by repressive measures from the employment of his undoubted talents for the benefit of the State, preys upon the community. He enriches himself by impoverishing the people, and more especially the peasant, who is the least able to protect himself.

When universal military service was first imposed upon the Empire, the Jew, who has an inveterate distaste for the conscription, set his busy brains (which the Russians say are all over his body) to work in order to circumvent the Act. On approaching the age of conscription his sons were sent abroad, mainly to Turkey, where no Christian or Jew is enrolled in the army, and after taking over the Turkish nationality, they returned home as foreigners. For a time, this form of evasion was successful, but, when discovered, the Russian Government repressed it by an enactment that no Jewish alien entering the country could remain longer than three days. Many of the Jews also fail to pass the medical test, receiving, on that account, certificates of exemption. These become of marketable value, the sound men purchasing them, and impersonating the defective to their own advantage.

The religion of foreigners must always be declared on entering the country, and, should they happen to be Jews, they must obtain a special permit, or leave again within the three days. Further, if they are of conscript age, entry is refused. It is nearly as difficult to leave, and large numbers desirous of quitting the country, apply for assistance to the frontier Jew broker, who is always equal to the occasion. Should the broker not have a passport ready to his hand, he will get a permit signed and sealed by the chief officer of the patrol for the passing of merchandise, or even of some animal, and this, when stamped and presented to some official in the pay of the broker, passes the person across the border. It is no uncommon thing for a man to pass as an ox, and the tale is even told of women having been passed as pigs. In fact, the amount of contraband smuggled into Russia through the ignorance of the patrols, who can neither read nor write, together with the venality of the officials, is so enormous that, if duty were received, it would make a very substantial increase to the budget.

During the reign of Alexander II, among the many beneficent reforms that he inaugurated, was the granting to the artisan Jewish classes, after examination under their several trades, the right to settle in any part of the Empire. The examination took place at certain frontier towns, where the so-called Tsek (labour guild) existed, and, of course, it was held under police supervision. Immediately on the issue of the Ukase, both the Jew and the examining authorities began to make use of it to lubricate the wheels, and it was commonly reported that, for a fee of three roubles, the necessary trade certificates would be forthcoming, without too keen an exercise of knowledge on the part of the Jew. Of course, the monetary consideration included, should any question arise, the fee for instruction, although it proved the easiest way to evade the law. I was credibly informed that in one week in Kharkov over 300 glass-cutters passed the examination, and obtained their certificates by the simple expedient of cutting a piece of glass with a diamond along a straight edge.

Any employer of standing was allowed to nominate artisans for whose efficiency he could vouch, and many a one of their own persuasion took occasion to extend his patronage to members of his own faith for a consideration. As the grant permitted the recipient to move from one part of Russia to another, it followed that when one place became too hot for him, he could easily remove his modest belongings to fresh fields and pastures new. These certificates are eagerly bought up by brokers within the Pale, the transfer of the name Abraham Goldberg to Moses Goldstein only requiring a stroke of the pen. A good supply of these documents is also available from the death of the original owner; they, in accordance with the law, should be returned to the police, but I am of opinion, were distinct control exercised, it would be found that the certificates returned were a very small percentage as compared with the death-rate.

Of course, these evasions of the law, both by the police and the Jew, exhibit a great lack of morality on both sides, and have an exceptionally far-reaching effect upon the community. It is an ingrained axiom with the lower-class Jew that it is his religious duty to cheat the Christian, and the keen, acute, sharp-witted, new, Jewish settler, who has purchased his certificate, has no other aim than to put this belief into practice, and, in very truth, for knavery, peculation, roguery, and disreputable dealing this type is unapproachable and unequalled. Some years ago a Commission was appointed to examine the working of the law. It found the proportion of those practising the trade for which they were certificated was exceedingly low, and advised the deportation of a number of them back to the Pale. I well remember how the sentiment of our English people was stirred, and meetings were held and deputations formed (though not received by Russia). The newspapers shrieked, in their boldest type, the shameful persecution of the Jew. I have often been led to consider whether it would be possible, and by what means, to infuse a new spirit into the conflicting elements, and replace the old era of religious and racial strife, at present existing, by a sound national spirit as a basis for internal reform, order, and prosperity. I do not believe the mere differences of creed and ritual stand in the way, but that the mutual distrust and antagonism arising from economic sources require drastic amendment.

Russia is a country that is mainly agricultural, with a climate of extremes, and on an average the peasantry, with their primitive mode of agriculture, can scarcely rely upon one good harvest in three. I do not know whether this proportion is accurate for the whole of Russia, but it certainly is for the south, and a succession of bad years means famine and destitution. But although the peasant is becoming poorer year by year, the exactions through the tax collector grow at an increasing ratio to his poverty, and the only source of aid in his distress is the Jew, who is a hard taskmaster, demanding in exchange the sale to him of his present and future crops. The accumulated interest virtually renders the peasant the serf, or even worse, of the Jew. I am glad, however, to recognize the great benefit which has accrued from the establishment of the Peasant Land Bank, which will greatly mitigate, if not eradicate, the power of the usurer.

It must be admitted that much of the peasant's distress is due to his intense craving for drink, and, in his bargaining, the Jew fosters this habit by giving him repeated glasses of vodka. Through the succession of bad harvests, the exactions of the Government and the usurer, the condition of the peasant is practically hopeless. He is ripe for any means of extinguishing his liabilities, and falls a ready prey to the rioter and the anarchist.

In dealing with the Jewish question, in my opinion, the first and most urgent need is to satisfy the cry of the peasants for land, and ever more land. One of their bitterest grievances is their belief that it was the wish of the Emperor Alexander II to return them the whole of the land, and that this wish had been frustrated by the proprietors. The vast plains of Siberia and Turkestan hunger for population, and their climates, so often vilified, are for the most part far superior to that in Russia proper. The soil is virgin and capable of bearing two or three crops in succession, and only awaits the labour that is running to waste in the congested districts of their Fatherland to bring forth rich and abundant harvests. I am fully convinced that it would be not only more humane, but far more economical, to spend money on their transfer, than to sell up their samovars and their poor simple belongings to satisfy the Government's demands for their arrears of taxation.

Again, a great and progressive safeguard would be a system of national education. Under present conditions, 90 per cent. of the whole Russian population can neither read nor write, whereas these attainments are partially enjoyed by every Jew, who is also instructed in grammar, and can read and write his jargon in Hebraic characters. This gives him an immense advantage over the totally ignorant peasant. Most important of all, the Government should, by increasing the salaries of the executive officials, grant a sufficient wage to entice into its service honest and reliable men, incapable of being influenced by bribery and corruption.

In summarizing the foregoing remarks, I must assert that this is only an honest opinion upon a subject which I know deeply occupies the thoughts of every patriotic Russian, and also has proved, and is still, a problem for the Government. I can foresee that, through the false sentiment which permeates the English people, a similar problem is brewing in our midst—not perhaps on the same lines, or to the same extent, seeing that by means of our national education assimilation is progressing. I see also with dismay the cream of our youth leaving us in ever-increasing numbers for the West, and the inrush of the scum and dregs of other nations pouring in from the East. I note, further, with deep apprehension, our own Government rendering the Aliens Act inoperative, the alien having only to declare himself a political refugee to obtain asylum in England, and receive help from this Government for their admission, thereby swelling the Ghetto already formed in the East End of London. They should, in my opinion, be compelled to furnish sufficient proof to our respective Consulates to receive from them a certificate of fitness for the right of entry into our country according to the alien laws then existing.

It must be remembered that at the present moment there is a Jewish population in London of 150,500, a large proportion of whom are fugitives fleeing their country, not for any political reason, but to evade the just laws to which each member of the community is subject. I have no desire in writing this opinion to depreciate the Jew. In his family relationship he is a model father, strictly temperate, and generous to the poor, of his own persuasion.

In an advanced State like our own, with education permeating every section of the community, public opinion demands that all classes, whether Jew or Gentile, must obey the laws that have been enacted for the common welfare. This, however, does not apply in a community where millions of the population have but recently emerged from a state of subserviency and serfdom. Such being the case in Russia, where 90 per cent. of its population can neither read nor write, and its peasantry is ever on the verge of destitution, it follows that full protection should be given against usury, extortion, and evasion of the law on the part of the Jew, and it is not for England to dictate when the special protective laws should be abrogated and emancipation from them be accorded. In my opinion, the time is yet far distant before equal rights can with safety be applied.

Amongst the many good works inaugurated by our religious societies is one aiming at the conversion of Jews to Christianity. Although I would fain bear testimony to success achieved, yet truth obliges me to state that in my opinion the results have not been commensurate with the efforts and resources employed. It is possible that there have been many really converted from Judaism to Christianity of the Protestant type. I may safely assert, however, of those baptized into the orthodox faith, that their conversion is not generally based on conscientious principle, but with a view to some material gain. The following incident will elucidate my meaning:

A Jew named Simeon Kotlinsky, resident in the town of Tambov, had early in life worked his way up from a menial position to become the business agent for a very well-known and respected firm, Messrs. Pavloff & Sons, established in that town. Suddenly, without giving any notice or reason, he left their employ and the town. Shortly afterwards, at a village on the Volga, a merchant reputed rich, also of the name of Pavloff, received a visit from a Jew, who requested him to act as godfather on his being received into the Orthodox Greek Church. Amongst the ordinary merchant class such action is considered of very high religious value, so that an application of this nature is seldom refused. While carrying with it a certain standing in the community, it also involves a material outlay ; the convert in baptism takes the name of the godfather, and thus the name of Kotlinsky was effaced, and the name of Pavloff substituted, while it must not be forgotten that this was also the name of the firm with which he had been employed in Tambov.

On entering into the Russian Church a further benefit accrues to the convert from his new relationship. Associated with his change of name and his new position as godson, he has become a Coom to the family—that is to say, a kind of cousin, second only to those of blood relationship, which in the Russian language are termed brothers of the second degree (cousins). On these occasions the baptismal festivities, when the change of name takes place, last long, and are attended by all the relatives of the godfather, who with the latter usually give generous gifts to the godson on his incorporation into the family.

Subsequent to these proceedings, a letter was received by one of the large wholesale houses in Moscow, written on the paper with the heading of the Tambov firm of Pavloff, announcing to them that within a day or two their nephew would arrive for the selection and the forwarding of goods to various parts of the country, which were required for the fulfilment of a large military contract they had undertaken. In the letter it was also stated that the purchaser was not to exceed the sum of 80,000 roubles (£8,000). Shortly afterwards, Mr. Pavloff (Kotlinsky) arrived, made his selection, and personally supervised the forwarding of the goods to various destinations only known to himself.

In the usual course of business between the two firms, the goods purchased were only bought on credit terms, and a certain time elapsed before the Tambov firm knew of the large order given in their name, the

Jew having the whole of the accounts in his possession. On the wholesale house forwarding the bills to be accepted to Tambov, the fraud was detected, but the Jew had disappeared. Eventually, however, he was arrested under his former name, brought to trial, and was sentenced to a long term of Siberian imprisonment.

The Russian Government, in their desire to find some solution of the ever-present Jewish question, settled a certain number of Jews in colonies on the land that was specially allotted to them, with a view that by their industry and enterprise they might set an example of economic prosperity to their co-religionists. The experiment, however, did not prove successful, at least during my stay in Russia. The colony that I visited in the Government of Kherson some few years after its foundation presented a picture of dilapidation difficult to describe. Most of the inhabitants had already let their parcels of land to the peasants, and on inquiry I found that they themselves were drifting back to the towns and to their former occupations of usury and extortion.

Previous to the establishment of the Government monopoly for the manufacture and sale of alcoholic liquors, the distilleries, which had been the property of the landed nobility, had passed into the hands of the Jews, the proprietors having been unable to make them pay. The Jews, by bribing the Government inspectors, were on the other hand successful, but at the same time sold the spirit almost immediately on its production; as at that stage it contained a large amount of fusel oil, it proved extremely deleterious to the consumers. Under these circumstances the Government withdrew the right of manufacture and sale of the spirit from the Jews, and later, in order to regulate the output and give a good quality of liquor to the people, established a monopoly. This has proved so successful that the income nearly equals half the taxation of the whole country.

It has generally been considered by the Russians that the Jews are a race of cowards, and they point to the employment of every illegal means to avoid military service. I do not, however, myself consider this view to be justified, seeing that they unhesitatingly plan Nihilistic conspiracies, in which great personal risk is involved. In illustration of their point of view, the Russians relate that during the Crimean War the Jewish community offered to the Emperor Nicholas I a whole regiment officered and led by them, an offer which was graciously accepted by the Emperor. On approaching Sebastopol, the tale goes that the Colonel interviewed the General in command of that town, requesting him to send a strong military escort in order to protect the advancing regiments from the dogs of the villagers.

AUTHOR'S NOTE

THE origin of the word Ashkenazim dates from the very earliest sources—the generations of the sons of Noah.

From Genesis x. 2 and 3 it will be seen that Ash kenaz was the eldest son of Gomer, who was son of Japheth, son of Noah.

See also 1 Chronicles i. 6 : " And the sons of Gomer ; Ashchenaz. . . ."

The contemporary German Jews claim direct descent from Ashkenaz, the son of Gomer, from whom they derive their name.

CHAPTER XVII

RUSSIAN POLITICAL PROBLEMS
PART II. RUSSIA AND THE POLES

Warsaw, the capital of Poland—Moral depression of city—Poland treated as conquered—Permanent martial law—Russian language obligatory in Universities—Oppressive land laws—Prohibition of public meetings—Economic neglect of city—Military disabilities—Racial and religious differences between Poles and Russians—Revolution of 1863—Deportation of Poles—Causes of downfall—Internal dissensions and election of kings—Insincerity of Poles.

IT is quite impossible for any intelligent traveller, visiting Warsaw for the first time, not to be impressed with the air of gloom and despondency that dominates the city. The unkempt streets, the sombre public and private buildings, and above all the mourning costumes worn by the women, ever sorrowing for the loss of their liberty, lend a touch of true pathos that impresses one's heart and feelings painfully.

In the eyes of Russia, Poland as such is non-existent; it is always under martial law and subject to the strictest discipline. The military Governor-General is in autocratic power, and every citizen is liable to heavy penalties for even the most innocent infringement of the passport system, domiciliary visits and deportations being also very frequent. The Poles are treated as a conquered nation, and every means is employed, even of a most brutal character, to incorporate them into Russian hegemony.

The following regulations which prevailed during my long sojourn in Russia, and which I am credibly informed have not since been abrogated, will indicate the extent of their treatment by their conquerors, and the cause of the hatred existing, mainly on the part of the Poles, against them.

(1) The old historic name of Poland, which until its partition in 1795 represented it as a nation, has been suppressed, and it is now officially designated the Vistula Province.
(2) The Russian language is obligatory in all the schools, whether elementary, advanced, or university, and speaking the Polish language even by boys in the playground is subjected to severe punishment. The university of Warsaw remained closed until 1869 after the revolution of 1863, and was then reopened on Russian lines, the lectures being given in that language and not a word of the Polish tongue being allowed within its precincts.
(3) The suppression of the Municipal Councils and the imposition of heavy taxation without representation.
(4) The exclusion of Poles from all service in Poland under the Crown, all those occupying such posts in 1863 being replaced by Russians.
(5) The prohibition of Polish land proprietors bequeathing their estate to any but their lineal descendants and the interdiction of the sale of them to all nationalities except Russian.
(6) The strictest possible censorship on all printed and written documents of every description.
(7) The prohibition of public meetings, and the imposition of penalties should an assembly of over fifty persons be proved without having been notified and allowed by the police. In addition the country is inundated with spies, and under administrative action no home is sacred, no citizen is safe, but may without trial be imprisoned and deported.
(8) Although so heavily taxed, I have noticed in my frequent visits that everything in the city of Warsaw is wretchedly neglected and that

nothing is being done in the way of restoration or repair, so that gradual deterioration is fast drawing near to ultimate decay. The Poles have yet another grievance—that under the law of universal conscription, their young men are drafted into the Russian regiments in eastern provinces of the country, whilst to the Polish provinces are sent the Cossacks, the wildest free-booters of East Russia. It is undoubtedly the above disabilities that have given rise to the deep antagonism existing between these two branches of the Slavonic race. Poland was a nation almost up to the close of the eighteenth century (1795), and the dominant power in South-Eastern Europe, whereas to-day its main portion stands a humiliated, dismembered province of the Russian Empire.

It must be remembered that previous to its first partition in 1772, Poland had been a free nation for 800 years, its boundaries at one time extending from the Baltic to the Black Sea, and from the Ukraine to Cracow, with a further line northward to the boundary of Brandenburg, thus enclosing an area of over 200,000 square miles, In 1795 the second partition took place, and the kingdom of Poland has become a memory.

Subject to the foregoing being correct, it is easy to understand the *fons et origo* of the distinct split existing between these two sister nations. The proud, self-conscious Pole, mindful ever of his former historical status, nurtures a deadly hatred against the Russian, and only submits with suppressed feelings of aversion, knowing his incompetency to break the bonds by which he is held. It is not strange that the women should be less tolerant of the yoke than the men, for with them the spirit of their lost nationality never grows old, and, like the Spartan mothers, they are ever ready to sacrifice their nearest and dearest to regain their liberties and obtain the restoration of their country's lost freedom.

The Poles as a race are built upon much finer lines

A DESCENDANT OF THE CRUSADERS.

than the Russians, and the feet and hands of the highborn ladies are recognized throughout Continental Europe as being unsurpassed for smallness of size and perfection of form. I have often heard it discussed amongst the Russians why the two sister nations should differ so materially in language, ideals, and physical characteristics. My own opinion is that the cause lies partly in the difference of the religion, the Poles being Roman Catholics and the Russians of the Orthodox Greek Church, but the physical differences from the fact that Poland throughout its chequered history had been engaged in wars, either within its own borders or when outside them, with an enemy their equal or superior in civilization and refinement. The Russians, however, having been engaged in their borderlands with uncivilized hordes, have probably incorporated with themselves some of their grosser elements. Whatever may be the cause, the fact remains that, under the present political conditions, no racial assimilation is possible.

Should the foregoing list of disabilities be correct, it follows that the imposition of brute force by the Russian over a long period of years requires strong justification. Nearly two generations have passed into history since the last abortive revolution of 1863 was so cruelly suppressed, and more than 50,000 of the youth of the nation were hurried off in chained gangs to Siberia. That fight for freedom was doomed to failure from its inception, seeing that the bulk of the population (the peasantry) had refused to join, leaving the nobles, or rather the proprietary class, to carry on alone the unequal fight against the mighty power of Russia. As the reward for their abstention, the peasants received their freedom from serfdom together with free grants of land from the confiscated estates of their late masters.

I can yet vividly recall the long line of prisoners, fettered from waist to ankles with connecting chains and joined up into a gang by one long chain passing down the line; I can feel once more the indignation aroused at seeing the main body as they clanged their weary march ten versts daily to the northern Siberian desolation. Still more do I remember the peasants' carts, laden with delicately-nurtured women, the whole being guarded step by step by brutal soldiery. Other pens and more skilled than mine have pictured in vivid colours the horrors of that tramp, which lasted from one to three years according to the distance to be traversed to their different places of settlement. Our hearts bled, however, in deepest sympathy for the poor women, most of them bearing on their faces the traces of suffering and the deep humiliation of their lot. An added pathos, in the case of many of them, arises from the fact that they had accepted the voluntary exile offered by the Government to women desirous of accompanying their husbands.

In the absence of railways or other means of communication on the Siberian route, all prisoners condemned to hard labour in the mines or as colonists were forced to trudge from station to station along the convict track. The almost daily passage of these chained gangs worked so upon my wife's feelings that her health suffered, and I had to forbid the slightest allusion to them by any one in her presence.

It seems quite certain that the rule by autocracy has been a failure, and that the repressive laws, now prevalent, require modification. Otherwise the continuance on the present lines will eventually cause just indignation amongst all civilized nations.

However much we may sympathize with the Poles in their harsh treatment, the main causes of their downfall have been internal dissensions and internecine strife amongst themselves, which together with the elections of their kings accentuated their constantly-divided councils. Instead of being a united people, they became disunited and a perpetual irritating danger to the neighbouring borderlands. Possessing Southern temperament, with restlessness and insincerity of character, they fell an easy prey to the ever-ready and watchful coalition of their enemies. Their form of government, together with their religious differences, produced political instability. The Constitution, though monarchical in its ruler, was republican in its policy, and the constantly-recurring elections, accompanied as they were by faction fights and party struggles, were of a disintegrating instead of a cohesive character.

In the cathedral of the city of Cracow lie interred many of their forty-six kings, dating from Mieczyslaw (962–992), who was the first of their kings. On reading the history of Poland, I was struck with the shortness of the reign of many of them, and also with the fact that it was the Poles themselves who invited the intervention of the Russians in 1794 against their own nobles. This action on their part, together with the presence of Russians in their land, led Germany and Austria to participate as co-partners in the division of the country. On this taking place, Russia retained the lion's share.

In a previous paragraph I have mentioned insincerity as an attribute of the Poles, and this I do advisedly from many instances arising from my business relationships with them. Some of my Russian friends have been of opinion that this is not only an attribute of the Poles, but had become engrafted in the Slavonic race by ages of oppression and the fear of consequences. If this be so, I think we must personally have been particularly favoured in our selection of many Russian friends, to most of whom this characteristic does not apply.

In illustration of the word given, insincerity, the following instance may illustrate to my readers the meaning of the word I have used. On one occasion, accompanied by my wife, we accepted an invitation to dinner at a friend's house, after which there was to take place a musical reception in which one of the greatest pianists of the day was to take part. The house to which we were invited was that of one of the leading Polish families in Kiev, noted, as most of them are, for their hospitality and kindly disposition.

The company expected being a mixed one, the medium of conversation was the French language. Dinner over, we were assembled in the drawing-room and awaited the arrival of Mr. Rubenstein, the world-renowned virtuoso, who was to give us an exhibition of his wonderful skill in piano playing.

Having been the guest of honour at dinner, the hostess invited me to take a seat on the sofa, between herself and a titled lady, when they began talking over me about a third person of the aristocracy of the city who, although she had accepted the invitation to dinner, had not deigned to come. The conversation was far from being complimentary, and I began to feel uneasy. Presently, however, the arrival of the said lady was announced, when on entering she was most effusively welcomed by the hostess, whereupon I rose and rejoined my wife, my place being taken by the new arrival.

I am of the opinion that whatever be the inner feelings of one English lady towards another, it would never enter her mind to give expression to them in the presence of a third person, and it would be still more impossible for her to receive a person with effusion whom she had but a few minutes before been unfavourably criticizing.

Of course Rubenstein's playing met with enthusiastic appreciation, but all that I can recall is my fear and the look on the face of our hostess lest the beautiful grand piano might collapse under the heavy hand of the performer. I have also the vision of a man with an unkempt mane of hair swirling about his head, bent on avenging with remorseless fury some great wrong inflicted by the inanimate victim of his vengeance.

It is a well-ascertained fact that just prior to the insurrection of 1863 Alexander II was preparing to grant autonomy of a wide-reaching character to the whole of Poland, which would have been placed under one of the GrandCed Dukes as Viceroy. But following on the ill-timed revolt, the disabilities were increased and the flower of the nation was deported.

I have had an excellent opportunity of studying the different characteristics of both sections of the Slavonic race. In our office in Kharkov, which was the centre of a Russian province, our staff was of Russian nationality, with the exception of two Jews whom we had taken young and trained to our service. In Kiev, however, we had only Poles as clerks, fourteen in number, together with a German manager whom we had transferred to Kiev from having been our chief book-keeper in Kharkov. Here we had very considerable work with sugar factories, distilleries, etc., and as head of this section of our business we had as manager a Pole who was a highly-cultivated gentleman and a first-class technical engineer. Owing to the educational disabilities existing in Poland, he had studied in Germany, was in possession of high-class certificates, and proved a most reliable and careful coadjutor. Kiev, being the metropolis and centre of the sugar industry, employed almost exclusively Polish managers in the 230 factories, and had we not employed their class in our business not a single order would have come our way.

What in my experience I found as an attribute both in the Russian and Polish character was the absence of initiative. In their early life up to a certain point they are extremely precocious, but a short period after attaining their majority they rapidly deteriorate, whereas with ourselves and the Western countries maturity may continue until middle age is reached.

Of the two sections the Russian is far more reliable and of firmer character; the Poles, on the other hand, are characterized by what I might term femininity, exemplified by the adulatory language the men employ in their social intercourse with women. On such occasions the most fulsome language is used, such as the oft-repeated phrase " fall at your feet," instead of " excuse " or " pardon me," which always struck me as an abnegation of manhood and an evidence of insincerity.

CHAPTER XVIII

A GEOLOGICAL TOUR IN SOUTH-WESTERN RUSSIA

Aim of journey—Berditchev—Jewish metropolis in Poland—Dubious methods by hotel-keepers—Incident on previous visit, and its sequel—Zhitomir—Visit cathedral and city—Labradorite quest accomplished—Hospitable invitation by Bohemian quarry-owner—Russian surprised at our visit—Journey by post-wagon—Character of quarry—Sudden storm on return journey—Interesting conversation with postmaster, and kind entertainment—Journey to Kiev by diligence—Our fellow-passengers—Terrible storm—Attitude of companions—Tree struck by lightning with terrific crash—Coach embedded in mud—Arrival at Kiev—Picturesque city—Mother church of Russia—Centre of sugar industry—Mazeppa—Dnieperian Cossacks—Pilgrimages to shrines—Pechersk monastery and catacombs—St. Sophia Cathedral—The monasteries—Visit to a monk—Incident of loan to Emperor—Nestor—Russian classical authors.

IN 1891, when, together with my son, I planned a tour through South-Western Russia, a special study was made of the geological maps prepared by Murchison, de Verneuil, and Keyzerling. Our attention was specially attracted to a small indefinite spot in Volhynia, marked vaguely as Labradorite Rock near the area where the important towns of Berditchev and Zhitomir are situated. It seemed a strange and somewhat dubious quest to found on so small an occurrence, but lying as it did not far from one of the great highways of entry into Russia, we decided to seek it.

Berditchev, the great modern capital of the Hebrew race, was to be the starting-point of our search; here 200,000 Jews dwell within the protection of the Pale, outside which their movements are attended with difficulty. There seems a strange unwritten law that those who attempt anything in faith, boldly, but not rashly, have the way opened up step by step before them, and such was the case with ourselves.

As we crossed the great plains of Germany, we had a Russian gentleman as a fellow-passenger, who, hearing of our intentions, gave us the name of the best hotel to be found in Berditchev. Well it was he did so, for as we drove away from the station, lean Jews came out from dubious-looking inns like birds of prey, stating that the paving was up between us and our destination, and inviting us to enter their own excellent establishment. Our Izvoschik, or driver, who foresaw reward for himself, helped them by drawing up as each appeal was presented, but we had resolved that no obstacle should prevent our reaching the place recommended.

It was a day of public holiday. The balconies of the low double-storied houses were crowded with men and women, and as we approached the desired haven the road was certainly up, and the carriage had to halt a hundred yards from its doorway. However, it was an easy thing to cross over and see the proprietor, who promptly sent men for the baggage, and we were soon installed in surroundings which, if not precisely luxurious, had some pretensions to cleanliness. The owner of the hotel, too, was not averse to giving information, and it was arranged that, as nothing was known at Berditchev about the rock we were seeking, we should go on next day by carriage to the town of Zhitomir, we being also supplied with the name of the best hotel there.

The remainder of the afternoon was spent examining the neighbourhood, and the parts of the town visited by me some years previously, when an incident occurred to me on a business visit to this city, which I have always associated with connivance between landlord and driver. At the time of my arrival, the droshky driver informed me that the hotels were all full, that military manœuvres were commencing, and every room was taken. We called at several places, the driver always bringing me word " No rooms ";

to this day I am of opinion that he never went farther than the entry, and when hidden from view for a few seconds returned with the same answer. At last I asked him if he knew of any place, when he said he thought a friend of his might give me a room. The night being on us, I ordered him to drive on, and so he did, until at last somewhere in the suburbs he stopped at a cut-throat-looking house in a most forbidding street. After a lengthened interview between the driver and landlord, the latter came forward and took my portmanteau. The only glance I had of him by the light of the carriage lamps gave me an impression that I must beware; but having my revolver with me, I was not over-exercised in my mind, being thus prepared against eventualities. The landlord led me under an archway to a side door which, on his lighting his candle, I saw led to a narrow, rickety, and eminently filthy stairway terminating at the very top in the cock loft under the roof, which was assigned to me as my bedroom. The furniture was indescribable—an iron bedstead that shivered at the touch, surmounted by a mattress that suggested thoughts too deep for words, a three-legged stool supporting a cracked basin encrusted with immovable dirt, and an oval mirror that elongated the features. The only decent piece of furniture was a table which proved of great use in barricading the door unprovided with either lock or bolt.

Before the man left the room I thought it advisable he should know I was armed, so amongst other impedimenta I ostentatiously placed my revolver on the table and observed he noticed it. He then left, after I had made him bring me another candle and matches. I then carefully barricaded the door with the whole inventory, placing the table-top in such a manner that the door being forced would bring the legs to the floor with a thud, and placing my revolver near my hand, lay down on the floor clothed, and soon fell asleep.

It must have been between three and four in the

morning when I was startled out of my first sleep by what appeared to me to be a shriek of agony, followed by apparently a series of choking sounds. Down came my barricade, and with a light and revolver in hand I hastened along the corridor to ascertain the cause of the distressful cry. I must explain that the corridor was formed by dividing the attic floor with boards which were not grooved into each other, but placed roughly, having interstices at intervals. All of a sudden another, but more subdued, sound occurred, when I discovered the cause. It arose from the fact that the landlord kept geese in the other half of the attic, and it was their greeting to the morn that had startled me.

Needless to say I left the place at early dawn, and driving to the principal hotel, found my surmise correct. My driver had made no inquiry there, and if he had, the required accommodation could have been had. The accommodation was ample, the reason of the boycott being that they refused to subsidize the drivers. This incident impressed itself indelibly on my memory owing to the fact that during that same year the circus had been burned down in the city, and hundreds of men, women, and children met their death by fire.

The town of Zhitomir, 120 miles from Berditchev, is a pleasant spot, the Cheltenham of Russia, where many retired officers dwell in comfortable homes. These stood bowered in trees on the slopes of a ridge, at whose base flows a wide and limpid stream. Our journey thither was uneventful, the only conspicuous feature being the number of carts met with on the road laden with china clay, which is used all over Southern Russia for the purpose of whitewashing the walls of the peasants' houses.

Then, with cracking of whip and the familiar mingling of threats and endearments from the driver to his horses, we sped up the hill and to the door of the hotel, from the portals of which a man hastened to assist us down. But a glance at the Jewish name above the door revealed the conspiracy, and, obeying a stern order, the coachman turned the horses' heads, and drove to the place which had been recommended to us. The hotel proved to be superior to most of those met with in the smaller towns of Russia, and, content to have reached such good quarters, we sallied forth to examine the town.

Our steps were first directed to the cathedral, and hope rose high, as the whole of the lower stonework proved to be made of labradorite, sparkling with its beautiful play of iridescent colouring. On leaving this building (which in its ornate character and wealth of decoration resembled the majority of Russian churches), we came to the yard of a monumental mason, and once again found the same stone being used for some of the more elaborate gravestones. On entering to make further inquiry, the owner of the work exclaimed, "You could not have come at a more favourable opportunity, for at this moment I have the proprietor of the labradorite mines with me, and I am sure he will be very pleased to meet you." Entering an inner chamber, we met a man of frank appearance, black bearded, differing in build from an average Russian, and who introduced himself as a Bohemian. He urged us to visit his quarry, assuring us that it was only twenty versts by post road and fifteen versts across country, a distance of about twenty-two miles. Before parting, we promised to come to him without fail, and were naturally very well satisfied at the way opening so readily.

On returning to the hotel, the incident was related to a Russian staying there, who exclaimed with astonishment, "Why, here I have dwelt, man and boy, these thirty-five years, and have never heard of this rock, yet here are two Englishmen come all the way from London in order to see it."

The next day found us ensconced on hay in the post-wagon, and moving rapidly over the dried steppe road. As we sped along, we met a cartload of Jews, whereupon our driver turned and said, "They toil

IN RUSSIA

not, neither do they spin, but God gives them richly to eat."

At the first station a change of horses had to be made, and during the wait we were courteously entertained by the station master. Then, seated on hay in a springless cart, a start was made across country, the journey being rendered extremely rough by the deep ruts in the trail. A hearty welcome, however, awaited us, and we were taken to inspect the quarry, a low scarp in which the rock was displayed in all its beauty. Here we stayed as long as possible with our hospitable host, exchanging experiences and receiving numerous specimens of the labradorite. This mineral is one of the felspar group, in composition a silicate of alumina and lime, which under certain circumstances possesses a beautiful play of colours, yellow, blue, and purple predominating. This portion of Volhynia is composed of gneissic rocks, with which this ornamental stone is intimately associated.

But it was time to leave, and already the gathering of dark clouds threatened one of those sudden and violent thunderstorms so familiar to all dwellers in prairie and steppe regions. We had not quitted the shelter of our host's roof when the rain began, rapidly increasing in intensity to a heavy and continuous downpour. There lay nothing before us but to face these pitiless weather conditions which had rapidly submerged all traces of the roadway, so that we drove over rut and ridge, jolting and bumping, while the wheels gave rise to continuous mud geysers as they splashed through the half-liquid soil. Finally, we arrived at the post-station bespattered and drenched, receiving on our arrival a hearty reception from the postmaster and his wife.

Excellent Russian tea was promptly provided, clothes were dried, and our host joined us to learn something of the great outer world in which he was deeply interested, though far removed from the main trend of its events. The famous Baccarat case, which was then of recent date, had especially attracted his attention, and he could not understand how King Edward (then Prince of Wales) could have consented to appear as a witness at the trial. In Russia the appearance of a member of the royal family in a court of law, under such circumstances, was something quite outside his experience

The Home Rule question had also been matter of thought with him, and it was strange thus to be introduced to the workings of an active mind, keenly following the course of history in spite of isolation and difficulties of communication. We learnt, too, from him, that somewhere still farther in the wilds dwelt a Scotsman, who, he thought, was burning charcoal in the depths of the forest.

Parting from our kind hosts, we sped quickly through the gathering darkness, flashes of lightning to the south showing the direction in which the storm had passed.

Next day we arranged to take the " diligence," or stage coach, a heavy, lumbering vehicle drawn by seven horses, our destination being Kiev. The journey was to take two days and two nights, and naturally, under such circumstances, our fellow-passengers were of considerable interest to us. There was room for six in the *coupé*. Two Russian ladies belonging to the class of smaller proprietors occupied two corners, while opposite me sat a long-haired and bespectacled Russian student. At a few stages farther on a tall young Polish priest came to bid his sister good-bye, she occupying the remaining seat. And thus this strange medley of human beings, representing such varied nationalities, creeds, and sentiments, passed forward toward the belt of forest in front and into the night.

It was soon evident that anything but a spirit of amity prevailed among those thus fortuitously thrown together, nor could it be so. The two ladies represented the class still dominant in Russia, the student, the Nihilistic seething discontent of those who have not, but long for power ; the young girl, not yet on the threshold of womanhood, was an embodiment of the pride and despair of once-powerful Poland; and we pulsed with the rich freedom of the great country which, with all its faults, has liberty in fact, and not only as a watchword. In religion, too, how different! Two members of the Greek orthodox faith, a young Polish Catholic, two to whom Protestantism meant freedom of conscience to worship God in spirit and in truth, and one to whom all creeds represented only mental slavery.

That night a test was to be applied which would reveal the effects of teaching and nationality, for already as night advanced the rumbling of distant thunder and flashes of lightning marked the unchaining of the elements ahead. Quicker grew the flashes, louder the moaning of the wind. Terror seized the two ladies in the corners, who crossed themselves, and finally, seeing a lighted cabin among the closely-set pine trees, pleaded to get out and stay there. The student, blanched with fright, spent his time between declaring that there was no God and terrified ejaculations. Grandly awesome as was the scene, on others the very sight of these panic-stricken people had an opposite effect. The Polish lady sat impassive and stern, a slight curl of the mouth marking her disdain for her companions. One of us, who has no love for thunderstorms, asked by one of the Russian ladies whether he were not afraid, answered lightly as though these events were common occurrences in his life; the other smoked his cigarette, the welcome gleam of which shone bright in the intervals of pitchy darkness.

Suddenly there was a terrific crash, a glow of fire, the vehicle came to a standstill, for only a few yards away the lightning had struck some mighty monarch of the forest. A few moments of awesome silence, and then the student sprang forward, seized the cigarette from the hands of his *vis-à-vis*, at the same time shouting "Do you not know that a cigarette attracts the lightning?" Then the storm, as though it had exhausted itself in one final supreme effort, rapidly died away.

We had driven on for some little time when we met the stage coach from Kiev to Zhitomir stuck axle deep in thick mud, from which it was impossible to extricate it by means of its own team of seven horses. First one of ours was taken to assist, and then a second, but nothing would persuade those responsible for the arrangements to take all our horses and so secure the desired result. Instead it was decided to send to the nearest village for bullocks ; and our further presence being useless, we drove on.

At a comfortable roadside station we were able to take an early cup of tea, and had an opportunity of studying several characteristics of modern Russia. Our driver, a man of a humorous spirit, held forth on the events of the night to an admiring crowd who were greatly impressed with the " bolt the size of a house " which had fallen in front of his horses. On the other hand, the student refused to sit down with us to tea in the spacious refreshment room, but paced up and down, holding forth on the theme that all Russia's great literary men had been martyrs, evidently himself being impressed with the idea that he was one of the immortals to whom suffering was a certainty. In him the ridiculous and the pathetic were strangely blended, for he was the living embodiment of the cry for some better condition than that enjoyed—a bitter cry where envy, desire, and dissatisfaction play strange tunes on men of weak body and intense imagination.

Here we also learnt that two Englishmen had passed that way two days before, who could not speak a word of Russian, and whose knowledge of the Russian money was so limited that they took a handful of silver out of their pockets, from which those who were to receive payments could take without any restriction. To us, it was very evident from this statement that they were indeed strangers and sojourners in the land.

" Okontchatelno " (finished), shouted the driver, Time to go ! But we, being in a country where hurry is almost a crime, continued our leisurely meal, and minutes elapsed before once again the summons came.

Once more no response, until at length "Okontchatelno" was uttered, with a tone of finality. Again the ill-assorted party found itself cramped within the narrow compass of the coach, and so, half waking, half sleeping, we jogged on through the night, till at break of dawn the golden domes of Kiev's famous churches came in view.

In the city, picturesquely poised on high cliffs above the river, and the centre of ecclesiastical Russia, we remained for some days, visiting the more famous sights, or studying the loess deposits of the neighbourhood, under Professor Armachevsky's guidance. Yet the contrasts in this strange land were again forcibly recalled by the fact that it is impossible to leave the lighted paths of the public gardens, even when full of people, for in the woods lurk men ready to rob and even murder those who enter them. My son, less experienced in the ways of the country, was attempting to view the river from a point which involved entering the side alleys, but realized instinctively that certain persons seen wandering in the shade of the trees were of dangerous character. On his return he found me in a state of great anxiety, and was warned that there was much risk in leaving the main track.

This town is one of the most picturesque cities of Europe, and certainly in European Russia there is none other to vie with it either for its beauty of position or for the interest attaching to it as metropolis of the mother church of the orthodox religion in Russia. It is situated on the River Dnieper, which has been spanned by a magnificent bridge over half a mile in length, at the date of its erection in 1848-53 considered unequalled for length and width of span by any other bridge in Europe.

The main central street of the city, the Kreshtchatik, lies in a valley, from both sides of which rises a series of hills, varying in height, and attaining a maximum of 500 feet in the centre. At the extreme end of the main street overlooking the Podol is the Vladimir Hill, 300 feet in height, the public promenade of the city, which is laid out in beautiful gardens and surmounted by a statue of the Prince of that name. On this spot he stood in A.D. 988, and watched his heathen subjects being driven by his soldiers into the river at its base, to be baptized into the orthodox faith. Tradition states that he adopted this form of worship after an examination of all other Christian creeds, owing to its gorgeous vestments, elaborate ritual, and psalmody. At the foot of this hill is the Kiosk, which marks the spot where a whole tribe was thus summarily converted from heathendom to Christianity. The hill overlooks a vast extent of country, and the Podol quarter of the city, which lies directly below on the river-side. This is the great commercial centre, both of the banks and of the river steamers. Here also the immense fairs are held, the business transactions in which dominate the whole sugar industry of the Empire. It is a fact that during the great fair of the year, the "Contract Fair," the turnover in accounts amounts to many millions of roubles. Looked at from below, the great cross borne by Vladimir, when illuminated on the great public holidays, has a most impressive effect.

The river, which near the Podol is divided into two branches by the Island Trukhanov, reunites at the southern end of the town, and has a breadth at that point of about 1,500 feet in summer; at the breaking up of the ice in the spring, it submerges the whole of the island, and has the appearance of an inland lake of immense proportions.

As already mentioned, this city is not only the centre of the great commercial activity in the interchange of the products from all parts of the Empire and abroad, but is also that of the great sugar industry, which from 230 factories supplies the whole of the sugar for the Empire. In order to prevent the introduction of foreign sugar into the country, the Government have assisted the industry by enacting special laws for its production, and it also fixes the selling price, which falls a heavy burden upon the peasantry.

COSSACK FORT, AND ROCK OF TAMARA.

Kiev is not only remarkable for its public buildings, which are solidly built of stone, but many of its private dwellings compete with those in the metropolis both for their solidity and structural elegance. Many of the large opulent sugar refiners have mansions equalling those of (in former times) the most prosperous of the Venetian towns, and all the more remarkable because many of their owners have risen from very low estate, or even from the ranks of the itinerant trader.

The city also contains a royal palace, which is of modern construction, and has rarely been inhabited by the emperors or even their relatives. The widow of the late Grand Duke Nicholas, who resided many years in the town, was located in a private house. The palace garden and the adjoining " Château des Fleurs," the public city grounds, form a very picturesque setting to the river flowing at their base.

The population, which when I first knew it in 1865 was computed to be 75,000, at the present time is no less than 590,000, one factor of increase being that in 1879 several outlying suburbs were brought into the municipal boundaries.

Like most border towns, its history has been an exceedingly chequered one. From being for 376 years an independent province of Russia, for 80 years it was under the Mongols, for 249 it belonged to the Lithuanian Principality, for 35 to Poland, and finally was united to Russia in 1686, in the year 1840 becoming subject to the civil law of the Russian Empire.

The history of Kiev is also inseparably connected with that of Mazeppa, who, born in 1644 and educated in Poland, was, owing to an intrigue, tied to the back of a wild horse and driven into the Steppes of the Ukraine. Rescued by the Dnieperian Cossacks, he became their leader, and subsequently was appointed by Peter the Great to be their hetman, great honours being bestowed upon him. On the invasion by the Swedes under Charles XII, owing to personal grievances against the Czar, and having made up his mind that Charles and not Peter would win, he refused to obey the orders of Peter to join forces against the Swedes. He conspired with Count Piper to close the Ukraine against the Russians, but the Swedes with their 80,000 men being thoroughly beaten, he accompanied Charles XII to Turkey with the 1,500 men who remained of the King's forces, and died at Bender on August 22nd, 1709. He had already been excommunicated as a traitor by the Metropolitan from the High Altar, and had been dragged in effigy through the mud at Kiev and publicly burnt by the common hangman.

Formerly the city was surrounded by bastions, earth-works, and ditches, the entry being provided with gates; but the only remnant of these defences is the ruins of the Golden Gate, situated in the central part of the city.

Kiev is also the great intellectual metropolis for South-West Russia. In addition to numerous public and private schools, it possesses institutions for the study of every literary and scientific subject, an Imperial College of Music, and its University gives instruction, on an average, to not less than 2,500 students. But beyond and above all, it is to all Russians the mother city, the Mecca of their faith. The deeply-seated religious instinct of the peasantry compels them even from the utmost confines of the Empire to make at least once, in their lifetime, a pilgrimage to their sacred city, and during the summer season the poor pilgrims are to be seen toiling ponderously along the roads and tracts of the country to prostrate themselves before the Holy Shrine of the " Mother of God " and beseech their angel to intercede for them. Of course the churches are numerous and large, but the centres for their worship and veneration are the Cathedral Church of St. Sophia, the Pechersk Monastery with the catacombs, and the Cathedral Church of the Assumption. Seen from a distance the gilded domes of many of the churches and the lofty Campanilla with its golden cupola have in the summer sun a marvellous effect, all the more so from the plain, green-painted, sheet-iron roofs of the private houses, which form so marked a feature of Russian towns.

The Pechersk, or cave district, from which it derives its name, is the meeting-place of the 300,000 pilgrims who yearly visit its monastery, receiving as they believe full redemption for all sins they have committed during their lives. Many of the churches and ecclesiastical buildings are undoubtedly of ancient origin. Thus St. Sophia was founded by Prince Yaroslav in 1037. The monastery was founded in the twelfth century and that of St. Michael in 1108. There are two sets of catacombs; the St. Anthony containing the bodies of eighty of their saints or martyrs, and the second, those of St. Theodosius, containing forty-three.

Up to a very recent period the pilgrim was allowed the privilege of viewing certain parts of the bodies of these sainted martyrs, who are supposed to be miraculously preserved, but this has been discontinued. On several occasions, when visiting them in former years, I have seen a hand or other portion of the upper limbs exposed, but they were to me not a very invigorating sight, the dark leather-like ligaments recalling the tanyard rather than miraculous intervention. There is no doubt whatever that a considerable number of these so-called martyrs became such mostly by self-infliction. For instance, you are shown cubicles where monks have passed years of their lives in darkness and seclusion. There is also a head protruding from the floor, but mercifully covered by a thick, ecclesiastical cover, where we were informed that the sainted owner had allowed himself to be buried alive up to his head " to the glory of God."

I once visited in a monastery a monk to whom his brother, a well-to-do proprietor, had given me an introduction, and found him in his cubicle, which was simply but comfortably furnished. He was a gentleman of birth and breeding who had taken vows for some reason, and was acting as one of the gate-keepers. We had a long conversation in French, and amongst other things he told me that at the time of the Crimean War the Emperor Nicholas I pretty well bled the monasteries of their wealth under the guise of loans; but not having, after repeated efforts, been able to obtain restitution, the monks took occasion, on Alexander II visiting them, to make him a present of the formal receipt which they had received at the time from the Government Treasury. The Emperor thereupon graciously handed them back the receipt to keep in their archives as a memento. He told me also that the bodies of the saints in the catacombs were in very truth miraculously preserved, and that at Easter time they were washed with much ceremony.

Amongst the more prominent of the ecclesiastics interred there are Nestor, the earliest of the chroniclers (1056–1114), who as the author of the Chronicle under his name still remains the earliest recorder of Slavonic times. The principal work by which he is known was the fulfilment of his mission to find the body of St. Theodosius. In his Chronicle he ascribes the foundation of Kiev to the year 864, and his own novitiate in the Pechersk monastery was undoubtedly 1073. In Russian literature there are many names of eminence, but it must be admitted that autocracy has not been a very exuberant field for the cultivation of genius, and many an author who might have added lustre to his fatherland has had to expiate his crime of too great a patriotism by deportation to the wildest regions of Northern Siberia.

Amongst the more prominent authors who were born during the reign of Catherine may be cited Derzhavin the satirist (1743–1816); Karamsin the historian (1760–1837); Krilov the fablist, the beloved of all Russian children; Zhukovski the poet, and translator of Gray's Elegy (1783–1852), the best that has ever been translated into any language; Pushkin (1799–1837), who, the descendant of a negro ennobled by Peter the Great, was the author of many poems, some of which are of great merit, such as the opera of *Ruslan and Liudmila*. He was killed in a duel with d'Anthé, the son of the Dutch Minister to the Court of St. Petersburg.

Other notable writers were Gogol the satirist (1809–1852), the author of the comedy *Dead Souls* and the *Revisor*, which are still favourites on the Russian stage; and Lermontov, the author of "The Dream" and also of "The Demon," surnamed "The Poet of the Caucasus." With the death of Nekrasov in 1877, and Ogorev, the era of classical Russian literature closed, and no successors of great merit have hitherto arisen. Dostoievski, Pisemski, Turgueniev, Goncharev, Saltikov, Ostrovski, and some others are representatives of the modern realistic school, whilst Tolstoi has struck the popular imagination, and found many disciples converted to his peculiar views of life. Of all these much might be written, but many of them have been translated and are familiar in English literature. In the main it may be said that these latter follow on the lines of the Western modern school, and have not the distinctive national character of their predecessors.

CHAPTER XIX

GEOLOGICAL JOURNEY FROM KIEV TO THE DONETZ MINERAL BASIN

Leave Kiev—Plan of journey—River Dnieper—Methods of landing—Sandbanks—Visit to Belgian ironworks—Hospitable reception—Krivoi Rog, great iron-ore quarries—Original discoverer—New Russia Company—Mr. Hughes—Jealousy of mining department—Visit of Grand Duke Constantine to works—Local newspaper comments—Prosperous career—Vast iron-ore resources—Folding of strata—Krementchug—Alexandrovsk—Scene of my first Russian experience—Original reaper still preserved—Meet two sons of early acquaintances—Arrival at Kharkov—Leave for Slaviansk—Borki, scene of disaster to Imperial train, 1888—Monastery of Svyatogorski (Holy Hill)—Great pilgrim centre—Apparition of holy pictures—Kharkov Virgin—Procession—Nicholas I forbids appearance of holy pictures—Order obeyed—Visit friends—Yasinovataya—Coal and iron region—Hughesovka and the works—Visit to Stiela iron-ore region—Bakhmut rock-salt industry—Alabaster Hill—Nikietovka cinnabar (mercury ore) mines—Return to Kharkov—Close of journey.

AFTER spending a few days in Kiev, visiting the many attractions of this metropolis of the mother church in Russia, and at the same time renewing acquaintances and enjoying the hospitality of several old friends, we left the city, taking passage by steamer on the River Dnieper. The plan of our future itinerary was arranged with a view to visiting and examining the mineral deposits with which South Russia is so liberally endowed, but which up to a very recent period had been absolutely neglected. The technicalities connected with them would, I am sure, not interest the general reader, so I must confine myself to reminiscences of localities recalling the scenes of many of my early struggles.

Our stay at Kiev having closed the first part of our geological tour, the second stage involved a visit to the iron mines of Krivoi Rog and the axis of ancient rocks, through which the River Dnieper cuts its way to the sea. This great stream is the most westerly of the important lines of water communication which extend through Russia from north to south, and connect the vast interior with the southern ports of the country. As it passed through the districts we wished more especially to visit, it was decided, as above stated, to take steamer from Kiev, leaving our plans to develop themselves as we proceeded.

Consequently, on a fine summer's day we found ourselves part of a motley crowd assembled on the deck of a good ship, the name of which has long been forgotten. Most of our fellow-passengers in the first class were probably small proprietors returning to their homes, or merchants on business bent; while the third-class deck was crowded with typical Russian peasants, here and there a bright touch of colour in head-dress or clothing bringing an agreeable variation in a somewhat monotonous scene. But at last we were off, and soon Kiev, with its gilded domes and the bold bluff on which it stands, had faded below the horizon, and now one saw only the steep, low cliff which forms the river's banks, and obtained glimpses of the broad Steppe-lands which lie on either hand. The method of landing at any wayside stopping-place is simplicity itself. The shallow-draught steamer simply backs into the steep bank, a platform on hinges is lowered to the shore, up which the departing passengers mount in turn, succeeded by those coming on board, bound for some down-river station.

It being summer, the river was shallow and sand banks numerous. As a result the steamer was constantly running aground. Under such circumstances the sailors and able-bodied members of the third-class community promptly jumped into the shallow stream. These, assisted by those on board, pulling with ropes, and accompanying their labours by a commendable amount of shouting, sooner or later succeeded in speeding the vessel on her somewhat devious way.

Two Englishmen travelling as we were could not but attract the attention and interest of their fellow-passengers. In course of conversation with one of these he stated that we would be passing one of the great Belgian foundries, and assured us that we would receive a most hearty welcome from the staff there. The suggestion was promptly adopted, and we found ourselves dumped at sunset on the pier of the works, whose outlines were already standing out grim and forbidding in the waning light. One or two workers, who had not yet left the buildings, shouldering our luggage, guided us to the office. Here we received a very kind welcome, and as it was already late, were sent on to the Company's comfortable rest house.

The programme for the next day included a visit to the works themselves, and it was arranged that on the conclusion of this inspection we should be driven over to the great mineral region of Krivoi Rog, there to be the guests of their chief engineer. It is not necessary here to dwell on the details of the foundries themselves, which present no features requiring special description, though they are laid out according to the best modern practice. On the other hand, it was very pleasant to be speeding once again over the boundless Steppe in a comfortable carriage drawn by two spirited horses, and, on arrival at the other end, to be welcomed in their pleasant bungalow by the Polish engineer and his beautiful young wife. Lavish hospitality was provided in this out-of-the-way home, and every facility was afforded us of visiting the huge open workings, which have been developed by companies of various nationalities in this locality.

The original discoverer of the iron-ore deposits appears to have been a Polish Prince, who had had a chequered and pathetic career, having been involved in the revolutionary movements of 1863 against the Russian Government. He had been condemned for many years to exile in Siberia, and the whole of his property had been confiscated. At the time of our visit he occupied a subordinate position where once all had been his own.

We were naturally especially interested in the huge workings of the New Russia Company, with which I had been intimately connected from its inception. Forty-six years have elapsed since Mr. Hughes (who was well known at that time in connection with the new industry of armour-plating) came to Russia in order to casemate the forts of Kronstadt. After completing this work, the Grand Duke Constantine suggested to him to form a company for the exploitation of coal and iron in the South of Russia. Fortified by the study of the great geological works of Murchison, Keyserling, and de Verneuil, in which these deposits were described, he sent a letter requesting me to accompany a Mr. Swan, who was to examine the locality.

The undertaking seemed a bold one, for at the first place we visited, Sofiefka, the beds were highly inclined, and in addition the head of the Mines Department in St. Petersburg, General Rochette, had already established and abandoned a smelting furnace, after the expenditure of a large sum of money. When it was abandoned, there was still an immense mass of iron in the furnace. Continuing our examination, we next visited the estate of Prince Lieven, where we found the coal measures exposed on the River Kalmiuss, in a favourable position, and with a low angle of dip. The general distribution of the coal was attested by the number of holes sunk by the peasants for its extraction, these having been abandoned when the sub-soil water-level was attained. On the spot where now stand the immense works of Hughesovka, employing from 20,000 to 25,000 men, and with a township of over 50,000 inhabitants, there was at that time only a shepherd's hut, with flocks of sheep grazing on the open Steppe.

Owing to the nature of the report sent in, it was possible for Mr. Hughes to enlist strong financial support in England, which ultimately led to the establishment of the New Russia Company. Mr. Hughes also decided, as a result of the report, to visit the locality himself, and I accompanied him to the spot, together with a Mr. Cameron, when he laid out the whole plan of the future works, and gave instructions for the erection of wooden buildings to accommodate the workmen.

Few could foresee the difficulties that would arise after the inception of the Company, and it was only by the dogged perseverance of all engaged that success was finally achieved. On the arrival of the heavy machinery at the port of Taganrog, autumn was far advanced. Then disembarkation had to be performed from a distance of many miles, owing to the shallowing of the Sea of Azov. Once on shore, the long transport of fifty-five miles (in a straight line) had to be carried out over a Steppe without roads and crossed by ravines and streams, unbridged, or with bridges only constructed for the light carts of the peasantry. All these had to be reconstructed, and in addition, owing to the late season's rains, the mud was so thick that the wagons were firmly embedded and remained so fixed throughout the winter. Only in the ensuing spring was it possible to move them, and finally to bring them to their destination.

This accomplished, the work rapidly proceeded, finally bringing down on the Company the envious notice of the Mining Department engineer, and of those who had failed at Sofiefka. It should be mentioned that the Russian Government was giving a subsidy for every pood of cast iron produced in the country, and there was a widespread report, finally mentioned in the press, that all the cast iron produced by the New Russia Company at their place Hughesovka had been imported from England, and passed as their own product. In the leading Russian comic paper, for instance, a caricature of Mr. Hughes was printed, showing him surmounting a hill on the way to England, with a large bag of subsidized gold upon his back.

These rumours finally reached the ears of the Grand Duke Constantine, who when visiting the Black Sea Fleet as Lord High Admiral also decided to inspect the Company's property. On this visit being announced, Mr. Hughes requested me to come over to the works so as to assist him at the interview, he having sent Mr. Cameron to Taganrog in order to meet and accompany the Grand Duke to Hughesovka. At the date named the Grand Duke came to the station of Constantinovka, accompanied by Admiral Popoff (the inventor of the circular battleship known as the Popoffkas) and the leading mining engineers, many of whom had been the authors of the criticisms. On his arrival it was evident that the Duke was in a very excited condition. When alighting he took not the slightest notice of Mr. Hughes, with whom he was well acquainted, and after pacing up and down the platform for a short time re-entered his carriage, which was shunted on to a side line for the night. Admiral Popoff having made arrangements for the visit to take place next day, we entered the special train that the Company had provided and returned to Hughesovka.

The next morning the Grand Ducal party arrived and were accommodated upon a trolley (on which chairs had been placed with the usual accompaniment of red baize) in order to go to the centre of the works, where carriages and a tent awaited them. Mr. Hughes had arranged that an inspection of the mine should first take place, after which they passed through every stage from the coke-ovens to the blast-furnace. This had been made ready for immediate casting on their arrival.

The furnace being tapped, the molten metal poured forth into the moulds, when the Grand Duke, after asking to see the ores from which it was produced, called the chief of the Mining Department to him, and in severe tones asked him whether the material pouring from the furnace had been derived from the ores which had been shown him. Seldom in my experience have I seen a man so thoroughly humiliated, while undergoing the stern and well-merited censure of the Grand Duke, after he had been forced to admit that all his previous statements had no foundation in fact.

After his departure, a Kharkov paper announced that he had been so disappointed with the condition of the works that he had refused the lunch provided for him. As a matter of fact he had lingered so long, and had been so interested over the inspection, that the railway time-table did not permit of his staying any longer. The express train had been stopped at Constantinovka specially for him. From that time forward the relations with the governing authorities became satisfactory, and the Government inspectors were withdrawn.

Geological Journey No. 2

These events marked the commencement of a long period of prosperity, though chequered from time to time by political and labour difficulties. The Company was the pioneer of a great iron industry in this district, in which many nationalities have since taken part; but since Mr. Hughes' death, under the guidance of his four sons, it has retained the leading position that was then established.

In the Krivoi Rog (Crumpled Horn) district this Company has enormous workings of very pure hematite and other rich iron ores over a very extensive area. At the forty-sixth annual meeting of the Company, held in 1914, the chairman, Mr. Balfour, informed the shareholders that the deposit of ore which they possessed was, so far as indication went, illimitable. The existence of this great source of supply gives every hope for the future success of the Company, in view of the fact that the coal and limestone deposits they possess are among the richest beds hitherto discovered in the Russian Empire.

We personally inspected the works under the guidance of Mr. Perry, the manager, who with Mrs. Perry entertained us on the Steppe in his English home. One of the most impressive features in connection with these ore deposits is the remarkable close-folding of the strata, which are thrown into most striking curves within a limited space, showing the great compression which they have undergone.

From Krivoi Rog we had to drive five miles to the station, and thence by rail to the river, where we took the boat to Krementchug. This town presents no features of interest, and we only stayed there till the time arrived when we could leave for Alexandrovsk by train.

CURVATION OF STRATA AS SHOWN AT KRIVOI ROG.

Alexandrovsk for me is a place of great interest, not only for its position and history, as one of the chief centres of the Zaporozhski Cossacks (one of whose triple-tiered forts is a conspicuous feature just outside the tôwn), but also as the locality connected with my earliest Russian experiences. It was just over the river that I erected the first steam mill that had ever been in the country, at the village of Keitchkass (Einlager), and next day a friend showed us the first reaping machine that I had brought into the country, forty years previously. He informed us that he was manufacturing a thousand of these per annum, exactly on the same model, and that he had given a new machine and fifty roubles in exchange for it.

The town is the key to the German colonies, and is on the main road of communication to Ekaterinoslav, which is now the centre of the South Russian mining industry. Alexandrovsk is also situated at the southern termination of the Dnieper rapids, Ekaterinoslav being forty-six miles away at their northern end.

Our next stage was the city of Kharkov, involving an uneventful train journey across the Steppe of 125 miles in a direct line. In the same compartment as ourselves were two gentlemen, who, in the course of conversation, to my surprise proved to be the sons of two of the most prominent colonists, who had given me hospitality in my earlier days. The unexpected meeting gave mutual satisfaction. Arrived at Kharkov, friends were on the platform to meet us, and we were comfortably installed in our own house, for a short period of rest before going farther afield.

The next journey was taken to the south in order to visit the salt, coal, iron, and cinnabar mines in the Slaviansk and Bakhmut districts. Leaving Kharkov for Slaviansk, we pass the station Borki, the scene of the miraculous escape of the royal family in 1888, the locomotive jumping the rails at a curve. Arrived at Slaviansk, we hired a side-seat car, or leneika, and drove away over lovely hills, the chalk formation cropping out on the slopes, and giving them the appearance of being covered with snow. As is usual in Russia, the town of Slaviansk was several miles distant from the station itself.

The reason for our alighting at the town was to visit the great monastery of Svyatogorski (Holy Hill), situated at the foot of a beautifully-wooded bluff. Perched on an extremely steep cliff, and reached by steps, stands the small church which is said to have descended from heaven with the holy picture in a single night, while yet higher the bluff itself is crowned by another edifice, with its gilded dome glittering in the sunlight, and reached by an ascent of 573 steps. Viewed from this spot, the River Donetz is seen to wind its way to the Don through beautiful park-like scenery.

Svyatogorski is visited by over 100,000 pilgrims yearly. It is well known that the peasantry of Russia have deep-seated religious instinct, which finds its expression in the fervent worship of holy pictures (ikons) and in strictly keeping fasts and festivals appointed by the Church, these amounting to over a hundred in a year. In every house ikons are to be found in the corners of the rooms, with lighted lamps hanging before them. To these the servants devoutly cross themselves morning and evening, and in a certain sense they are regarded as the guardian of the house; for if a domestic wishes to steal, he or she turns the picture to the wall during the process.

In our city of Kharkov was a very holy picture that appeared in a field which a peasant was mowing. The tradition is that he had heard a sudden cry proceeding from an ikon of the Virgin, which he had slashed with his scythe, and blood was issuing from the wound; he was therefore told to take her to the neighbouring monastery, which became immediately the gathering-place of devoted pilgrims.

This ikon has two resting-places, her winter being spent in the cathedral of Kharkov, and the summer at the Kaurish monastery, about three miles distant from the town. The procession in and out is of the most impressive character, and as it passed our office followed by thousands of devotees the mind became absorbed in the contemplation of its incidents. It is preceded first of all by church lanterns, bearing various ikons of saints, the whole being on long poles, and supported on the shoulders of pilgrims. Next to the lanterns passes a shrine on which glow a dozen tapers (the unaccustomed movement causing them to smoke). This is followed by that of the holy picture—a huge case of church architecture, with a glittering gold cross on the top, and the sides adorned with paintings of the Virgin's life. Around and within are precious stones and jewels, the gifts of the faithful (those mostly of the poor), and it is a pathetic sight to see women lifting up their children, risking the crushing crowd, in order that the little ones may touch even the poles that bear the holy shrine.

The ikon is but a small one, 16 inches square, and is not within the shrine, but is carried by the police master, followed by the Governor of the city and the Governor-General of the province. Behind these come the priests dressed in all their gorgeous and varied church costumes, then the aged Archbishop supported by two priests (one on each side), with his golden and jewelled mitre upon his head, the rear being brought up by the choristers, clad in light-blue robes with silver-lace trimmings, and singing a Gregorian chant.

The procession is led and closed by large troops of soldiers, who are followed by a dense crowd. It is a heaving, seething mass of humanity, the watching of which causes the eye to grow dim and the head to swim as the apparently interminable throng moves on. On they come, young and old, professors of the University (among them several who in private deplore these superstitions, while still fostering them by taking part in the ceremonies), officers, merchants, and peasants. All are there, but busier than them all are the high-capped monks, with their money plates upon which is already heaped a good pile.

About two hundred years ago a trade sprang up in Russia, commenced and carried on by monks, and connected with miraculous appearances of the pictures of the Virgin or saints in localities possessed by the church or interested communities. These generally made their apparition near wells, or in woods, and always in a place suitable for a monastery. The abettors or dupes of these monks were peasants or small landed proprietors, who were interested parties in carrying out the fraud. The ikons, on making their appearance, often spoke, requesting the finder to have the shrine erected to its honour on a certain spot. Pilgrims soon began to congregate, miraculous cures of various diseases were speedily authenticated, the monks settled on the spots, and in a very short time a monastery was raised from the money subscribed by the faithful.

Many of the sacred pictures change their residence, remaining in the cathedral during the winter, and migrating to a monastery during the summer. A tale is told that the Kharkov Virgin had had her day of departure changed from the accustomed April 23rd to May 1st. She apparently disapproved of the alteration, and, to the immense despair of the monks, her

CAUCASUS MILITARY ROAD AND DARIAL DEFILE.

niche in the cathedral was found empty on the following day. Their anxiety, however, was speedily allayed by a messenger hastily arriving with the happy intelligence that she had been found safe and sound in her summer home at the Kaurish monastery. She had evidently been offended at not having been consulted and had removed herself without waiting for the escort. Since that time her wishes have never been disregarded, and the crowds have always been punctual and assiduous in their attendance.

The trade in these ikons grew to such an extent, so many of them continually appearing and bestowing miraculous cures, besides performing gymnastic feats by climbing trees or being discovered in wells (thereby producing healing waters and other wonders), that the Emperor Nicholas issued an Ukase forbidding them to appear. The greatest miracle of all followed, namely, the saints themselves obeyed the edict and remained quietly at home.

Returning to Svyatogorski, we visited friends in a pleasant summer residence among the trees, and had a refreshing bathe in the deep waters of the Donetz. Then the long return journey to Slaviansk lay before us. These pilgrim roads are not altogether devoid of danger in the dark, owing to the bad characters which infest them, and the Jewish companion of our travels was in a terrible state of fear whenever we came to a wood.

From Slaviansk we travelled to Yasinovataya, in order to visit the great coal and iron region of the Donetz. Here horses were waiting to take us to Hughesovka, and we were at the same time able to render assistance to a gentleman, who had waited seven hours for a carriage which had not arrived. The night was weird and dark, and in the direction of Hughesovka the reflection of the flames from the huge blast-furnaces against the black background suggested an entry to a vast Inferno. Our fellow-traveller, fearful of robbers appearing on the road (as robberies with violence were of frequent occurrence, held his knuckle-duster ready in his hand.

The visit to the works was of great interest, more especially to my son, who, in pursuit of his geological studies, visited the principal deposits of the neighbourhood, and was surprised at the immense possibilities of the strata displayed. He descended the principal coal-mine at Hughesovka, at that time 1,000 feet deep, also obtaining coal-measure plant collections from the borings in the surrounding localities. A visit was also paid to the Stila iron-ore (limonite) deposits, situated over twenty-three miles southward of Hughesovka, where the ore occurred in pockets in the carboniferous limestone. The region here is a fine example of the broken rocky type, owing to the development of volcanic formations. The Steppe between Stila and Hughesovka is of the character, and possesses the fauna, described in a previous section.

On leaving Hughesovka our itinerary took us to the town of Bakhmut, the centre of the rock-salt industry. The distance to this place from the nearest station, Constantinovka, was about fifteen miles, over which we journeyed on a dark night, with lightning flashes of a gathering storm in the distance, but we arrived at a friend's house before it burst. Here we were again hospitably received. Our friend, who hailed from Staffordshire, was the head manager of the great Scaramangar salt works, which we visited next day. The salt water is pumped up from the salt measures below ground, and is then evaporated in large pans, the amount of heat employed determining whether the salt be coarse or fine. The works are carried on by prisoners, who seem not to have a particularly hard life.

In this neighbourhood is a hill entirely composed of alabaster, though but little of this material can be seen at the surface. This rock, which is beautifully striped, is being worked out in huge chambers with pillars left to support the roof, which give them the appearance of the vaults of some great cathedral.

From here we also drove to Nikitovka, eighteen miles south-west of Bakhmut, in order to visit the cinnabar (mercury ore) mines there. The road thither lies above the valley of the River Bakhmutka, the banks of which, lined with trees, relieve the monotony of the Steppe-land. The mining centre itself is of the ordinary character. The mineral was being used, until its value was discovered, as gravel for the station, but in 1879 M. Minenkoff perceived its true character, and since then it has been continuously worked. The cinnabar crystals are very beautiful, small in size, but of a rich ruby colour. Specimens of these brought by us are now in the collections of the Natural History Museum of London.

Our southern tour finished by a visit to the two principal salt mines of South Russia, which are being worked on the same lines as Wieliczca, near Cracow, but have not attained the depth or grandiose proportions of the Galician mines already described. They were at that time 350 feet and 630 feet deep respectively. Roof, floor, and walls were all of salt, which has very fine dark lines running through it in a wavy manner about four inches apart, and giving it a beautiful striped appearance. The main galleries are 56 feet high by 50 feet broad, and several hundred feet in length, being totally unsupported by pillars. At one spot there is a life-sized model of the Emperor Alexander II entirely cut out of the salt.

Our journeys having thus successfully finished, we returned to Kharkov and thence home.

CHAPTER XX

INCIDENTS OF TRAVEL: FROM KHARKOV TO TIFLIS ACROSS THE CAUCASIAN MOUNTAINS

Programme of journey—Slaviansk salt springs—Borki—Enthusiastic reception of Emperor after accident—Taganrog—Silting up of Sea of Azov—Scene of death of Alexander I—The Don Cossacks—Land held subject to military service—Cossack horses—Feats of horsemanship—Cossacks a frontier guard—Rostov—Circassia entered—Various races at station—Armenian fellow-passenger—Armavir—Change in scenery—Plains replaced by hills—Mineral-spring centres—Nizoblania and its horse fair—Picturesque tribesmen—Armed escort at Kavkaz—Train robberies—Vladikavkaz—" Ruler of the Caucasus " — Caucasian tribes — Burnous — Hôtel de France — The Elbruz — German brewery — Beer not forbidden by Koran — Revelry of Circassian Prince — Quaint notice—Scotch colony—Russian dissenters—Special passport—Varieties of dialects—Insecurity in the mountains—Surrender of Schamyl—Principal tribes—The Ossitinski—Descendants from Crusaders—Procession to Table Mountain—Blood feuds. *Through the Caucasian Mountains :* Military road—Russian troika—Station of Lars—Special luxuries—Balta station—Grandeur of Darial defile—River Terek—Devil's Bridge—Postboy's impressions—Cossack fortification—Castle of Tamara—Lermontov's " Demon "—Table Mountain—Kazbek—Prometheus legend—Young Englishman and Bass's beer—Mountain road from Kazbek—Danger from snow avalanches—Cossack fort—Kobi—Chalybeate spring—Caucasian chamois — Gudaur — Magnificent view — Avalanche — Boundary between Europe and Asia—Apex of watershed—Zigzag road to Mleti—Passanaur—Orchards, honey, and bears—Ananúr—Fortified church of Kitobel—Mtzkhet, the " Meeting of the Waters "—Cathedral and Georgian Regalia—The seamless robe.

In the spring of 1887, I started for a journey through the Caucasus to Baku, passing by way of Vladikavkaz to Tiflis, through the mountain range that separates the two towns. My return journey was over the minor range from Baku to Batoum, thence by sea to Sebastopol, terminating by rail at Kharkov.

On the evening of April 28th, I started from Kharkov on the Kharkov-Azov line, arriving at three o'clock the next morning at Slaviansk, a well-known town owing to the large and important salt springs. These rise from artesian borings 5 to 100 feet in depth, and contain 30 per cent. of the mineral. The baths are being now much frequented owing to the pronounced benefit for patients suffering from rheumatism. Between these two stations is one named Borki, the scene of the miraculous escape from death of the Emperor Alexander III and his family on October 29th, 1888, the train having jumped the rails on a curve owing to excessive speed; twenty-one persons in the train were killed, but the whole of the imperial family escaped with only a severe shaking. On the arrival of the Emperor and his family at Kharkov, they received a most enthusiastic reception, and the scene as they passed our offices was of a most extraordinary character; the populace, having unharnessed the horses, dragged the carriages through the streets to the cathedral.

The next station of importance is that of Taganrog, the main port of the Sea of Azov, which is gradually silting up, to the great detriment of the town. Within it is the palace in which Alexander I of Russia died, and his statue occupies the centre of the square, near which he ended his days.

Leaving Taganrog, the railway follows the course of the Don, a river from which a celebrated branch of the Russian military service takes its name. The Don Cossack is a figure as prominent in military history as the Bashi-Bazouk, and on account of the same qualities. Scarcely tinged with civilization, he is as much the enemy of friend as of foe. Wherever he goes, his natural instinct for robbery and pillage asserts itself, and he is therefore dreaded by the peaceful villagers of the interior. If a body of Cossacks enters a market-place, its appearance is the signal for a general rush to clear all portable goods from the stalls, and the women hasten to hide themselves. In the Caucasus they and the natives are open foes, and destroy each other without the least compunction.

These tribes hold their lands subject to military service, and the males are trained from their early infancy to manage horse and lance, as also the short carbine of this service. Their horses, not above the height of ponies, are wiry and hardy, living on the Steppe thistle which no other animal will touch, and going for hours without water. In addition to this they are as sure-footed as the goat, and never give in on the longest journey. Obeying the rider's voice or sign with wonderful precision, they stop short when in full canter, pirouette on their hind legs, turning almost in their own length, and in many of their own movements seem to be instinctively guided by the will of their master. They form on the Steppe a race apart, the Cossack horse having become the type of a distinct breed. The animal is always the property of the rider, and is generally, if not invariably, treated with the greatest care. He is patted and played with by the children, washed and cleaned by his owner, whom he will follow like a dog.

The Cossack's saddle is a structure of wood, high in the pommel and back and deep in the crutch, with a leather bag strapped to it. A well-known figure on the Russian frontiers is this wild son of the Steppe, with his dirty blue clothes (except on parade), his hat, resembling an inverted saucepan without a handle, his long knee boots perched upon the high saddle,[1] his lance in rest, and the little animal beneath him jogging along, a large net filled with hay dangling on either flank.

They are very fond of performing various feats of horsemanship called the "Djigitoffka." A number of them form up in line, the spectators being at a distance of two or three hundred yards in front. Turn by turn they advance, their horses going at fullest speed. One rushes along with his head nearly to the ground,

---

[1] They generally ride with naked feet, carrying their boots in front of them.

righting himself as he passes; a second stands on his head upon the saddle; a third stands upright; a fourth is stretched lengthways across. Next you see a barebacked steed coming, and as it passes, the report of a gun draws your attention to the cavalier hanging along its side, and firing from beneath its neck. Now come two together at furious speed, the foremost one with loose clothes fluttering in the wind—this one represents a woman and the man behind is in pursuit. As they pass, the pursuer rushes up, whips the other from the saddle and bears him off. Others, in full career, pick up coins and perform various antics too numerous to mention; suffice it to say, these sons of the Steppe are consummate horsemen. It is a very open question whether such savage hordes of irregular cavalry are of very great value in real warfare, their discipline being of the laxest. They have always been employed by Russia as a frontier guard, and their settlements extended throughout the Ukraine, where they formed the boundary between Russia and Crim Tartary. On the eastern frontier they people whole districts, and as conquest follows conquest, their "Aouls," or villages, are pushed forwards, gradually encircling the enemy in a network impossible of being broken through.

Returning to our journey, we next arrive at Rostov, a trading port of very great importance, the emporium for the whole of the Cis-Caucasian districts, and the great centre for the sale of their corn and wool.

Crossing the boundary line of the Cossack territory, Circassia proper is entered at the station Kavkaz. The whole of this region from Rostov had but recently been colonized, and representatives of many different races are now peopling the Steppe. At the various stations on the line one meets with Lettish, German, Cossack, Russian, Little Russian, and Armenian travellers, who jostle each other, and there is a regular Babel of tongues in consequence.

At one of the halting-places we were joined by an Armenian gentleman travelling to the town of Armavir.

He possessed large estates in the neighbourhood of Ekaterindar, the major portion of which was devoted to the cultivation of tobacco. In addition he had a herd of horses numbering over two thousand head and had that year supplied the Rumanian Government with 400. An Armenian by birth, he said he had read many foreign works on their people and their religious rites, but he could not recall a single one that could even be called passably correct, and added that if any writer visited Armavir, he would be able to gather most valuable information from old manuscripts concerning their race. Owing to persistent persecution by the Turks, they petitioned the White Czar, who gave them their present settlement. They formed a community of 522 families, possessing churches, schools, hospital, and other institutions, the town being generally considered to be prosperous and improving.

After crossing the River Kuban, the character of the scenery changes. Instead of the plains, we enter upon a more hilly region, and here at the post station all traces of Russian harness are lost sight of, everything reminding us of Turkish rather than European manners and customs. We now arrive at the centres of the mineral springs, which descend from the mountains at a temperature of 30° R. (99° F.). They are of four qualities, occurring respectively at Pyatigorsk (five mountains), Essentuki, Kislovodsk (bitter water), and Zhelyeznevodsk (iron water). All these localities are increasing in importance for people suffering from poorness of blood (anæmia) and rheumatism, and should they be provided with the conveniences of foreign watering-places, so far as Russians are concerned, the latter would speedily be superseded.

The next station of importance is Nizoblania, the centre of the great Caucasian horse-fair which takes place in the month of September, when from 12,000 to 20,000 horses are assembled, most of which find purchasers, not only for use in the interior, but for export. We are now well within the lands of the Circassian tribes, and far more picturesque costumes grace the natives. Here you find the men broad in shoulders and slim in waist, with their outside coats loosely fitting the body, hanging over a blue or red silk shirt. In a leather strap fastened with silver buckles is fixed their kinjal, or dagger, and on either side of their breasts hang silver-bound cartridge cases, all adding to the picturesque appearance of the wearer.

At the station of Kavkaz we were boarded by armed Cossacks, the train having been held up the day before by Circassian raiders, who had killed the driver and robbed the travellers of all their belongings, making their escape without let or hindrance. Our defenders appeared to us quite as wild as the marauders themselves, but no untoward event occurred, and we arrived safely at Vladikavkaz.

This town, whose name translated means " Ruler of the Caucasus," is a strategic point, guarding the entry to the mountain range, which in fine weather appears to overhang it, and of which the highest peak is Kazbek (16,000 feet). It is the meeting-place of all the various tribes inhabiting the northern districts of Circassia. Here foregather the Tchinshitze, Karbadentze, Tcherkess, Kuban Tartars, Cossacks, and Ossitinski, all similar in appearance outwardly, but whose distinctive dress for each tribe was pointed out to us by fellow-travellers.

As we entered the town, the rain was pouring down in torrents and the natives were clad in burnous, or native cloaks, which are extremely valuable for mountain travelling, being warm and rainproof, and whilst being loose at the top, stand out well at the bottom owing to the stiffness of the material, thus allowing the rain to pour off from them. They thus make, therefore, a good covering at night during journeys, and a warm and comfortable refuge against rain and cold at all times. The ordinary ones consist of a skin with wool inside, and can be bought for about ten shillings, whereas the highest quality, made of camel hair and extremely light, cannot be purchased at less than ten pounds. We ourselves were glad, owing to the inclement weather, to seek refuge in the Hôtel de France, which stands in the main street of the town.

Between the stations of Kavkaz and Vladikavkaz we notice the snow-capped Elbruz, the highest mountain in Europe (18,526 feet).

On the road from the station I had noticed the name of Lucké over a brewery, and remembering a former acquaintance of mine of that name, called to ask, being gladly welcomed by the good man and his family. When I knew him in Kharkov, he was the representative of a very important electro-plating manufactory in Warsaw, but becoming ill, he was advised to leave that city and live in a more bracing air in the Caucasus. He therefore placed his savings in the building of a brewery (which was his original profession) in Vladikavkaz. This greatly surprised me, seeing that this was the very centre of the best wine-growing district, where a quart of the finest juice of the grape costs only sixpence. On giving expression to this feeling, he told me he was doing a very good business, for the simple reason that the followers of the Prophet, who are in immense majority, by the law of the Koran are forbidden wine, but beer and vodka not being mentioned, they indulge in them *ad libitum*, remaining conscientious Mohammedans all the same.

Vladikavkaz is a military outpost, the head-quarters of two army corps, which are necessary to keep the most savage mountaineers of the Caucasian races in check.

At the time of our visit rain had been pouring continuously for five weeks, and the corn, which had grown very high, had become laid by the wind, and was rotting. The next day was one of brilliant sunshine, and looking out of my bedroom window, the mountains appeared as though just over the bridge which spans the Kura, a quarter of a mile distant. The night had been a very uncomfortable one, owing to a Circassian prince with his companions (a motley lot) holding high festival in the adjoining room. The partition between us being very thin, their loud talk in a foreign tongue and the continual popping of corks made sleep impossible. Under these circumstances the framed notice in the dining-room can be understood, which translated reads " Gentlemen are requested not to get into bed with their boots on."

A curious incident occurred while talking with Mr. Lucké, he asking me if I were aware that a Scotch colony had once settled near Pyatigorsk. Although the remnant had lost all knowledge of their mother tongue, individual members still retained Scotch names. On telling him I was unaware of the fact, he called in a workman, who on my inquiring his name replied " Styles," but he could give me no information how his ancestors came there, nor any other particulars. He only knew that he was " Inglesi."

Vladikavkaz was formerly a place of banishment for all sects which started in opposition to the Greek Church, known in Russian under the general term Raskol (Dissenters). Here we find the Molokhani, a prosperous community practising Biblical tenets, allowing of no drinking or smoking, and engaged in agricultural pursuits. The Sabbatarians follow the orthodox rites, but keep Saturday instead of Sunday. The mountain Jews practise polygamy and seclusion of their women. The Klisti, or Self-torturers, whip themselves with thongs, and mortify the flesh. Here also are the Dukhobortsi, or Fighters for the Spirit, and heathen who have gods, mythology, and rites of their own. All these, together with the Gregorian and Nestorian Churches, form a motley assemblage, representing all the forms of dissent from the Orthodox Greek Church, and it seemed to me strange to find all these various religious forms being practised in the depths of mountain fastnesses.

The time, however, had now arrived for us to leave, but it was necessary for us to obtain a special passport for traversing the mountains. This gives the name and particulars of the traveller, stating that there is no objection to his departure, and giving directions to the various postmasters on the route, the permit being duly signed by the Vice-Governor and Treasurer of the province. These passports have one great advantage, enabling the traveller passing through a disturbed district to be easily traced, his name with date of arrival and departure being duly noted at each station. Journeying as I was with my own carriage, hired for the whole distance, three horses were noted on the documents as to be supplied on demand, but as a matter of fact four or even five were harnessed on ascending the zigzag to the top of the pass.

A few words with regard to the region may be of interest, it being unknown to Europe and one where no adventurous Cook has yet advertised his cheap accompanied trips. In this district the Russian language is only used as the medium for petitions to the Government making known the wants of the inhabitants. The tribes are numerous, speaking as many as fifteen different dialects, the dwellers in neighbouring villages often understanding each other only by means of interpreters, and none of them being provided with a grammar or written characters. I was told that there were many places in the recesses of these mountains where Cossacks dare not venture, no taxes could be levied, and the inhabitants owned no allegiance to the Emperor. Indeed the place was still unsafe, Cossacks constantly patrolling the route, and only five years before our journey frequent fights took place in which the soldiers did not always come off the conquerors. For more than a hundred years the Russians vainly fought to subdue the tribes, and it was not until the year 1858 that by the surrender of Schamyl at Gunib the conquest was completed, and the people cowed though not subdued.

The principal tribes are the Ossitinski, the Inguishi, the Immeritinski, the Abuzenki, the Karbadentzi, the Gruzinian, the Karatchaiefski, and the Gourietsi, and had they held together Circassia would have remained free up to the present day. Of these various tribes, the Ossitinski (or better known as Ossetes or Ossetians) are perfectly distinct from the others, being fair-haired, of light complexion, with blue eyes and European features. They are Christians, who state that they are the descendants of some Crusaders, who wandered to the spot after the wars in the Holy Land, and it is a fact that many coats of arms, breastplates, suits of chain armour, casques, etc., of those times have been handed down from generation to generation, and are still preserved in various families. It is interesting to note that on a certain day in the month of June of each year the men of the tribe assemble, clothed in white kaftans (having a cross embroidered on back and front), and proceed in procession to the Table Mountain, twelve miles from Vladikavkaz, and there offer up burnt offerings of sheep and goats in expiation of the sins of the past year.

Among these tribes blood feuds are rife, and if by accident or design one takes the life of another, the relations of the murdered man follow as avengers, to kill the murderer remorselessly wherever they may meet. So ingrained is this custom among them that the laws in force more or less recognize its existence, and while ordinary murderers are punished with several years of chain labour, the avenger is let off with but a few months' imprisonment.

Through the Caucasian Mountains

Having often traversed the military road of which the following pages are a description, I was on this occasion accompanied by an English gentleman, a Mr. D., who was desirous of seeing the country. All the formalities being concluded, we gave instructions for horses and carriage to be brought to the hotel, which on arrival we found to be a Russian troika—that is, a carriage with three horses, the centre one being the only one between shafts joined by a bow, from which hangs a bell, while the two side horses are loose, and have their traces attached to the axles of the front wheels.

To the music of the bell and with a cheery shout from the driver we start on our journey for the second station, Lars. This post-station bears the reputation of being the best on the road, having an excellent cook and being supplied with every luxury, such as wild boar's head, ass's meat, bear's hams, wild-goat cutlets, salmon roe, etc., none of which are palatable to a European taste, except the salmon roe. Gradually ascending through wooded scenery along the valley of the Terek, we pass Balta station. Three miles from Lars we enter the Darial defile, and words absolutely fail to describe the wondrous grandeur of the scene. Before us is the River Terek, rapid and turbulent in its onrush to the Caspian Sea, with its passage obstructed by massive boulders against which the waters swirl, breaking into thick clouds of spray. The ravine culminates in the narrow passage at the Devil's Bridge, on which the vehicle stops; and on our looking upward, only a narrow strip of sky is visible, the cliffs rising to a height of more than 5,000 feet. These towering precipices are so steep that they appear as though some giant hand had suddenly rent them asunder. They are so awe-striking and threatening in their solemn grandeur that together with the roaring, foaming torrent at their base they form a sight never to be forgotten.

Wishing to know the opinion of our postboy, I asked him his impression of the scene, his answer being: "I am a child of the Steppe; confined in these mountains, I cannot breathe. How happy I should be if I could return to the free air of heaven!"

Within a short distance of the station is the crenulated Cossack fortification, and during our visit the garrison was practising with mountain guns. The effect was most extraordinary, the reverberations seeming to fly from rock to rock, re-echoing from every crag, dying away in the distance, only to be again repeated, finally closing as if from sheer exhaustion. Here we are on classic ground. Above the fortress stands a celebrated ruin, perched on the summit of an apparently inaccessible rock known as the Castle of Tamara. The legend has been embodied by Lermontov in his poem of "The Demon," in which he has represented Satan as having fallen in love with mortal woman, the most lovely of her race, and the daughter of one of the bravest warriors of the Caucasus. Being foiled, however, in his endeavours, he waylaid her betrothed when on his way to his marriage, and killed him. Tamara, on hearing the news, threw herself in despair from the battlements. In close proximity is the Table Mountain, to which, as already described, the Ossitinski resort in pilgrimage.

Leaving Lars we reach Kazbek (or the White Mountain). This hostelry is situated on the flank of the mountain, 16,546 feet high, and on which, according to heathen mythology, Prometheus was chained, condemned to eternal punishment by birds continually tearing at his vitals, but ultimately pardoned by the god Zeus. His crime had been drawing down fire from heaven.

An incident occurred at this station. When we arrived there we found a young Englishman vainly endeavouring to make his host understand that he desired a bottle of Bass's beer, hoping to do so by repeating the word Bass in an emphatic manner. On our arrival, he recognized in us fellow-Britons, whom he promptly called to his assistance. On being informed that the desired beverage could not be supplied, he expressed incredulity, stating that it was obtainable at Tiflis. It had to be gently pointed out to him that Tiflis and the heart of the Caucasus Mountains were not the same thing.

Here we stayed the night, and had much conversation with our new-found friend, who informed us that he had repeatedly failed in his examination for the army, whereupon his grandmother, who had brought him up, had sent him on a Continental tour with a tutor in order to improve his general education. They had been to Constantinople, and from there had gone to Tiflis with the intention of going to Baku, and his tutor, having been taken ill with fever at Tiflis, had advised him to come on and see the mountain where " some Johnny " had been chained, as his grandmother would be sure to ask him about it. We got much interested in the young man on account of his innocent fatuity, and he accompanied us back to Tiflis, much strengthened in mythological lore.

The road from Kazbek is extremely narrow, cut out from the mountain-side ; and the awful precipice, which tends to cause vertigo, is only separated from it by posts painted white on the top and placed at short intervals. This road, which is only wide enough for the passage of one carriage, follows the contour of the mountain, and is provided with side cuttings or turn-outs. On arrival at these, a horn is blown, and if no answer is received the traveller proceeds. The journey, however, is very trying to any nervous person, and my servant said to me, " Master, if I ever get out of this place alive, I will never come to it again."

We now arrive on the snow line, and by a succession of terraces reach the top of the pass from Kazbek to Kobi. This is the most dangerous part of the journey, especially in spring time. The road is cut through snow, which during the winter stands like walls 15 to 20 feet high. In these flags are stuck, white, red, or black, the white signifying that the driver may proceed at a sharp trot, the red at a slower pace, and the black walking. High up on the mountain stands a Cossack fort, on the watch-tower of which is a sentinel who by means of flag signals notifies the driver as to the movements of snow avalanches. Accidents owing to this cause often occur, and only a few years before a whole battalion of Cossacks was swept into the ravine.

The next station, Kobi, is built into the mountain, and on approaching it we pass a waterfall or small

MAIDEN'S TOWER, BAKU.

cascade, which pours from a great height in an effervescing state into a natural basin. The rocks throughout the whole line of its fall are of a red colour, the result of a large solution of iron salts in the water. We had a good view here of the Caucasian chamois, or toura, leaping from crag to crag.

We now continued to rise by a steep road cut in parallel suntil we reached the summit of the pass at Gudaúr. From the balcony of the station a magnificent view was obtained of a vast bowl-shaped circle of mountains, abruptly rising from a deep valley to a height of 12,000 to 15,000 feet. It was from this station that I had my first view of an avalanche. The officer in charge of the station pointed out a cloud, as of steam, creeping gradually down the slopes. The movement at first was slow, but increasing in intensity and size, until at last, with a terrible roar, a mighty mass of snow thundered down into the valley below, a sheer fall of some thousands of feet.

Between Kobi and Gudaúr an inscription let into the rock informs travellers that they are 7,719 feet above sea level, and that it is the boundary line between Europe and Asia. In England it is quite possible to stand in a room with each foot in a different parish or even county. Here, however, this can be accomplished for two continents. This is also the apex of the watershed; on the one side the Terek flowing to the Caspian and on the other the Aragva joining the Kura, which passes through Tiflis.

At Gudaúr we cross the snow line, which in the Caucasus is much higher than in the Alps, and vegetation also flourishes at a much higher elevation than in the Swiss mountains. From this summit of the pass we glance down several thousand feet to Mleti Station, and so precipitous is the mountain face that it appears possible to throw a stone into the yard below. For the descent a zigzag road has been constructed, supported on the rocky face of the cliffs, and only one horse is now harnessed to the carriage.

These animals are well trained. Each section terminates abruptly at a parapet wall on the edge of the abyss, on reaching which the horse rears itself on its hind legs, suddenly swerves round and continues its career down the next parallel until we are landed at the station. On reaching Mleti, which is a favourite resting-place for the night, we find the same notice about sleeping in one's boots in Russian, Turkish, and Georgian. Here fresh salmon caviare is a very favourite dish.

The next station is Passanaur, one of the most ravishingly beautiful spots I have ever visited. The River Aragva divides it from the mountain spurs, which are clothed with foliage to their very summits, while fruit trees (grapes, apples, pears, etc.) are very plentiful, as also bees, producing honey which is a great attraction for a large number of bears. On one occasion a large specimen of the latter was brought in on a Tartar cart, and the skin offered me for 6s., but as I had no accommodation for it, the bargain had to be declined.

At the next station, Ananur, we visited the most celebrated archæological curio of the Caucasus, the fortified church of Khitobel, built in the fifteenth century. This is surrounded by a crenulated wall, and flanked with strong towers.

We are now in Georgia, and the next station is Mtzkhet, the "Meeting of the Waters," where the Aragva joins the Kura. Their waters flow side by side for many miles before they mingle. Formerly the capital of Georgia, it is now only a poor village. The Georgians declare that it was founded by Mtskethas in the fifth century, but in the fifteenth was taken and destroyed by Tamerlane, and the seat of government removed to Tiflis. Once a noble city, nothing now remains but the Cathedral Church of the Twelve Apostles. Here is a portion of the old Georgian regalia, and the verger informs you that a Jew of Mtzkhet was present at the Crucifixion of our Lord, and brought back the seamless vesture gained in the casting of the lots. This he presented to his sister Sidonia, who on putting on the divine relic fell dead, and was buried in the garment. When, under the influence of St. Nina, Mirian was converted to Christianity, the place of interment of Sidonia was revealed by a dream. The body, when exhumed, had all the appearance of life, and exhaled delicious perfumes. The most precious of all the relics is a crucifix supposed to have been made from a piece of the true cross.

CHAPTER XXI

INCIDENTS OF TRAVEL: FROM TIFLIS TO BAKU, BATOUM, AND SEBASTOPOL

Arrival at Tiflis—Capital of Georgia—Hotel London—Bazaars—Zion Church—Mount Ararat—Depressing railway journey to Baku—Kurdish raids—Capture of bandits—Copper works of Ekhptala—Locusts stop train—Arrival at Baku—Its railway station—Increase in population—Its harbour—Black and White towns—Balakhani—Artesian oil fountains—Burning of wells—Temple of Zoroaster—Fire-worshippers—Firm of Nobel—Visit to gas geysers in Caspian Sea—Return journey to Batoum—Lower Caucasian Range Mountain Railway—Mud volcanoes—Liquorice factory—Tremendous storm near Elisabetpol—Use of Fairlie engines—Glorious views—Vast forests—Mountain plants—Tunnel being built—Dangerous descent—Rion Station—Circassian women—Variety of headgear—Phasis—Large size of fruit—Gori resembling Athens—Meet a Circassian Prince—Croaking of frogs—Fireflies—Poti—Hotel Colchide—A pleasant surprise—Mr. Wilson Sturge—The " Baboshka "—Progress of Batoum—Wooded hills near Batoum—Ruins of Pitzunda—Voyage on the *Juno*—Fellow-travellers—" The captain cannot understand French "—Lifelessness of Black Sea—Anapa—Shipping of Circassian slave-girls—Kertch—Greek influence—Tumuli—Mithridates—Theodosia—Old fortifications—Russian Riviera—Sebastopol.

Mtzkhet is the last station on the road before we arrive at TIFLIS, the capital of Georgia. This city is now of great importance, with a very large cosmopolitan population, it being the meeting-place of all the tribes and nationalities inhabiting Circassia. Our resting-place was at the Hotel London, where our young traveller rejoined his tutor, whom we were glad to find was much better.

The town is divided into the Asiatic and European quarters, which are separated by the Vorontzoff bridge over the River Kura. On the Asiatic side are the bazaars and the open shops, and where each street is devoted to its own special trade; here also is the Zion Church, the oldest Christian edifice in Asia still extant, founded in the third century. Tiflis being under martial law, special permits for visiting it have to be obtained.

From Tiflis, Mount Ararat, the centre of Armenia, and around which cluster traditions and memories from the Deluge to the present time, is visible on fine days. Its hoary head has looked out over centuries of change, and while generations and dynasties have passed away, it still stands as a sentinel and watchman over the cradle of the human race.

From Tiflis to Baku

This journey by railway has an extraordinarily depressing effect, and life at the railway stations must not be worth living, the only recreation possible for the officials being the one or two daily trains that bring them a supply of food and water. Occasional excitement is also provided by the raids of wild Kurds from the neighbouring frontiers of Persia.

At the station of Kara Su (Black Water) several prisoners were entrained, accompanied by some of the frontier guards, armed with Peabody guns, with long pronged bayonets. It appeared that an Armenian, living near a station, had been raided and murdered by a horde of Persian bandits under the leadership of a man named Rhamadan. The cause of the attack arose from the victim having informed the Government of the robbers being in the neighbourhood. On going down his garden one morning, he was ambushed by men hidden in the bushes. These were observed by his son, who hastily took his father's gun. Two shots rang out; with one his father fell dead, and with the other he had shot the murderer.

On the road we pass Elisabetpol, near which are the copper works of Siemens Brothers at Ekhptala, known to have existed and to have been worked for several hundred years, but in a very small way, until taken in hand by William Siemens, German Consul at Tiflis. He got his brothers interested, since when the mining operations have been successfully carried on.

Ten miles from Baku our train was stopped by locusts, which came in such numbers that the sky was darkened, and they struck against the carriage like hailstones. Owing to millions of them being crushed by the wheels of the engine, the rails became so greasy that it was impossible to proceed, and a delay of two and a half hours was caused while the permanent way was cleared and sanded.

BAKU

The railway station at Baku, erected in the Oriental style, stands as a fine entry into this progressive city. Forty-five years ago a village of 1,400 inhabitants, now it has a population of between 200,000 and 300,000. This increase is due to the oil wells in its vicinity, which have brought wealth and prosperity to the town. Its magnificent harbour, lined with wide and solid quays eight miles long, is filled with shipping bringing produce from Persia, the Tekki Steppes, and all parts of Russia to barter for the produce of other countries.

Baku is divided into two towns, the White and the Black. From the former all the smoke-yielding oil factories were summarily removed to the Black Town by the Governor Staroselski. This, however, is not the centre of the oil-well district proper, which is at Balakhani, five miles distant and reached by railway.

Seen from a distance the wells have the appearance of a forest, due to the erection of derricks or towers to which is affixed the machinery for raising the naphtha from below. I have often seen, when the wells have been sunk, the phenomena exemplifying the marvellous pent-up forces of nature, these giving rise to the artesian oil fountains, which frequently spout to a height of 150 to 200 feet. The whole district at the wells reeks with natural gas, which forms one of the greatest dangers of the place, I myself being witness of the burning of one of these when in full blast.

Adjoining Balakhani at Surakhani, is the temple of Zoroaster, which has been placed by the Russian Government, for protection, under the refinery of Kokoroff adjoining. This temple for over 2,500 years was the sacred resort of the Quebers, or fire worshippers, whose descendants are the present Parsees. Formerly a flourishing monastery, it is to-day a decaying monument of a dying religion. It consists of a large courtyard enclosed by cells for the monks, with a double-stoned erection for the chief priest. In the chapel cell the eternal fire burned on rude stone altars ; and in the centre of the courtyard, in an arched recess at the base of four flanking towers, the bodies of the faithful were cremated.

We had been very hospitably received and entertained by various firms to whom we had had letters of introduction, and especially I would name the firm of Nobel, who most kindly received us. Also through the kindness of Messrs. Dubois and Aksakoff, we were invited to join a party who were going out that evening in their pinnace, to a place where the gas rises from the surface of the sea in such quantities that the water can be literally said to be set on fire. This invitation we cordially accepted and the rendezvous was made for eight p.m.

The company consisted of a party of officers and ladies ; the pinnace was elegantly arranged with Chinese lanterns and comfortable cushions for the trip, refreshments of various kinds being provided. It took about half an hour to reach the place from the quay, it being some few miles from the Bay of Baku. As it was a grand Mohammedan holiday, all the hillside surrounding the town was lit up with small lamps, which, together with the revolving light from the Maiden Tower, made a most impressive picture.

When well out to sea the boat was turned towards a headland on which stand the works of Mr. Targaeff, an Armenian merchant. On approaching the spot, we saw the appearance of a large number of powerfully-working geysers of gas, when the skipper, lighting some tow, threw it into the midst of one of the most conspicuous of these. At once the whole surface burst into flame, tongues of fire leaping from point to point until a very large area was affected. To obtain a maximum effect, the boat was put head on to the flames, which swept up on both sides far above the deck. Mr. D., leaning over the side trying to set his handkerchief on fire, had one side of his whiskers, eyebrows, and moustache well singed, most of us, however, escaping by quickly drawing back when the flames came rushing up the side.

While thus engaged, a large steamer with a band of music on board came up and lit up another portion of the sea, so that the effect was doubly grand. We were told that on a dead calm night the burning would continue for over four hours. As we left the spot the other steamer stood out, dark and gigantic against a background of leaping, writhing fire flame, and the band seemed playing an accompaniment to some sacrificial rite of the water gods. The dark sky, the bright flames, the pale faces gazing over the bulwarks made a weird picture never to be forgotten. Mr. D., who had been for some years in India, said it was an enchantment, and he had never seen anything like it before.

Appendix

The town of Baku had, from its inception as a municipality, the privilege of having for many years the above-named governor, a man of enlightened and progressive views. He was of Polish nationality, and whilst courteous in his manners, was a man of strong individuality, and had been able to impress himself upon his surbordinates and the municipal authorities. Amongst the reforms which he introduced was that of the necessity for carrying out a complete system of town planning. At my first visit this was in progress but not completed, but on a later occasion I found it had eventuated in a new city that may now be fitly termed the metropolis of the Caucasus.

Armed with an introduction from the Prefect of Kharkov, I called upon him, and besides being hospitably entertained, he invited me on any occasion that assistance might be necessary to come to him personally for advice. In the course of conversation he himself told me that on taking up his appointment the oil refineries were located in the White Town, over which there hung a dense, black, pungent cloud of smoke, which, besides creating an intolerable stench, rendered habitation in the centre of the town impossible. Thereupon summary removal of the refineries was ordered to their present location in the Black Town, about three-quarters of a mile distant, the former rights in the White Town being allotted as commercial and residential quarters. So great an autocratic revolution could scarcely have been carried out in our own country, but it had proved an immense beneficial advantage to the town.

Baku is situated on the shores of the Caspian Sea and is encircled by a range of hills, in ancient times the boundary of the Caspian itself. The view from the cemetery hill is very effective: before one's gaze lies the whole stretch, eight miles in extent, of the well-built solid quays that are bordered by the mercantile establishments, the commercial offices, and the large, spacious harbour crowded with shipping, and it is of ever-increasing interest to watch from there the moving, restless crowd of many nationalities in their varied costumes, consisting of Persians, Tartars, Turcomans, Armenians, and many others.

In Baku there are many relics of the Persian domination; for instance, there is the "Ancient Palace of the Khans," now a museum, but formerly the Court of Justice which was presided over personally by the Khan. A trap-door is still shown close by his seat, where, under the rough-and-ready system of justice at that time prevalent, prisoners condemned to death were precipitated into the sea below.

About the central portion of the quay stands a tower called the "Maiden's Tower," now used as a lighthouse. The tradition connected with it is, as usual, one of the love affairs between a Khan's daughter and a youth objected to by the father, culminating in her throwing herself from its summit into the sea below. In the custom-house yard is to be seen an obelisk erected to the memory of the conqueror of Baku, who, in the moment of victory, fell on that spot.

The climate is exceedingly arid, the rainfall during the year being almost a negligible quantity, but it is replaced by strong north winds descending from the Caucasian range, which often blow for ten days consecutively. These cool the atmosphere, and on their cessation the whole scene changes; the air becomes cool, spring-like, and genial. During their occurrence, however, they are an unmitigated nuisance, the sand being blown through the thickest walls, filling the eyes, ears, and nostrils, and covering the whole town as if with a fog.

The only place of outdoor public recreation is the Club grounds, which were formed by importing the soil from Persia, and the shrubs grown are all of semitropical character.

On a previous visit my arrival preceded by a few days the arrival of the late Shah of Persia, who was proceeding on a visit to the Czar at St. Petersburg. A suite of rooms had been obtained at the Grand Hotel where I was staying, and on his arrival he was received with much ceremony. The guard of honour was placed opposite the hotel, and he was received by the high officials deputed by the Emperor to invite him to the capital. As customary on such occasions, the guard of honour was drawn up for inspection, and after the Shah had been consulted a number of the soldiers came forward to receive promotion as non-commissioned officers.

In consideration of the honour conferred upon the hotel, the landlord had decked out the hall porter in a gorgeous uniform, and it caused among the guests much merriment as they looked down from the corridors above at seeing the Shah grasp the hand of the porter under the mistaken notion that he was the highest official of the lot.

Baku to Batoum

The return journey now takes us by the Lower Caucasian Range mountain railway over the apex of the Suram Pass at Varvarino, a height of 2,480 feet above the sea. At the first station after leaving Baku is a series of mud volcanoes, which, having been quiescent for several generations, had again become actively eruptive. One of the Russian Ministers had visited Baku during our stay, and had thence returned by the Volga, so we were fortunate enough to secure seats in the carriage which had been placed at his disposal, but was now being returned to Batoum. These were disposed on a platform at the end of the train in such a manner that the whole of the scenery could be observed without hindrance, and truly it was worth the journey to come and see it.

Repassing the route which we had traversed on our outward journey to Baku, we recross the waterless plain, white with salt, and only notice as we approach Elisabetpol the Udzarri liquorice factory that had been erected there by some enterprising Scotsman. The whole of the district is infested with bands of brigands from the Persian frontier, and we were able to be of some assistance to our fellow-countrymen by giving them shelter in Baku when their works were sacked and burnt down by Kurds.

Seen from the railway, the Karabagh range of mountains rises very prominently in the distance, and again we pass Elisabetpol, the station for the Kadabek copper mines.

Four days after our arrival in Baku, a tremendous storm broke over the district of Elisabetpol, when the water fell in immense sheets, rushing like a wall down the ravine through which the railway passes, and literally sweeping away eleven miles of the road. We were in the second train that had passed since its reconstruction, which had occupied 3,800 men eleven days to complete. As we passed I noticed that chasms over 100 feet in depth had been excavated and the bridges carried bodily away. The rails were twisted and turned into the most curious shapes, and reduced to a perfect state of chaos. It almost passes belief that this could have been done by a single storm. Happily no lives were lost, nor train wrecked, the watchman being in time to signal the disaster.

From this spot we begin to rise between rounded hills which appear to overlap each other, and are seamed by beautiful glades. Their slopes are clothed with the greenest of verdure, and vineyards are planted along their sides up to a great height. At the station of Mikhailovo two double engines of the Fairlie type are attached, one behind and one in front, and it takes a full half-hour to do six miles. The engines, not seeming to relish their task, snort and roar, the steam issuing from their funnels in short, sharp snaps, like successive explosions of small charges of gunpowder, but still they drag us on to the summit of the defile, between 5,000 and 6,000 feet above the sea.

From here the view is glorious: within the range of vision hill tops hill, and peak succeeds peak, the whole backed by mountains clothed with eternal snow that glistens like diamonds in the sun. Up to the snow line the slopes are clothed with vast forests, the home of the bear, the wild boar, the stag, and even the aurochs. Here the walnut tree grows to an immense size, blocks eight feet in diameter being seen by us on the quay at Poti awaiting shipment.

We passed for six hours through the spurs of these mountains, which are clothed to their snow line with mountain plants of almost every species; rhododendra are in immense numbers, with variously-coloured flowers. The wild azalea scents the air, and gentian, ferns, and travellers' joy are amongst the most notable forms.

On descending, we note the commencement of a tunnel, which is being pierced by Italians, and which when completed will be six miles long, but alas! it will do away with the splendid panorama through which we have just passed. At the present time the engineers have carried the boring half a mile into the mountain, but one of them, a young Swede who with his sister joined us at Shipka station, stated that they hoped to complete it within four years. The descent on the other side is far more difficult and dangerous than the ascent; the brakes being put on hard make the wheels scream in agony, and are excruciating to the ear. Our young friend the engineer tells us that on more than one occasion trains have toppled over the precipices with their freight. Fortunately we have escaped this time, and have reached the station of Rion.

This is a place of some note, it having been the chief town of the most ancient of the southern Circassian tribes—the Immeritinski, who claim that they were the first to embrace Christianity in the Caucasus and, like the Ossitinski, had taken part in the Crusades. The women are said to be the most beautiful in Circassia, and we had every opportunity of observing them. The arrival of the train being the main event in their monotonous lives, the station there forms a promenade. From the number that we noted on the platform, we came to the conclusion that the statement is more or less justified. They had very large black eyes, oval faces, dark hair, very fair, almost white skin, with none of the coarseness which so often accompanies the types of southern lands.

Very noticeable is the variety of headgear worn by the different tribes. Here may be seen the bachlik of the Immeritinski, who know how to fold it in the most coquettish of styles, with its two ends hanging gracefully on one side or behind. We certainly thought this headgear very becoming and practical, it being impervious to rain and warm for mountain wear. Then there is the low round black cap of the Armenian, the taller one of the Ossitinski and Lesghian, and the highest-peaked one of the Persian, all of Astrakhan skins. Again, there are the fez of the Turk, the mushroom-shaped sheepskin hat of the Tartar, and the turbans, varied in form and different in colour, from the green badge of the Mecca pilgrims to the white ones of the Shiite Persians who have made the pilgrimage to the holy city of Kerbalek in Khorassan.

The town of Rion takes its name from the river which rises in the mountains through which we have just passed, and is flowing its way westward to cast itself into the sea at Poti. We are here on classic ground, it being the ancient Phasis, intimately connected with Jason and the Argonauts in their search for the Golden Fleece.

The mountainous region through which we have just passed exhibits most luxurious vegetation, which clothes the hills to their very summits. At every station we are invited to buy apples over a pound in weight, water melons of over forty pounds, and grapes whose immense clusters of berries rival those of Syria. From these are made the wine famous throughout Russia under the name of Kakatinski, which, being quite unadulterated, is very palatable, and far better to drink than the water, which very often engenders fever.

Blackberry bushes abound on the mountain-sides, and the barberries lend vivid colours to the landscape. These, rising from a bed of green velvety mosses, and associated with large ferns, laurels, and even the humbler yellow and white gorse, make up to my mind a perfect picture of natural scenery.

On our way from the station of Suram to Samtredi, we pass the beautifully-situated town of Gori, which I consider to be a thorough reproduction of Athens, only instead of its central hill being surmounted by a Parthenon, it is crowned by an ancient stronghold that even now in its ruin looks down grimly upon the surrounding plain, a fit residence for the half-tamed mountaineers that are even at the present day its inhabitants.

One of their princes travelled with us to a station near Batoum. A young man of about thirty years of age, with a frame lithe and supple as an Indian's, he had not a spare ounce of flesh on him. His fine, handsome, beardless face with flashing eyes and coquettish moustache was surmounted by a fez, round which was wound, turban fashion, a bashlik, its gold-fringed ends hanging down behind. His vest of light-brown colour fitted closely to his body like a jersey, the front being adorned with cartridge cases, as is usual in Circassia. Round his waist was wound a splendid silk shawl, in which was stuck a brace of silver-mounted breech-loading pistols and a silver-handled Circassian Kinjal or dagger. These, together with baggy-looking Turkish trousers and jackboots, caused Mr. D. to exclaim "What a magnificent brigand!" We found, however, that he could speak Russian fluently, was an officer in the Guards, and a most courteous gentleman.

Rapidly descending, we follow the course of the Rion, now flowing more sluggishly and bordered by immense banks of reeds; the croaking of the frogs is perfectly deafening, the tree frog adding his bass note to the sharper one of his brother in the fen. As darkness comes on, we enter forests lit up by thousands of fireflies constantly darting backwards and forwards, and appearing like continuous sparks from a locomotive in motion. We arrived at the station Samtredi, where I parted with my companion for a season, it being the junction between Batoum and Poti. I had promised to visit Mr. Wilson Sturge at Poti on my return journey, and as there are only two steamers a week from Batoum to Odessa I had given Mr. D. a letter of introduction to our Consul, Mr. Peacock, while I went to Poti to fulfil my promised visit.

As we approached the Black Sea, the light from the lighthouse standing upon the mole became visible as the rays fell shimmering white upon the gently-rolling waves breaking upon the shore.

While upon the road I had inquired of a fellow-passenger as to the nature of the accommodation available, but the reply was discouraging—the one possible place, the Colchide, being much infested with nocturnal vermin. To my great surprise and pleasure, on arriving at the Colchide I found myself ushered into a room which was beautifully clean, with all the appurtenances and comforts of civilized life. From the information given me I found that this change was due to the fact that a French lady and her daughter had taken the house, and had had it thoroughly renovated, their efforts being rewarded by a considerable custom.

On calling upon Mr. Sturge, I met Mr. Gardner, a member of the well-known Liverpool firm. The name of Wilson Sturge is familiar to a wide circle, owing to the interest which he took in the sect of the Doukhobors. The Quakers, to whom he belonged, aided these people to emigrate first to Cyprus and then to Canada, Mr. Sturge superintending these undertakings. The reason for the departure of the Doukhobors was their noncompliance with the conditions of universal military service. I spent three very pleasant days with them, and retain a warm memory of their hospitality.

Poti while under Turkish rule was nothing but a Turkish swamp and its port perfectly neglected; now it is an important centre for the export of maize, walnut wood, oak, and manganese ore worked by a French company in the hills at Kirila near Borzhom.

Having bidden good-bye to my excellent landlady, I took passage to Batoum on a boat called the *Babushka* (*Grandmother*), an old rickety tug not so big as a Gravesend steamer and rotten throughout. It took five hours to do the twenty-four miles, and rolled the whole time, although the sea was quite calm. However, we arrived safely at our destination, where I rejoined my friend, who was anxiously awaiting me, and found we had six hours to wait before the boat started.

I found that great progress had been made since

BALAKHANI. OIL WELL ON FIRE.

it was in possession of the Turks. The harbour is a creek running up into the land. On its north side many petroleum tanks of immense size have been erected, and instead of the dirt and filth that used to be visible everywhere (although there is much yet to be desired) tolerably good hotels have been erected. Amongst the best are the Imperial and the Colchide. The smells, however, are still intolerable, and the heat was suffocating.

The Turkish fez is still the most prominent headgear, and two large steamers flying the English flag were in the port, as also a French Messageries and an Austrian vessel. I found a large company of English and Americans assembled to bid adieu to Mr. Chambers, the American Consul.

The hills in the neighbourhood of Batoum are richly wooded, and are still the home of the wolf, wild boar, and the stag, while pheasants are very cheap, and quite common at the table. The name of the bird is derived from Phasis, the ancient name of the Rion. Twenty miles from this town is a celebrated monastery, visited during the year by thousands of pilgrims. It is built near the ruins of one named Pitzunda, which was erected by Justinian in the sixth century. Owing, however, to these ruins appearing dilapidated to the Governor at that time, he had them whitewashed, much to the disgust of the Governor-General, Prince Dondukoff-Korsakoff. The latter ordered the delinquent to restore them to their original condition, which proved to be an almost impossible task.

The boat by which we travelled from Batoum to Odessa was the *Juno*, a sister ship to the *Mithridates*, my old vessel, and the captain was a former acquaintance. There being very few passengers on board, we each had a separate cabin. Among our fellow-travellers were two nieces of the celebrated Polish poet Mickiewicz and Prince Schervashadze, the representative in the direct line of the former Abkhasian rulers. He owns most of the land along the shore from Soukhum to Redout Kalé, about 200 miles in length.

His former subjects were deported, after the Russo-Turkish War, into Turkey because they took part against the Russians, he himself only just esc ping the same fate. He was dressed as a Russian general, and his son, a fine young fellow in the Guards, as a captain. The latter confided to me that he had a high regard for the great English nation.

It was very amusing to listen to the efforts at conversation between Mr. D. and the captain. They had mutual tastes on the subject of photography, and both spoke equally vile French. The captain interlarded his speech with Russian words, and Mr. D. with English, which he used without a stop, only putting a French-like termination to them. Thus " If you take a lens " would be rendered " Si vous takez a lensé," or " the mountains are well wooded " became " les collines sont beaucoup woodé," and the captain's face was a study as he politely tried to show he had fully comprehended. When the conversation came to a sudden stop for lack of word fuel, Mr. D. would say, " I say, Hume, just tell the captain what I am saying in Russian ; he does not understand French very well," which of course I did with the addendum, much to the captain's astonishment and amusement, as he on his part was perfectly and rightly persuaded that D. was far more hopelessly ignorant of the French language than he himself.

A striking feature of our passage was the utter lifelessness of the Black Sea ; no fishing boats, no sailing boats, no steamer, not an object to obstruct the view seaward, but to the east or land-side are high mountains, many of them snow-tipped, but no living thing moving to be seen with a telescope.

We called in turn at Soukhum, Redout Kalé, Anapa, Novo Rossisk, and finally Kertch. It was from Anapa that the Circassian slave-girls were formerly shipped to supply the harems of Constantinople. It is, in common with other ports of call, only a member of the fortified coastal defences.

Kertch is situated on the Straits of Yenikale, and

was formerly the capital of the Grecian kingdom of the Bosphorus, and is even now not only Greek by tradition, but numerous Grecian colonies still remain round the Sea of Azov. Above the town is a series of hills, studded with tumuli, many of which having been opened have yielded up treasures of Grecian art in the shape of lamps, statuettes, tear bottles, vases, gold and silver ornaments, coins, etc., which now adorn the museums of various parts of Russia, as well as Kertch itself. The main historical points of interest, however, are those connected with Mithridates, the King of ancient Pontus, whose tomb and so-called arm-chair are pointed out to visitors. Since the Crimean War, Kertch has been strongly fortified, and now absolutely protects the Sea of Azov from invasion.

Leaving Kertch, we arrive at Theodosia, the ancient Kaffa which two centuries ago was a town of 80,000 souls, but to-day is only a second-rate watering-place. The main features along the coast are the ruins of the old fortifications erected by the successive conquerors of the Crimea, Phœnicians, Romans, and Genoese. The whole southern shore, owing to its health-giving mild climate in the winter, has received the name of the Russian Riviera.

Our last shipping-place is Sebastopol, which has already been described in these pages, and which was the parting-place of Mr. D. and myself, he proceeding to England through Odessa, while I returned to Kharkov. With my arrival there, this very interesting and instructive journey was brought to an end.

CHAPTER XXII

CONCLUDING REMARKS

SIDELIGHTS ON RUSSIAN LIFE

FROM frequent remarks made by me in these reminiscences it will be surmised that in my opinion a great future lies before the Russian Empire. Situated as it is in a ring fence, although composed of a number of nationalities, it has great colonizing instinct and will be able eventually under liberal institutions to mould them into a homogeneous whole. Under the circumstances it would become a solid buffer between the Eastern and the Western civilizations. At present it is a nation in the making and presents a very interesting subject for study. I entertain a sanguine hope that, under judicious laws and a system of national education, the country will progress along the paths of peaceful evolution, avoiding reaction and revolution.

The Russians possess many pleasant and bright qualities. Hospitality, kindness, self-sacrifice, family affection, and strong religious instincts are dominating features in their social life. I have used in this work the words "religious instinct," which has a very different meaning to "personal religion." Although they are very strict in the outward observances, such as genuflections, adoration of the ikons (or pictures of saints), fasting, keeping the holy days prescribed by the Synods, keeping their names' days (saints' days), they have not the slightest compunction to call on God to witness to a lie, and one of the great difficulties that has arisen in the introduction of the jury system into the courts has been that they cannot be believed on oath only when it suits their purpose. These remarks do not refer to the *intelligencia*, but only to the uneducated peasantry. In short, the religion as practised by them is a fetish one, and not a religion that affects the conscience.

In my many visits to the country houses of the proprietors, their hospitality may be fitly compared with that of our own land. Every attention is given to the guests, and at the same time the latter have full liberty in their actions. Before the abolition of serfdom, when their means were much larger than at present, it was no uncommon thing to hear at mealtimes several different languages spoken. I have heard nine, each being spoken by representatives of their nationalities.

During the period of serfdom, a great regard had often sprung up between the serfs and their master's family, whose children they had nursed or served from their infancy; so much was this the case that on the promulgation of the abolition many refused their freedom.

In Russian family life there are some very pretty customs. After the meals the children kiss the hands of their parents, and before going to bed receive the accolade and blessing of their mother and father. A further custom is the assembling of the family and friends to wish " God speed " to a departing guest ; on such occasion all remain seated round the room, offering for a few moments silent prayer for a safe and successful journey.

On one occasion I had been staying at the house of a very dear friend whose husband was Marshal of Nobility. Before my departure, the lady of the house approached me with a request on the part of the butler to allow him to kiss me before leaving. He was an old man verging on eighty years of age who had served three generations of the family from their infancy. Of course I gave my hearty consent ; and when I went into the anteroom ready to depart, he stood at the door, and on my going up to him to wish him good-bye, with streaming eyes he put his arm round my neck and kissed me three times, using the word "Proschaite," meaning in Russian a last farewell. He also added. "I shall never see your face again, Barin"—and he never did.

Going out to the carriage, the footman stood at the door; and as I was going to enter, he, not to be outdone by the butler—much to the amusement of all assembled and to my great surprise—also suddenly kissed me. Between the footman and the butler there had always been a certain feud as to who should wait upon me during my stay; on no account would the latter allow the footman to serve me.

My stay in Russia was brought to rather an abrupt conclusion owing to a complete breakdown in my health, resulting from overwork and the effects of the climate of Baku.

The raw rice for our mill came from Persia through the Port of Baku, so that we had lately built a mill and established a business in that city. This necessitated frequent journeys into Persia, where rice was grown under swampy conditions giving rise to attacks of ague fever. Under the doctor's advice I had to leave the city, after which I took a round journey up the Volga from Astrakhan and by the River Oka to Berm in Siberia, visiting on my return Nijni-Novgorod, Moscow, Petrograd, etc., etc.

The liquidation of so extensive a business lasted over three years, and would have been more extended had not my partner together with his two sons taken over the milling. In the meantime it became necessary for me to take a complete change, as my health was becoming rapidly worse, and upon my arrival home I was so ill that I had to take to my bed and be for a considerable time under the doctor's care. The reviving climate of England eventually restored me, so that I have been able on several occasions to revisit Russia and renew my acquaintance with my many old friends.

The experiences herein narrated will, I trust, indicate what openings exist for British enterprise in Russia, the difficulties to be overcome, the success to be obtained by initiative and perseverance. From the reign of Elizabeth for many years onward England was predominant in commerce with this country, but owing to the lack of adaptability of our business men, we have long been outrivalled by Germany. As an instance it may be mentioned that while Germany's imports increased from 1893 to 1910 by £26,910,000, during the same period the British have increased only £1,032,000. In further proof of my contention I may mention that my firm was for many years an importer of the best indiarubber tubing for steam purposes, but never on any occasion have we been visited by an English traveller in that class of goods, whereas almost every week some representative of a German house called upon us, the result being that we were forced to obtain British goods through a Berlin firm, they being so superior for our business to those of any German manufacture.

It has been said that lessons are to be learned from every casual stranger, and in my experience this may truly be said of every separate nationality and often under the circumstances that are connected with one's daily life. For instance, in directing a letter in Russia, the name of the town to which it is sent takes precedence of that of the person addressed. Again, a dwelling-house is not made ridiculous and desecrated by being endowed with a name called from some aristocratic or invented name; this in Russia takes the name of the owner with the street number attached, such as " Hume House," etc.

The Eastern custom of combining the Christian name of the father with their own is universal, the surname only being used in documentary papers or in correspondence. In commencing a letter a fine distinction is made according to the status of the person written to; thus to your tradesman it would be " Dear sir," to your friend and equal " Very greatly esteemed " or " High born," to your superior " Very high born, and above that in various degrees according to their civil or military rank. In all business houses the reckoning board is used for addition and subtraction, owing to their money being in the decimal system.

It may interest future Russian students of street nomenclature to know that the "Hume Street" in the residential quarter of Kharkov was an honour conferred upon me by the municipality.

The introduction of agricultural labour-saving machines into those far-distant and almost unknown regions had eventually a most stimulating effect on the development of the farming industry of the country. It supplied a long-felt want; the same number of workmen who formerly immigrated during harvest time enabled the farmer to greatly extend the area under cultivation. It also introduced a new and permanent industry into the country; and if the aphorism holds good that a man deserves well of his country who causes two blades of grass to grow where only one did before, so much the more, I am of opinion, are my colleague and myself justly entitled to, and should claim, that same distinction.

APPENDIX

The map accompanying this book well illustrates the extent of the area over which extended the operations of our firm. The district in question includes the best part of the black-earth region known as the Garden of Russia, and throughout the whole of that part of the country a stone the size of a finger-nail is a rarity.

In the centre of this vast region, the so-called Ukraine or Borderland, is situated the city of Kharkov, the centre and the metropolis of the great agricultural industry of South Russia. It was here that were established the main central offices of our firm, which by gradual gradation extended its bounds both to east and to west.

To give the reader some idea of this country of vast distances, I may mention that the other centres of our activity were Kiev, Taganrog, and Baku. Of these Kiev was 300 miles distant to the west, Taganrog 427 miles, and 1,300 to Baku on the east. It will therefore be understood that the harmonious working of these component parts necessitated efficient organization and involved a great strain upon my physical powers, having under my control the executive, whilst my companion, Mr. Lister, carried on the office work. If often happens, as with empires so with businesses, that the exigencies compel them to undertake responsibilities which otherwise they would willingly forgo, and the same condition caused us to extend our organizations.

Russia is not only a country of vast distances, but it is also one of climatic extremes, ranging from Arctic conditions in the extreme north, the home of the reindeer and the Samoyeds, to the swamps and forest of Linkoran in the south, the prowling-ground of the tiger.

In my opinion, the centralization of the power in one authority in Petrograd seems an anachronism, seeing the differences that exist from climate, nationality, and economic conditions.

Take for example the schools. These reassemble after vacations throughout the whole empire on August 1st, which is quite appropriate for the northern provinces, but finds the southern ones in the full heat of summer.

In addition it gives rise to great slackness in the administration of the law in remote provinces, where the Crown administrators too often act on their own initiative on the principle of the Russian aphorism that " God is high and the Czar afar."

It may be that in the near future the promise given by the Czar to Poland to form it into a separate province under a Russian viceroy may be extended, and that in the womb of time there may be born, following the example of the United States, a series of responsible provinces with limited powers of self-government.

The change from the present order of Zemstvos might form a nucleus for the transition without involving any great evolutionary effort, and, in my opinion, this would greatly strengthen the power of the Central Government as the United States of Russia.

INDEX

Agricultural labour-saving machines:
  effect on industry, 312
  my introduction of, 50–60 *et seq.*
Agriculture:
  animal pests, 101, 102
  Caucasia, 290, 302
  drought, effect on crops, 77, 94, 96
  insect pests, 100, 104
  irrigation Steppe lands, lack of, 78, 96
  lease of Government lands, 96
  Mennonite colonies, 55–61
  nomad tribes, 93
  peasant life and labour, 81–87
  primitive methods, 56
  primitive windmills, 56
  the Steppes, 93–108
  see also Peasant life
Alcohol, government monopoly, 236
Alexander II, xv, xvi, 215, 221
  assassination of, xviii, 221
  speech on Nihilism, 139
Alexandrovsk, 269
Alupka, 104
Alushta, 104
Ananur 290
Anapa, 306
Ararat, Mount, 293
Armavir, Armenian settlement, 280
Army, 161–170
  compulsory service, xviii, 161–164
  exemptions from service, 163
  employment of veterans, 162
  Jews' attempt to evade compulsory service, 229
  Mennonite exemption from military service, 55, 62, 64
  military reserves established, xviii

Army, reorganization of, xviii
  the Cossacks, 164–166
  the Opolchénie, 163
  terms of military service abridged, 163
Artel system of labour, 150
Artesian wells, 95
Autocracy, Imperial, 218–219
Autocratic government by officials, 146, 160–161
Avalanches, 289
Azov, Sea of, desiccation of, 51

Bakhmut, 274
Bakounin, theories of, 138
Baku, 294–299, 313
  see also Balakhani
Balakhani, 294–296
Banking, Russian methods, 123
Bankruptcy, Russian methods, 121, 199
Bashkirs, 93
Batoum, 304
Beggars, professional, 128
Berdiansk, 51, 55, 89
Berditchev, 246
Bird life of the Steppe, 56, 81, 102
" Black Earth," the, 94, 96, 313
Black Sea, storms in, 49
Black Sea Treaty, clauses abrogated, xviii, 33
Borki, railway accident at, xix, 277
Breslau, 191
British imports, 311
British trade, opportunities for, 311
Bulgaria and Russia, contrast in political status, 146
Bulgarians, settlements in Crimean Tartary, 93
Burian bushes, nitrate in, 99
Bustards, 81

315

Cattle-breeding, nomad tribes of the Steppes, 93
Caucasia, passports in, 283
Caucasian mountains, military road, 285–291
Caucasus, 276–307
  see also Circassia
Chamois, the, 289
Cinnabar (mercury ore), 275
Circassia, 279
  see also Caucasus
Circassian tribes, 281, 284, 301
  picturesque costumes, 281, 301, 303
Climate, extremes of, 96, 313
Cloud effects, the Steppe, 98
Coal mines, Hughesovka, 265, 268, 274
Colporteurs, special facilities, xxi
"Contract Fair," Kiev, 256
Copper works, Ekhptala, 293
Cossacks, 140, 164–169
  Don, 277
  Zaporozhski, 168, 269
Country life, isolation of, 90–92, 127
Cracow, 191–193, 243
Crimean Tartary, the Steppe, 93
  see also the Steppe
Crimean War, 38–42
  effects of, xv, 40, 215

Darial defile, 286
Doukhobors, 304
Drought. See Agriculture
Dukhobortsi, the, 283
Duma, representation in, 127

Easter Sunday festival, 38
Education, 314
  want of, 145, 232
  Zemstvos' attitude, 144
Ekaterinoslav, 89, 112, 269
Ekhptala copper works, 293
Elbruz, 282

Family life, 309
Famine, the great (1891), xix
Field cookery, 85
Forestry, Government plantations, 111
Fuel, dried manure as, 92

Genghis Khan, 93
Geology, South-west Russia, 246–255, 262–275
Georgia, 290–291
German imports, 311
Gori, 302
Gounib, 43, 284
Graham, Mr., my partnership with, 50
Grecian art, ancient remains, 307
Grecian forts, remains, 104
Gregorian Church, 283
Gudaúr, 289

Hessian fly, 100
Horse-breeding, nomad tribes of the Steppes, 94
Horse-fair, Nizoblania, 280
Horsemanship, Cossack, 278
Horses, Tartars' care of, 80
Hospitality, examples of Russian, 91, 308
Hospitals, revenue from municipal stamps, xix
Hughesovka, coal and iron works, 265–268, 274
Hume, G., autobiography. See chapter headings, v–xii
Hungarian beetle, 100

Ikons, 270–273, 309
Iron-ore quarries, Krivoi Rog, 263, 268
Iron-ore, Stila, 274
Iron works, Hughesovka, 265–268
Irrigation. See Agriculture and Steppe

Jerboa, the, 102
Jewish pale, 224, 225, 246
Jewish problem, 223–237
Jewish race in Russia:
  Ashkenazim, 224, 225, 237
  Karaim, 224
  Sephardim, 224
Jews:
  disabilities and repression, 227–230
  the mountain, polygamy, 283
  unscrupulous character, 228–237

INDEX 317

Jitomir. See Zhitomir
Justice, courts of, 146

Kalmucks, 93
Kazbek, 281, 287–288
Kertch, 306
  tumuli, 41
Kharkov, 115, 313
Khitobel, fortified church, 290
Kiev, 255–260, 313
  pilgrimages to, 258
Kirghizes, 93
Klisti, the, 283
Kobi, 288–289
Komaroff, General, xviii
Krapotkin, Prince, murder of, 139, 220
Krivoi Rog:
  iron mines, 263–264
  strata, 269
Kurgans, Scythian burial-places, 75, 95, 103

Labour, Artel system, 150
Labradorite, 246, 250
Land, lease of Government, 96–97
Land question, 232
  see also Peasants, and Serfs
Lars, 286
Law procedure, Bureaucratic action, xvii
Laws, Russian, basis of, 137, 146
Lister, Mr., my partnership with, 119 et seq.
Livadia, 104
Locusts, 104–108, 294
Lutherans, settlements in Crimean Tartary, 93

Malotchnaya, R., 55, 90
Manure, use as fuel, 92
Marmot, the, 101
Martial law:
  country under, 140–151
  Poland, 238
Mazeppa, 257
Mennonite colonies, 37, 55–66, 93, 111
Merchants, three guilds, 121
Military insurrection of 1825, 214

Mineral springs, Caucasia, 280

Mir, the, 217
Mirage, the, 102
Mithridates, tomb of, 307
Mleti, 289
Mohuls. See Kurgans
Molokhani, the, 283
Mtzkhet, 290

Nestor, 260
Nestorian Church, 283
New Russia Company, 118, 265–268
  see also Hughesovka and Krivoi Rog
Nicholas I, autocratic character, 215
Nihilism:
  its origin, aims, and growth, 138–151, 219–222
  public insecurity in the towns, 125–127
  students' support, 219–220
Nikitovka, cinnabar mines, 275
Nitrate:
  burian bushes, 99
  manufacture of, 75
Nizoblania, 280
Nobility:
  degrees of, 127
  impoverished, 126, 127
Nomad tribes of the Steppe, 93

Odessa, 34–38
Officials:
  apathy of Russian, 195
  autocratic government, 146, 160–161, 314
  salaries of, xvii, 233
Oil gas, Caspian Sea, 295
Oil refineries, Baku, 294, 297
Oil wells:
  Baku, 294
  Balakhani, 294

Partridges, 81
Passanaur, 290
Passports:
  Caucasian mountains, 283
  martial law, 140–142
  peasants', 140
Peasant Land Bank, 232

318 INDEX

Peasant life in S. Russia, 81–87
  Jewish moneylenders, 230–232
  land question, 216–217, 232
  national education required, 145, 232
  poverty, 231
Peasant religion:
  ikons, 270
  pilgrimages to Kiev, 258
  pilgrimages to Svyatogorski, 270
  religious instincts and observances, xxi, 86, 270, 308
Peasant superstitions, 60, 87
Pechersk monastery, 259
Pedlars, Hungarian, 128
Penjdeh incident, xviii, 159–160
Perekop, Isthmus of, 40
Pilgrimages:
  Kiev, 258
  Svyatogorski, 270
Pilgrims:
  Christian, 43
  Mohammedan, 44
Pitzunda, 305
Plague, measures to stamp out, 194–195
Playing-cards, tax on, xix
Plevna. See Russo-Turkish War
Poland, 238–245
  ancient kingdom, 240, 242
    disunion of, 242
    Poniatowski, 211
    promised reconstitution of, 212, 314
  coercive treatment by Russia, 212–213
  political problem of, 238–245
  racial and religious differences between Russia and Poland, 240
  revolution of 1863, xviii, 241
  Russian attempts to destroy nationality, 238–240
  under permanent martial law, 238
  see also Cracow and Warsaw
Police, autocracy of, 146, 160–161
Police supervision, 147–150, 160–161
Poll tax:
  abolition of, xviii
  peasants', 140

Poltava, 110
Poor relief, institutions for, xx
Popoff, M., 70 *et seq.*
Poti, 303
Pottery, prehistoric mounds, 104
Printing press, censorship, 146

Railway travelling, incidents of, 195, 205–211
Reaping and thrashing machines. See Agriculture
Religion, Orthodox Greek Church, xxi–xxii
  church services, xxii, 54
  clergy, xxi, xxii
  Easter Sunday festivities, 38
  "Intelligencia," the, xxii
  peasants, the. See Peasant religion
Religion:
  Dukhobortsi, 283
  Gregorian Church, 283
  Jews. See Jews
  Jews, mountain, 283
  Klisti, 283
  Mennonites, the, 61–66
  Molokhani, 283
  Nestorian Church, 283
  Sabbatarians, 283
  Stundists, 65
Rostov, 279
Russian Empire, future of, 308, 313–4
Russian life, sidelights on, 308–312
  see also Country life
Russian literature, 260
Russian Riviera, 104, 307
Russian Steam Navigation Company, 32, 42–50
Russo-Turkish War, xviii, 152–159

Sabbatarians, the, 283
Salt (brine), Scaramangar, 274
Salt mines:
  Bakhmut, 274
  S. Russia, 275
Salt springs:
  medicinal properties, 277
  Slaviansk, 277
Scaramangar, salt works, 274
Schamyl, 43, 284

INDEX 319

Scythian burial-places, 95, 103
Scythians, 103
Sebastopol, 38–42
  siege of. See Crimean War
Serfdom, abuses of, xv
Serfs, emancipation of, xvi, xviii, 78, 144, 215, 219
  land question, xvi, 79, 215–217
Sheep pasturage, 97
Siberian exile, horrors of, 242
Slaviansk, 277
"Smell of the villages," 90, 92
Snakes, 108
Snipe shooting, 52
Snowstorms, 89, 90, 208
Social unrest, causes of, 226–227
Souslik. See Marmot
Steam, superheating apparatus, 30
Steppe:
  black earth, 94
  character, 93, 94, 95
  cookery, 85
  Crimean Tartary, 93
  fauna, 93, 100–102
  history, 103
  isolation in winter, 92
  lack of irrigation, 96
  law, 110
  nomad Oriental tribes, 93
  population, 93
  primitive roads, 113
  riders. See Tchumaks
  Tchumak landmarks, 90, 112
  travel, difficulties of, 89–92, 113–115, 116
  underground water supply, 95
Stila, iron ore, 274
Student riots, xix, 145
Students and Nihilism, 219–220
Stundists, the, 65
Sudak, 104
Sugar industry, Kiev, 256
Superstitions, 60, 87
Svyatogorski, 270

Taganrog, 51, 277, 313
Tamara, castle of, 287
Tarantula spider, 108
Tartars, 93, 103
  love of horses, 80
Tchatuir Dagh, 39

Tchin. See Nobility
Tchinovniks, xvii
Tchumaks' (Steppe Riders), landmarks, 90, 112
Terek, R., 286
Theodosia, 39, 104, 307
Tiflis, 290, 292
Todleben, General, xviii, 64
Tolstoy, Count Dmitri, reactionary policy of, xix
Trading:
  English risks, 122–123
  points for English merchants, 120
Travel:
  Caucasian mountains, 285–291
  difficulties of, 53, 89–91, 250–255
  see also Steppe and Railway Travelling
Trepoff, General, attempt on life of, 220
Trial by jury, introduction of, xviii, 136
Troika, 285
Tumuli, 41, 75, 307
  see also Kurgans

Village communes and their powers, 217
Vladikavkaz, 281–285
Volunteer fleet, its formation, 159

Warsaw, 211, 239
Water supply, underground, 95
Wedding ceremonies, 54
Wieliczka, salt mines, 191–193
Wild flowers, the Steppe, 98
Wild geese, shooting, 52
Windmills, primitive, 56
Wine districts, 104, 302
Witte, M., 124
Wool Fair, Kharkov, 115

Yaila Dagh, 39, 104
Yalta, 39, 104

Zemstvos, xviii, 144–146, 218, 314
  attitude to Nihilism, 139, 144
  on education, 144
Zhitomir, 249
Zoroaster, Temple of, 295